LIVING TOGETHER

ENGLISH FOR HOUSEKEEPING AND SOCIAL CARE

von
Maureen Bamming
Horst Beckmann
Gisela Machunsky
Elsa Toben-Vollmer

4., durchgesehene Auflage

Dr. Felix Büchner – Handwerk und Technik · Hamburg

Vorwort

Living Together ist ein Lehrwerk für das Unterrichtsfach Englisch. Es ermöglicht Schülerinnen und Schülern der Hauswirtschaft und Sozialpflege, in zwei Jahren vom Grundlagenbereich bis hin zum Erwerb des erweiterten Sekundarabschlusses I zu kommen. Es entspricht den Lehrplänen des Faches Englisch in den beruflichen Schulen.

Die Themenbereiche in Living Together wurden so zusammengestellt, dass sie zum einen hauswirtschaftliche und sozialpflegerische Kenntnisse vermitteln, zum anderen die Lebensprobleme der Jugendlichen in diesem Alter ansprechen. Die bereits vorhandenen englischen Grundkenntnisse der Schüler werden durch integrierte **Übungen zur Grammatik** (grün hinterlegt) wiederholt.

Das Buch legt Wert darauf, zahlreiche Möglichkeiten der **fächerübergreifenden Arbeit** im Bereich der Hauswirtschaft und Sozialpflege anzubieten. Denkbare Themen sind z. B. die Herstellung eines englischen oder amerikanischen Frühstücks, die Herstellung von Badezusätzen aus Kräutern, die Erstellung von Einladungskarten mithilfe des Computers, die Besichtigung eines Altersheimes.
In diesem Lehrwerk wird die englische Schreibweise verwendet. Es finden sich jedoch auch Redewendungen, die aus dem amerikanischen Sprachgebrauch stammen.

Weitere Elemente von Living Together
- **Zahlreiche Aufgaben** und Impulse ermöglichen eine Binnendifferenzierung durch die Lehrkraft.
- **Die Revisionsseiten** (blau hinterlegt) greifen die Kapitelthemen mit vertiefenden Texten auf und ermöglichen eine wiederholende Vorbereitung auf Klassenarbeiten.

- **Die Methodenseiten/Activities** im Anhang
  - bieten spezielle Themengebiete wie Umgang mit dem einsprachigen Wörterbuch oder Informationen über Lautschrift, Werbung u. v. m.
  - ermöglichen kommunikationsfördernde Unterrichtsformen wie Planung von Quizveranstaltungen, Feiern, Diskussionen und schaffen Ideen für andere Lernorte. Beispielsweise ermöglicht die Küche als Lernort die Kommunikation über die Umsetzung von Hygienevorschriften und Rezepten sowie die Planung von Feiern. Im Computerraum können Textprogramme und Tabellenkalkulationsprogramme z. B. für Nährwertberechnungen genutzt werden. Das Internet soll als Quelle für Information zu gezielten Themen eingesetzt werden. Ebenso bietet sich eine Kontaktaufnahme mit englischsprachigen Schulen via Internet an, um an gemeinsamen Projekten zu arbeiten oder Partnerschaften aufzubauen.
- **Verweise auf die Methodenseiten** (Symbol 🦶) schaffen Impulse zur Verknüpfung von Kapiteln und "Activities".
- Nach jedem Kapitel folgt ein **Vokabelverzeichnis** der neuen Wörter inklusive englischsprachiger Umschreibung und Lautschrift. Alle Vokabeln sind im Anhang noch einmal alphabetisch zusammengefasst.
- Ein **grammatikalischer Anhang** stellt grundlegende Regeln der englischen Grammatik zum Nachlesen in deutscher Sprache zusammen.
- Spezielle Kommunikationsspiele (**"Talking Games"**) für die Partnerarbeit wiederholen spielerisch Wortschatz und Inhalt.

Das Autorenteam und der Verlag wünschen allen Lernenden und Lehrenden viel Spaß und Erfolg mit Living Together. Learning English is fun!

ISBN 978-3-582-01621-8

Verlag Dr. Felix Büchner –
Verlag Handwerk und Technik G.m.b.H.,
Lademannbogen 135, 22339 Hamburg;
Postfach 63 05 00, 22331 Hamburg – 2005
E-Mail: info@handwerk-technik.de
Internet: www.handwerk-technik.de

Umschlaggestaltung:
Harro Wolter, Hamburg
Reproduktionen: Reprostudio Winterhude, Hamburg
Druck: Druckhaus Thomas Müntzer, Bad Langensalza

Inhaltsverzeichnis

Inhaltsverzeichnis

IV

Unit 1
Free Time

Look at the pictures. How do these people spend their free time?

1.1   Gina and Ken at Home

"I'm Gina. I'm twenty-two. I'm a baker. In my spare time I like to read fashion magazines and I spend a lot of time with my computer. The computer is my hobby! On the weekends I usually work in a fish and chip shop."

"I'm Ken. I'm twenty-three. I'm a shop assistant and I work in *Penny's Supermarket* in the food department. Gina and I live in a flat in Birmingham. My hobbies are going out with friends, watching television and cooking."

At the moment Gina and Ken are relaxing at home. They are not watching television. Ken is in the kitchen. He is wearing an apron. Gina is sitting at her computer.

Gina: "What are you doing, Ken?"
Ken: "I'm cooking. I'm testing a new recipe for cheese scones."
Gina: "Oh, that is nice. I'm looking forward to them."
Ken: "How are you getting on with your computer?"
Gina: "Well, it's not easy. At the moment I'm learning how to use the Internet. I'm sending Jim and Fiona an e-mail to test the software."
Ken: "What do you think, wouldn't it be nice to invite them to see our new flat?"
Gina: "Oh yes. I'm inviting them in this e-mail to visit us next Friday."

Subject: Invitation
Date: Tue, 2 Jan 20.. 14:28:16 + 0100
From: "Gina Hartnett" <hartnett@gbdirect.uk>
To: "Jim Kelly"<J.Kelly@gbdirect.uk>

Dear Fiona and Jim,

I hope you are both well. I have got a new computer! It was quite cheap. I bought it at Woolworth's, so I have to install the programmes myself. It is exciting to see how fast this computer is working. I am sending you this e-mail to find out if the software is working properly.
Ken and I moved into our new flat last week. There is still quite a lot of work to do. If you don't mind a little chaos for the moment, we would like to invite you to have supper with us on Friday.

Let me hear from you soon.

See you,
Gina

A Read the text and the e-mail.
Choose one of the alternatives (a, b or c) below and complete the sentences.

1 Ken's hobby is
   a sending e-mails.
   b cooking.
   c reading fashion magazines.

2 Gina spends a lot of time
   a going out with friends.
   b watching television.
   c working with the computer.

3 Gina's computer
   a is working very fast.
   b was very expensive.
   c is twenty-two years old.

4 Gina
   a works at *Penny's Supermarket*.
   b is a shop assistant.
   c is a baker.

5 Ken is
   a testing a new recipe.
   b inviting Jim and Fiona to come next Friday.
   c testing whether the software is working properly.

6 At the moment Gina is
   a wearing an apron.
   b looking forward to Ken's cheese scones.
   c visiting Jim and Fiona.

B Do you have a computer room in your school? Ask your teacher about it.
Use the computer and write an e-mail to one person in your class. Tell this person in your e-mail what you are doing right now.

Present Progressive

When do you use the present progressive?
The *present progressive* describes an activity that is happening right now.

I am cooking.
Ken is testing a recipe.
Gina is learning.
Gina and Ken are relaxing.

Past	**Now**	Future

Statement Clause			
I	**am**		
He She It	**is**	test**ing**	a recipe.
We You They	**are**		

Negative Clause			
I	**am**		
He She It	**is**	**not** wat**ching**	television.
We You They	**are**		

Question			
	am	I	
	is	he	
		she	
What		it	**doing?**
	are	we	
		you	
		they	

Spelling Rules:

Verbs that end in -**e**:

make	→	making
writ**e**	→	writing
driv**e**	→	driving
etc.		

Verbs that end in -**ie**:

l**ie**	→	lying
d**ie**	→	dying
t**ie**	→	tying
etc.		

Verbs that end **in a vowel (a, e, i, o, u) with a consonant (p, t, g, m etc.)**:

sto**p**	→	sto**pp**ing
ru**n**	→	ru**nn**ing
ge**t**	→	ge**tt**ing
swi**m**	→	swi**mm**ing
etc.		

In the meantime … black humour:

A What are these people doing right now? Use the verbs in the box to form sentences in the *present progressive*.

> to walk – to play – to climb – to cycle – to check – to swim – to wait – to have (breakfast)

Tony and Mick

Jane

Barry

Bill and Jack

Jennifer

The Dixons

Anne, Jill and Esther

Gary

Example:
*Tony and Mick **are** playing **soccer**.*

1. Jane is … with a knapsack.
2. Barry … on a mountain bike.
3. Bill and Jack … up a mountain.
4. Jennifer … for a bus.
5. The Dixons … their breakfast.
6. Anne, Jill and Esther … in a swimming pool.
7. Gary … the lotto numbers.

→ For rules see page 153

B Put the words in brackets into the *present progressive* tense.

Examples:
It's five to one. Ken (have) lunch.
*– It's five to one. Ken **is having** lunch.*

Gina (not work), she (play) tennis.
*– Gina **is not working**, she **is playing** tennis.*

What a surprise, Fiona! Where you (ring) from?
*– What a surprise, Fiona! Where **are** you **ringing** from?*

You don't seem to be interested. You (listen) at all?
*– You don't seem to be interested. **Are** you **listening** at all?*

Why Sarah (not, come with) us to the cinema?
*– Why **isn't** Sarah **coming** with us to the cinema?*

1. There is something wrong with my car. Where is Ken? – He (work) in the garage.
2. Look, Sarah (teach) her brother how to ride.
3. Why Ann (not wear) her new dress?
4. It (rain)? – Yes, it (rain) very hard. You can't go out yet.
5. What you (read) now? – I (read) *The Forsythe Saga*.
6. Why you (make) a cake? Someone (come) to tea?
7. Why you (run)? Are we late?
8. There are some strange noises in the sitting room. What Tom (do)?
9. I don't know what Gina (do) at the moment. She (not repair) the computer.

1.2   A Phone Call from Fiona

Fiona: "Hello, Gina, Fiona here."

Gina:　"Hello, Fiona, what a surprise! Where are you ringing from?"

Fiona: "I'm ringing from Manchester."

Gina:　"You're in Manchester! Where are you staying?"

Fiona: "I'm staying at the *Watts Guest House*. It's much cheaper than staying in a hotel."

Gina:　"What are you doing there in Manchester?"

Fiona: "I'm taking part in a practical course for nurses."

Gina:　"Oh, I see. Did you get my e-mail?"

Fiona: "Yes, I got it. Thank you for the invitation."

Gina:　"Can you and Jim come on Friday?"

Fiona: "Yes, we would like to come. At what time?"

Gina:　"Let's say 7:30 p.m.?"

Fiona: "That's fine."

A Read the dialogue between Fiona and Gina out loud. Let's talk about it:

1. Where does Gina live?
2. Where is Fiona ringing from? What is she doing there?
3. Why is she staying at the *Watts Guest House*?

B Look at this picture. What is Gina doing?
Write sentences about Gina and use 'She is …-ing' or 'She is not …-ing'.

Examples:
Gina/watch/television
*- Gina **is watching** television.*

She/have/dinner
*- She **is not having** dinner.*

1. She/sit/on the floor
2. She/read/a book
3. She/play/the piano
4. She/laugh
5. She/wear/a hat
6. She/write/a letter

1.3   An Evening with Fiona and Jim

It is Friday evening. Fiona and Jim arrive at a quarter to eight. Gina offers tea and coffee. The guests prefer tea. Gina serves apple crumble and scones with cream and jam. The television is on, there is a report about a soccer match. There are also commercials on the programme.

Question: Is he working?

Answer: It doesn't really seem like it, but the man in the picture is working.

Ken: "Well, Jim! I have not seen you for a long time. What are you doing at the moment?"

Jim: "I am doing a one-year course in catering. I want to be a chef, so I am learning about food and cooking. I find it easy because my parents are caterers. Look, Arsenal London is playing really well against Manchester United. Isn't that great! A goal for Arsenal! My team is winning!"

Fiona: "You cannot talk to Jim when there is a live transmission of a soccer match or something about cooking on television."

Gina: "What about you, Fiona. What are you learning?"

Fiona "At the moment I'm doing the second part of a nurse's training. I'm learning some practical skills like giving a bedbath and taking a patient's temperature and pulse-rate. Look at that commercial! Karl Lagerfeld is presenting his new collection. Isn't that exciting? I'm going to buy the new fashion magazine tomorrow. By the way, this apple crumble is delicious. Did you make it yourself?"

Gina: "Ken made it."

Ken: "Thank you. I will give you the recipe if you like."

A Read the dialogue between the four friends. They are talking about their professions. What are the names of the following professions? Form complete sentences with the words in the table. Be careful, they are not in the correct order! Start like this: Somebody who … is a ….

Example:
Somebody who goes to school is a student.

goes to school	fashion designer
bakes bread and cakes	teacher
designs new clothes	baker
works in a shop	chef
teaches students	trainer
cooks meals in a restaurant	nurse
looks after people in a hospital	student
trains a soccer team	shop assistant

B Hobbies and Professions – Make a list of the hobbies and the professions of ten people. Write down a table like this:

Name	Hobby	Profession
Ken	cooking	shop assistant
Gina	computer	baker
Jim	sports	
Fiona		
My mother		
My friend Ruth		
etc.		

7

1.4   In Ken's and Gina's Kitchen

Although Gina and Ken don't have much money they have a modern kitchen in their new apartment. Look at the photograph. What objects can you see?
Try to complete the following text. Use the words in the box to fill in the gaps.

> cupboards – cooker – dishwasher – sink – pot – flowers

It's a big kitchen, nice and clean with a lot of _cupboards_ ... There is a _sink_ ..., a fridge, an oven, and a _cooker_ ..., but there is no washing machine. There are some lovely _flowers_ ..., but there aren't any pictures. On the cooker you find a large silver _pot_ ... – Ken wants to prepare the dinner. Ah! And there are some glasses and plates next to the _dishwasher_ ..., and even some bottles of wine.

1.5   Fiona and Jim Are Making an Apple Crumble

Oven setting:
200 °C
(gas mark 6)
20–30 minutes

To make an apple crumble is very easy. Here is the recipe:

Ingredients	
For the filling:	**For the crumble:**
900 g apples	175 g flour
50 g brown sugar	50 g sugar
1/2 teaspoon of cinnamon	75 g butter
2 tablespoons of orange juice	a pinch of salt

A Translate the ingredients into German.

B Why not try to make an apple crumble in school? Talk to your teacher about it. Work together with other students and follow the instructions on the next page.

Preparation:
1. Peel the apples.
2. Cut the apples in half. Cut out the cores. Slice the apples.
3. Cook them in a saucepan with the orange juice, cinnamon and brown sugar until soft.
4. Pour the cooked apples into a one-litre pie dish and spread them out evenly.

Making the Crumble:
1. Put the flour and salt into a mixing bowl. Add the butter and cut it into small pieces with a knife.
2. Rub the butter into the flour with your fingertips. Keep lifting your hands high above the bowl. This lets the air into the mixture and makes it light. Continue until you have an even, crumbly mixture, then stir in the sugar.
3. Put the crumble over the apples in the pie dish. Spread the crumble out with a fork but do not press it down.
4. Bake the crumble for about 25-30 minutes until the top has browned a bit. Check it while it is cooking.
5. You can serve it with hot custard or ice cream.

→ Are you in the mood for a game? There are "Talking Games" you can play with a partner on page 144 ff. Have a look!

Jim and Fiona are at home.
Jim suggests to test the recipe they got from Ken. Here is a part of their conversation:

An old saying:

Jim: "Fiona, I would like to test the recipe which we got from Ken. Do you know where it is? I can't find it."
Fiona: "Well, I don't know either. You should ring Ken and ask him. He will not mind."

After the phone call:
Jim: "So, now I know what I need. Ken and Gina reminded me not to forget cinnamon. They think it really makes the flavour. They send you their best regards."
Fiona: "Thanks. Where are the apples?"
Jim: "They are on the fridge. Will you peel them, please?"
Fiona: "Yes, sure."

After a while:
Fiona: "Hm, the apple crumble is really very nice. Just smell it! I will ask our next door neighbour Mary to come over. She will enjoy it. I will just ring her."
Jim: "That's a good idea. You remember, she has invited us several times to her home."

9

Personal Pronouns

A noun is a naming word.
A *pronoun* is a word that you use instead of a noun. It replaces the noun in the sentence.
There are pronouns in the subject form and in the object form.

<u>**Subject form:**</u> We use a pronoun in the subject form when the pronoun is the subject.
The pronouns in the subject form are *I, you, he, she, it, we, you, they*.

<u>**Object form:**</u> We use the object form of a pronoun when the pronoun is the object.
The pronouns in the object form are *me, you, him, her, it, us, you, them*.
→ For rules see page 157/158

Personal Pronouns		Examples
Subject Form	**Object Form**	
I	me	Jim to Fiona: "**I** know everything I want. Ken and Gina reminded **me** not to forget cinnamon."
you	you	Jim: "Fiona, do **you** know where the recipe is?" Jim to Fiona: "Ken and Gina send **you** their best regards."
he	him	Fiona about Ken: "**He** will not mind." Fiona to Jim: "You should ring Ken and ask **him**."
she	her	Fiona about Mary: "**She** will enjoy the apple crumble. I will just ring **her**."
it	it	Jim about the cinnamon: "**It** really makes the taste." Fiona about the apple crumble to Jim: "Just smell **it**."
we	us	Jim to Fiona: "Shall **we** go to Mary?" Mary invited **us** several times.
you	you	Gina to Fiona and Jim: "I hope **you** both are well. I'm sending **you** this e-mail."
they	them	Fiona asks where the apples are. Jim answers: "**They** are on the fridge." The apples have to be peeled. Jim asks Fiona: "Will you peel **them**?

A Fill in the gaps in the following sentences. Use the pronouns in the box.

> me – him – you – them – it – us – her

Example:
"I have to peel these apples. Will you help …, please?"
*– "I have to peel these apples. Will you help **me**, please?"*

1. I will give you the money next week. Believe …, please.
2. You need some money for the ingredients. I will give … £10.
3. What about Ken? Where is he? We are waiting for … .
4. And Gina? Is she coming? Yes, this is … now.
5. What about the taxi? Where is it? I can't see … .
6. We are coming. Don't forget … .
7. Where are the others? Are they coming? Tell … to come now.

B Read the dialogue between Jim and Fiona on page 9. Look for personal pronouns and write them down.

C There are some personal pronouns in the directions for the apple crumble on page 9 as well. Look for them and write them down, too.

1.6   Fish and Chips

Gina and Fiona are talking about earning money in their free time.

Gina: "Do you have a part-time job, Fiona?"

Fiona: "Well, at the weekends I usually work in *Bizzie Lizzies*, a fish and chip shop. The shop belongs to my mother's friends. They're nice, friendly people."

Gina: "What do you think of your job?"

Fiona: "I like my job and I love fish and chips. I know that a portion of fish and chips hardly looks like a good meal. But believe me, Gina, it tastes delicious and doesn't cost a lot! The only problem is, fish and chip shops smell. And I smell, too. So I always need a good bath when I get home. I know it's not the best job in the world, but the payment is good. I think I will keep it until I leave school."

Gina: "Well, that sounds quite good. I would be interested to see the menu of *Bizzie Lizzies*."

Fiona: "Oh, that's no problem because *Bizzie Lizzies* has got a homepage on the Internet. You will find it when you search in the Internet with the search engine *Yahoo* for it. – Look, there you are! Well, isn't a 'mouth-watering' piece of fish fried in crispy batter with bread, tea or coffee for £3.85 a very good offer?"

A Read the following sentences. Each of them has a mistake in it. Find it and correct the sentence.

Example:
At the weekends Gina works quite often in Bizzie Lizzies.
– At the weekends **Fiona** *works quite often in Bizzie Lizzies.*

1. Fiona is looking for a part-time job.
2. Fiona thinks that a portion of fish and chips costs too much money.
3. The shop belongs to Fiona's friends.
4. When Fiona gets home from her job, she needs a good meal.
5. A piece of fish fried in crispy batter with bread and tea costs less than £3.
6. It is a big problem to see the menu of *Bizzie Lizzies*.
7. The friends of Fiona's father are nice, friendly people.

B Do you like riddles? Then find out the answer to the one with the pea, carrot and tomato. The answer has something to do with fish and chips ...

MENU

Back to the Main Page

Chips :   - 85p

Chicken Sandwich :   - £1.50
Spicey Chicken Sandwich :- £1.50

Fish & Chips :   - £3.10
Fish Bite & Chips :   - £2.00
Fishcake & Chips :   - £1.40

Pizza & Chips :   - £2.10

Baked Potato :   - £1.00
Toppings :   - 50p

Pie & Chips :   - £1.85
Pasty & Chips :   - £1.85
Sausage & Chips: - £1.35
Jumbo Sausage & Chips :   - £1.75
Chicken Nuggets & Chips :- £1.70

Buttered Baps :   - 35p
Tea :   - 65p

Curry & Chips :   - £1.45
Gravy & Chips :   - £1.45
Baked Beans & Chips :   - £1.55

Coffee :   - 80p
Hot Chocolate :   - 85p
All Cans :   - 60p
Soft Drinks – small bottles : - 35p
Soft Drinks – large bottles : - £1.00
Perrier :   - 60p

Beef Burger :   - £1.10
Quarter Pound Burger :   - £1.50
Cheese Burger :   - £1.25
Quarter Pound Cheese
Burger :   - £1.65
Hot Dog :   - 85p
Jumbo Hot Dog :   - £1.40
Jumbo Bacon Roll :   - £1.45
Breakfast Roll :   - £1.70
Egg Burger :   - £1.50
Vegeburger :   - £1.20

Dairy Ice Cream - single :   - 80p
Dairy Ice Cream - double :- £1.35
99's :   - 90p

5 Fresh Home-made
Doughnuts :   - £1.00

C Look in the Internet for offers of fish and chip shops. Write down some addresses that you
find.
You may use the search engine *Yahoo* (Internet address: http://www.yahoo.com) and
then search for "fish and chips".

Enjoy **DELICIOUS** **FISH&CHIPS**

GOOD FOOD   GOOD SENSE

★ ★ **MR CHIPS** ★ ★
Take-away and Cafe
MEYRICK STREET, PEMBROKE DOCK ☎ 682699

QUALITY FISH BAR

Roast Chicken   Spare Ribs
Fish Cakes   King Ribs
Cod & Plaice   Lasagne
Burgers (80% Beef) Pizzas
Jumbo Sausages   Bacon Rolls
Faggots & Peas   Pies
A Selection of Curries

ALL WITH FRESHLY COOKED CHIPS

We also have a fine selection of Take-away Sweets:
Hot Doughnuts, Apple Pie, Gateau etc.

Map:
Police Station
Water St
YOU ARE HERE
LEO'S Gordon St
Dimond St
Laws St
Bush St
Barclays Bank
Mr Chips
Meyrick St
Modern Print
NatWest Bank

1996 Gold Award for Quality & Excellence

10.30am ★ **OPEN DAILY** ★ **EARLY TILL LATE** ★ 10.30pm

We Cook in Low Fat for Good Health

THE LANTERNS RESTAURANT

MORNING COFFEE
LUNCHEON and EVENING MEALS: Local Beef, Turkey, Steak, Gammon etc.
AFTERNOON TEAS: Home cooked Scones, Gateau, Trifle etc.
MEALS ARE SERVED WITH LOCAL VEGETABLES (As available)
★ PRIVATE PARTIES CATERED FOR ★

D Go onto the homepages of the shops that you found. Find out if they offer menus like the menu on the left page. Maybe you have the possibility to print the menus? Ask your teacher about it.

E Use the Internet again and compare the offers of *Chippy in the Middle* with the offers of the fish and chip shop *Carlos Fryery*.
(This is the Internet address of *Carlos Fryery*: http://www.carlos-fryery.co.uk/fryery.htm)
Answer these questions: Which of these two shops offers a bigger variety?
In which is the food more expensive?

For more information how to search for something in the Internet, look on page 138.

Vocabulary

1.1 Ken and Gina at Home		
department [dɪˈpɑːtmənt]	a section or room within a large building	Abteilung
spare time [speətaɪm]	free time, leisure time, time for hobbies	Freizeit
fashion [ˈfæʃn]	up-to-date way of dressing; nice clothes that everyone likes	Mode
(to) relax [rɪˈlæks]	to rest	(sich) entspannen
an apron [ˈeɪprən]	something you wear when you are cooking	Schürze
recipe [ˈresɪpɪ]	It tells you how to cook something.	Rezept
an invitation [ˌɪnvɪˈteɪʃn]	when someone asks you nicely to come somewhere, for example to a party	Einladung
(to) be well [bɪ wel]	to feel good or healthy	gut gehen, gesund sein
proper, properly [ˈprɒpə]	correct, right	richtig
(to) move into [muːv ˈɪntə]	to go into	einziehen
an alternative [ɔːlˈtɜːnətɪv]	another way, an option	Möglichkeit, Alternative
complete [kəmˈpliːt]	finished	vollständig (auch als Verb to complete = vervollständigen)
expensive [ɪkˈspensɪv]	to cost a lot of money, to have a high price	teuer
department store [dɪˈpɑːtmənt stɔː]	a large shop selling lots of different things	Warenhaus
lake [leɪk]	on a lake you can go for a boat trip	See
constable [ˈkʌnstəbl]	a policeman	Polizist
(to) drown [draʊn]	to die in water	ertrinken
spelling [ˈspelɪŋ]	to write a word correctly	Schreibweise
(to) die [daɪ]	to stop living	sterben
(to) tie [taɪ]	to fasten together two ends	etwas binden
surprise [səˈpraɪz]	something that happens without knowing before	Überraschung
(to) ring [rɪŋ]	to telephone someone, to call someone by phone	anrufen
(to) seem [siːm]	to look like	scheinen, den Anschein haben
raining very hard [reɪnɪŋ ˈverɪ hɑːd]	Many drops of water are falling from the sky.	sehr stark regnen
strange [streɪndʒ]	different, not familiar	fremdartig, komisch
1.2 A Phone Call from Fiona		
✗(to) take part [teɪk pɑːt]	to be a part of, to be involved in	teilnehmen
nurse [nɜːs]	someone who looks after sick people	Krankenschwester
1.3 An Evening with Fiona and Jim		
scones [skɒns]	often served for tea time in Great Britain	Waffeln, Hörnchen
jam [dʒæm]	fruit cooked with sugar until it is thick	Marmelade
catering [ˈkeɪtərɪŋ]	to cater means to provide someone with food	Bewirtung von Firmen, Veranstaltungen
chef [ʃef]	someone who cooks food as a profession	Koch, Köchin
skills [skɪls]	the things you know	Fähigkeiten, Kenntnisse
commercial [kəˈmɜːʃl]	an advertisement on TV	Werbespot
exciting [ɪkˈsaɪtɪŋ]	very good	aufregend, spannend
by the way [baɪ ðə weɪ]	By the way, I wanted to tell you …	übrigens
delicious [dɪˈlɪʃəs]	tasty	köstlich, lecker
1.5 Fiona and Jim Are Making an Apple Crumble		
ingredient [ɪnˈgriːdjənt]	a food used with other foods to make a meal, part of a recipe	Zutat

Unit 2
Earning Money

A Here is a list of things this boy would like to do or have. Which wish is which number? The wishes are not in the correct order.

a) a ski course	d) holiday	g) go to parties
b) my own telephone	e) a racing bicycle	h) a new computer
c) a TV set	f) go to pop concerts	i) a computer course

B Make a list of your own wishes. Then tell the others in your class what you would like to have or do.
Start like this:
I would like to have/go on/attend/ …

2.1 Money Problems

Sue, Liz and Peter go to a College of Further Education. They study full time. It is a school for domestic science, and they want to become housekeepers. Right now they are sitting at a table in their school cafeteria. Peter is having a sandwich and a coke, and Sue and Liz are having an ice cream and a cup of tea.

They are talking about money, because they are always short of it. What do they think

about their money problems?

Sue: "My parents give me some pocket money every week. I get £10, but I must buy the bus ticket and pay for my writing paper with it. If I want a new piece of clothing, they say: 'You must save your pocket money.' If I want an ice cream, then I cannot buy a new pullover. This is really hard."

Liz: "I think you are quite lucky! My parents pay everything for me, but I must ask them whenever I want to have money for an ice cream or a new T-shirt. They often say 'No'. My Mum works in a supermarket, but she does not earn a lot of money there. And my father is unemployed. So I always have a bad conscience when I ask them for money. And look, I am wearing really old clothes."

Peter: "My mum is divorced. We are five children in the family, and so my mum cannot go working. We live on social allowance. Money is a really big problem for us. My dad lives abroad and he does not send very much money. I must try to earn some extra money, that is why I help an old couple and do some odd jobs for them. For example I go shopping for them and clean their home and do the garden."

A Do you like to fill in puzzles? Find out what the writing below means. Each symbol stands for a letter, the same symbols are the same letters. You will find the correct words in the text above.

1. A large shop where you can buy everything ✦◆□⋔□○⌣□&⋔◆
2. Someone who works in a household ⌇□◆•⋔&⋔⋔□⋔□
3. The pay which you get for an odd job ⋔⊠◆□⌣ ○□■⋔△
4. It is a cold, sweet food, tastes of chocolate, vanilla, etc. ℋ⋔⋔ ℔□⋔⌣○
5. A school on which you train for a job ♭□●●⋔℔⋔ □↗ ☞◆□◆⌇⋔□ ☞◔△◆⌣◆ℋ□■
6. T-shirt, pullover, trousers, socks, shoes are ℔●□◆⌇⌇ℋ■℔
7. He has no job, he is ◆■⋔○□■□□△⋔△
8. No longer married ◔ℋ❖□□⋔⋔△
9. If you only work for a few hours, you do an □◔◔ ℯ⒯□𝒩

Solution: ◔⌣■ △□◆ ◆⌇ℋ■& □↗ ⌣■ □◔◔ ℯ⒯□𝒩 ⌣■△ ⋔⌣□■ •□○⋔ ⋔⊠◆□⌣ ○□■⋔△ ?

B Look at Sue, Liz and Peter. Answer these questions on the text.
1. Find out what the young people have in common.
2. Why is Sue not happy with her pocket money?
3. Why must she be careful with her money?
4. Can Liz save her money better than Sue? Why or why not?
5. Why do Liz' parents often say "No" when she asks for money?
6. Why does Liz get a bad conscience when she asks her parents?
7. Do you believe that Peter asks for money, too?
8. Which of the three students can solve his or her money problems best? Why do you think so?

2.2   Looking for an Odd Job

In the United Kingdom a lot of young people are looking for odd jobs before or after school to make some extra money. Sue, Liz and Peter are discussing how they can find a good job with a fair pay.

Peter: "Before we make a big mistake and work like dogs for just a few pence, let's interview some fellow students who have odd jobs."

Liz: "That's a good idea. Let's start with you, Peter. You often help an old couple. What do you normally do for them?"

Peter: "Well, I go shopping for them. Then I clean their home and sometimes I even cook. But I do not earn much money. They both do not have a lot of money, you know."

Sue: "Well, then you are a nice boy, but it doesn't help you much! I don't want a job like that. My friend Peggy works on a farm every weekend. That is better."

Liz: "And what does she do there? Does she milk cows or does she plant potatoes?"

Peter: "Or does she breed kangaroos?"

Sue: "You two are making jokes. No, Peggy usually does household chores. The farmer's wife is lying in hospital for a couple of weeks."

Liz: "Well, that job sounds good. What exactly does she do?"

Sue: "Oh, she cooks meals and she washes the clothes. She also looks after the two children."

Peter: "Not bad. This is exactly what we are learning in school at the moment. So she is making her own experience and she is getting a fair pay, too."

Liz: "It is really good, but in this case it is no job for a longer period of time. Look, there is my friend Sara. – Nice clothes she is wearing. Hey Sara, do you own a clothes factory? You are wearing the latest fashion."

Sara: "No, but I work in a restaurant. I normally serve food from 9 p.m. to 12 p.m. The manager is really nice, and he is looking for young waiters and waitresses. Are you looking for a job? Why don't you ask him?"

A Read the dialogue and answer the questions.
1. Why do many young people look for odd jobs?
2. When can students do odd jobs?
3. Is Peter's job a good one? Why do you or why don't you think so?
4. What do you think of Peggy's odd job? Is it better than Peter's?
5. Why can Peggy's job be good for her training at school?
6. Why does Sara wear such nice clothes?
7. What makes an odd job a good job for you? Name things which are important for you.
8. What problem might Peter, Sue and Liz get if they take an odd job like Sara's?
9. How can you find out if an odd job is good for you *before* you take it?
10. Are the jobs on the right good ones? What do you think?

> Who wants to mow my lawn? Saturdays, Bath; call 8744332

> Can't go **shopping** anymore. Boy or girl wanted twice a week. Box No. 3344

> **Garage wants help** – Car wash, tidy up. Good for students. Pay: £2.50 per hour. Call Bristol, 4949493

> **Babysitter** wanted in Bristol Knowle. Good pay, Box No. 3345

B   Think of a good odd job which you would like to do. Tell your classmates about it:
1. What do you do? What time do you work?
2. How is your boss?
3. How much money do you earn?
4. How can you 'juggle' job and school?

The Simple Present

In the text on page 17 Peter, Sue and Liz **are** discuss**ing** how they can find a good job with fair pay. They are doing it **right now**. And remember: For things you are doing right now, you use the *present progressive* (see unit 1).

They are also talking about the odd jobs which they and their friends **usually** do. If you speak about things you usually do, you use another aspect – the *simple present*.
Signal words: often, never, seldom, sometimes, usually, always, normally

Example:
Peter *is* drink**ing** a coke **at the moment**, but he **usually** drink**s** tea.
→ For rules see page 153

Statement Clause			
I	never	drink	alcohol.
I	always	help	my mother.

CAUTION!
In sentences with third person (he, she, it) you add an 's' to the verb: verb + -s

He	sometimes	cook**s**	meals.
She	usually	bake**s**	cake.
It	always	rain**s**.	
Peter	normally	go**es**	shopping.
We	often	help	people.
You	never	breed	kangaroos.
They	seldom	drink	whiskey.

Remember that the 's' must be especially with 'he' and 'she', and those who are extremely fit add also 's' when there is 'it'!

Spelling rules:
Verbs that end with -o, -s, -sh, -ch, -x have a different ending in the third person (he, she, it): **verb + -es**
Consonant + -y: **verb + -ies**   vowel + -y: **verb + -ys**

Examples:

go – he/she/it go**es**	do – he/she/it do**es**	miss – he/she/it miss**es**
fish – he/she/it fish**es**	touch – he/she/it touch**es**	mix – he/she/it mix**es**
cry – he/she/it cri**es**		have – he/she/it **has**
can – he/she/it **can**	try – he/she/it tri**es**	play – he/she/it pla**ys**

A   Why not play a game?
Form two teams. Use the table „Statement Clause" and form sentences like *She seldom drinks whiskey*.
Then you change something in the sentence. You say, for example: bake a cake.
Now the other team must quickly say: *She seldom bakes a cake*.

Now they may say: They never
Your team must say:
They never bake cake.
If you or they can't form a sentence in five
seconds, the other team scores one point.
Play this game faster and faster. Your
sentences must make sense!
The losing team has to tidy up the kitchen
after the next cooking lesson.

B Now form sentences in the simple present with the words below.
Remember the spelling rules on page 18!

1. Peter/often/help/old people.
2. Sara/serve/food/in a restaurant.
3. I/work/in a hamburger bar.
4. Peter/fry/potatoes/every evening.
5. Sara/go shopping/with her friend.
6. My sister/never touch/the stove when
   it is hot.
7. My father/mix/very good drinks.
8. Peter/always/fish/in this lake.

Before he eats in a restaurant, he always looks
through the kitchen window. Then he often goes
somewhere else ...
Be honest – would this person eat in the restaurant
where those students work?

Negative Clause			
I	do not	eat	eggs.
You	don't	drink	milk.
He	does not	take	drugs.
She	doesn't	sell	clothes.
It		smell	good.
We	do not	eat	fat.
You	don't	sleep	much.
They		work	hard.

C Have a look at the following statements.
Correct them if they are wrong.
Use the simple present.

Example:
Peggy milks the cows.
*- Peggy **doesn't** milk the cows.*

CAUTION: Before you make mistakes, look
up the rules for "To do" on page 23.

1. Peter wants to work for a few pence.
2. Many people offer a good pay.
3. Many students wash their clothes themselves.
4. Peggy's farmer breeds kangaroos.
5. Sue owns a clothes factory.
6. Peggy has a job for a longer time.
7. Sue works in the evening.
8. Peter is happy with his job.
9. Peter has got much money.
10. Peter can buy expensive clothes.

If the weather is quite fine – dry washing on the clothes
line!

Questions in Simple Present

How **do** the English form questions?
Do you know that?
Does your teacher tell you?
Look at this table.

If you leave the *question word* (wh-word) out, you will get an answer with ‚Yes, ...' or ‚No, ...'. We call those questions "Yes-/No-questions". If you use a *question word*, you will get a longer answer. We call those questions "Wh-questions".

Question word				
Why	do	I	smoke	cigars?
When		you	work	there?
What	does	she	eat	... ?
Why		he	drink	milk?
How		it	help	you?
Where	do	we	do	that?
How much		you	earn	a week?
When		they	clean	the grill?

E Now form Yes-/No-questions in the simple present and give matching answers.

→ For rules see pages 153/154

Example:
you/smoke? – Do you smoke? – Yes, I do or *No, I don't.*

   CAUTION: *Do not make a mistake - Look up the rules for "To do" on page 23.*
 1. you/work/in a kitchen? – No, ...
 2. she/do/the garden? – Yes, ...
 3. they/help old people? – Yes, ...
 4. Sara/serve food? – Yes, ...
 5. they/want/a job? – Yes, ...
 6. the old people/go/shopping? – No, ...
 7. it/work/automatically? – Yes, ...
 8. Peter/is/at school? – No, ...
 9. Sue/can/cook well? Yes, ...
10. They/are/in the cafeteria? – Yes, ...

F Now form Wh-questions and give the matching answers. For your answers look in unit 2.2 "Looking for an Odd Job".

Example:
Why do you work in a restaurant?
– Because I need the money.

1. What/Peter/do/for the old couple?
2. Why/Peggy/work/on a farm?
3. When/Sara/serve/meals?
4. What/Liz, Peter, and Sue/want?
5. How much/the three/know/about household chores?
6. What/Sara/can/do/with her money?
7. What training/you/get at school?

2.3   Hi Jean – No Idea of Hygiene?

Liz is happy. She has got a job in *The Old Crown*, an old restaurant in the city. She works there as a waitress. Her working hours are from 7 p.m. to 10 p.m. from Monday to Friday. On Saturdays she works from 11 a.m. to 6 p.m., for seven hours. On Sundays she works from 10 a.m. to 2 p.m. So she works more than 20 hours every week. She gets £3 an hour. That means she is able to buy nice clothes, and she can go to the cinema or to the pub every now and then. She does not spend all her money – she wants to save £15 every week because she wants to get a driving licence and buy a small car, a Mini.

It's Monday evening, her first day in *The Old Crown*. She is serving the guests and is carrying trays with food and drink. Another girl named Jean is working in the kitchen. Jean is preparing the meals. The waitress must tell Jean what the guests have ordered.

Look at the picture above.

Right now Liz is not serving the guests. She is waiting for the meals inside the kitchen. The kitchen is really looking dirty. Liz knows: Jean doesn't work very well. Liz remembers what her domestic science teacher has told her. She is getting angrier and angrier.

Liz: "Hey Jean, what are you doing there? Why are you wearing rings on your fingers?"

Jean: "Why – I always wear these rings. They are really hip, aren't they?"

Liz: "But your kitchen is not. You must never wear rings when you work with food. And this kitchen doesn't look very clean. It's a rubbish tip!"

Jean: "Well, I never clean the kitchen when I have to cook. I can do that later."

Liz: "After your guests have eaten the dirt? Hell, no! And why don't you wear a hygienic hat? Do you wear that later, too?"

Jean: "Yes, much later. I never wear a hygienic hat, because I am not an old lady."

Liz: "Look, some of your nice long hairs are swimming in the soup. I am not serving hairy soup. Believe me: old or young, a hairy cook is never nice."

A   Are the following statements on the text true or false? Say why!

Example:

*The Old Crown is a country pub. – No, that's **false** because it's a restaurant in the city.*

1. Liz has a fulltime job.
2. She gives people something to eat and something to drink.
3. Liz works as a cook.
4. Liz needs all her money for living.
5. Jean is a good cook.
6. Liz is happy about the kitchen in the restaurant.
7. You must clean things right after you used them.

B Answer the following questions on the text on page 21.
1. What does Liz want to do with her money?
2. How much money does Liz get every week?
3. Why does Liz want to save some money?
4. Why must Liz go into the kitchen?
5. What does Liz know about hygiene?

C Do you want to have a clean workplace? Then you can draw posters for your kitchen and illustrate them with icons like this one on the right:

Form sentences with words from the two boxes.
Be careful, the words are not in the correct order.

not wear	the kitchen clean
wash	dirty utensils for cooking
wear	in a dirty kitchen
not taste	head scarf
keep	rings on your fingers
not work	food with a dirty spoon
not use	your hands after toilet

For example, the icon on the right can mean:
Do not wear rings on your fingers!
Now it's your turn to do the others:
Wash … ???
Do not … ??

D "Waitress, the bill, please!"
Liz must add up the prices very quickly. Look at the price list below. Read what the guest had, and tell the guest what he or she must pay.

The Old Crown's Price List

beer, 1 pint	£1.85	steak	£3.90
orange juice	£1.60	chicken	£1.90
lemonade	£0.60	fish'n' chips	£3.90
coke	£0.55	hamburger	£0,75

Example:
"Two pints of beer: three pounds seventy pence, three cokes: one pound sixty-five, two fish and chips: seven pounds eighty. That's thirteen pounds fifteen, madam/sir."

1. 2 glasses of orange juice, 3 hamburgers, 1 chicken
2. 2 pints of beer, 2 cokes, 1 steak, 1 chicken
3. 2 cokes, 5 beer, 12 hamburgers

E Design a better menu for *The Old Crown*. You can even convert the pounds into new euro prices.

F Look at the pronouns. Copy the table „Pronouns", write down the German meaning of the words and learn them.

Pronouns		
Subject Case	**Object Case**	**Possessive**
I	me	my
you	you	your
he	him	his
she	her	her
it	it	its
we	us	our
you	you	your
they	them	their

G The landlord of *The Old Crown* is a nice man. He tells Liz what she must do, so Liz can learn her job quickly.
Replace the underlined noun by the right **pronoun**. Choose them from the table on the bottom of page 22.

Example:
"Liz, I am thirsty. Bring <u>the landlord</u> a cup of coffee, please."
- *"Bring <u>**me**</u> a cup of coffee, please."*

landlord: "Liz, I am hungry. Bring <u>the landlord</u> a hamburger, please."
Liz:　　"Yes, sir. And shall I bring <u>the landlord</u> a coke, too?"
landlord: "Yes, please. There are my friends. Make five pints of beer for <u>my friends</u>."
Liz:　　"Yes, sir. Who will pay <u>your friends</u>' bill?"
landlord: "They are <u>the landlord's</u> guests. Give <u>the landlord</u> the bill."
Liz:　　"That man is drunken, sir. Shall I give <u>that man</u> another beer?"
landlord: "No, call <u>the man</u> a taxi. <u>The man</u> cannot drive <u>the man's</u> car."
Liz:　　"The telephone. <u>The telephone</u> is ringing. - It's <u>the man's</u> wife."
landlord: "Tell <u>the man's wife</u> that the <u>wife's</u> husband has just left. Then <u>the landlord and Liz</u> will have no trouble."

H Do you love puzzles?
Find out the right word for these descriptions.
1. A school restaurant
2. A girl or a woman who serves food in a restaurant
3. It gives dirt no chance
4. The day before Sunday
5. The place where you cook meals
6. A sweet non-alcoholic drink
7. If you combine the fields with the question marks (= ?) in the right order, you get what girls look for when they go shopping.

1.	?	✌	☞	☜	❄	☜	☼	✋	✌
2.	☥	✌	✋	?	☼	☜	◆	◆	
3.	?	✡	☝	✋	☜	☠	☜		
4.	?	✌	❄	✝	☼	👎	✌	✡	
5.	☺	✋	❄	👍	✍	?	☠		
6.	?	☜	◆	?	☠	✌	☜	☜	
7.	?	?	?	?	?	?	?		

To Do or Not To Do?

→ For rules see page 154

The answer to this question isn't really difficult.
There are three questions and easy answers:

1 **When do you use "to do"?**
　　a) with negations
　　b) with questions
2 **In which tenses do you use "to do"?**
　　a) only in simple present and
　　b) in simple past
3 **What exceptions are there?**
　　a) Don't use "to do" with forms of "be":

　　b) Don't use "to do" with modals like can, must, may, will, shall, … :

　　c) Don't use "to do" with "who" or "what":

Examples:
I don't smoke.
Do you smoke?

Do you help old people?
Did you help them?

Is she in the kitchen? No, she isn't.
Are you English? – No, I'm not.

Can she help me? No, she can't.

Who works in the kitchen today?

Vocabulary

	2.1 Money Problems	
College of Further Education [ˈkɒlɪdʒ əv ˈfɜːðə ˌedjuːˈkeɪʃn]	a school for learning a job	Berufsbildende Schulen (in Great Britain)
domestic science [dəʊˈmestɪk ˈsaɪəns]	housekeeping	Hauswirtschaft
housekeeper [haʊsˈkiːpə]	someone with a housekeeping job	Hauswirtschafter/-in
(to) be short of money [bɪ ʃɔːt əv ˈmʌni]	You have not enough money.	mit dem Geld knapp sein
(to) save money [seɪv ˈmʌni]	not to spend so much money	Geld sparen
piece of clothing [piːs əv ˈkləʊðɪŋ]	something you can wear	ein Stück Kleidung
(to) be lucky [bɪ ˈlʌki]	Lottery winners were lucky.	Glück haben
(to) be unemployed [bɪ ʌnɪmˈplɔɪd]	to have no job	arbeitslos sein
(to) have a bad conscience [hæv ə bæd ˈkɒnʃəns]	You feel bad because of this.	ein schlechtes Gewissen haben
(to) be divorced [bɪ dɪˈvɔːsd]	no longer married	geschieden sein
social allowance [ˈsəʊʃl əˈlaʊəns]	The money that poor people get from the government	Sozialfürsorge
old couple [əʊld ˈkʌpl]	an old man and woman	ein altes Paar
an odd job [ɒd dʒɒb]	a job you do for some hours, usually not regularly	Gelegenheitsarbeit
(to) do the garden [duː ðə ˈɡɑːdn]	to work in the garden	den Garten machen
in common [ɪn ˈkɒmən]	We have something in common!	gemeinsam

	2.2 Looking for an Odd Job	
(to) discuss [dɪˈskʌs]	to talk and share opinions with someone	diskutieren
fellow students [ˈfeləʊ ˈstjuːdntz]	your classmates	Mitschüler
(to) dig the weeds [dɪɡ ðə wiːdz]	to clean the garden and the lawn	Unkraut jäten
(to) mow the lawn [maʊ ðə lɔːn]	to cut the grass	Rasen mähen
boring [ˈbɔːrɪŋ]	dull, not interesting	langweilig
(to) breed kangaroos [briːd ˌkæŋɡəˈruː]	to raise kangaroos	Känguruhs züchten
household chores [ˈhaʊshəʊld tʃɔːs]	the work you do in a home	Hausarbeiten
(to) sound good [saʊnd ɡʊd]	Something seems to be good.	gut klingen
experience [ɪkˈspɪərɪəns]	You get it automatically when you do something.	Erfahrung
fair pay [feə peɪ]	enough money for your work	angemessene Bezahlung
clothes factory [kləʊðz ˈfæktəri]	a place where shirts and other pieces of clothing are made	Textilfabrik
(to) serve food [sɜːv fuːd]	to take the food to the guests	Essen servieren
waiter, waitress [weɪtə] [ˈweɪtrɪs]	people who work in a restaurant	Kellner, Kellnerin
team [tiːm]	a group of people working together	Mannschaft
(to) tidy up [ˈtaɪdi ʌp]	to clean everything and put things back where they belong	aufräumen
somewhere else [ˈsʌmweə els]	in another place	woanders
rubbish tip [ˈrʌbɪʃ tɪp]	place where all the dirt goes	Müllhalde

	2.3 Hi Jean – No Idea of Hygiene?	
every now and then [ˈevri naʊ ænd ðen]	from time to time	ab und zu
tray [treɪ]	a board on which you put the food	Tablett
Hell, no! [hel nəʊ]		Zur Hölle, nein!
hygienic hat [haɪˈdʒiːnɪk hæt]	a cloth to cover your hair	Kopftuch
hairy [ˈheəri]	full of hairs (auch: unpleasant)	haarig (auch: unangenehm)

Unit 3
Textiles

Why are these people wearing their specific clothing?

3.1   Laura and Mark are Buying a Pullover

"I'm Laura. I'm nineteen. I attend a vocational school for domestic science and I live with my mother. My parents are separated.

At the moment I'm on holiday, and I'm shopping at C & A. I'm looking for some bargains, because the sales are on.

Mark is with me. He is my boyfriend, and we're getting married next month. Mark is twenty–two. He is a social worker, that means he usually works in the evening. Mark helps students with their personal problems. At the moment he is in the men's wear department, because Mark is looking for a new pullover."

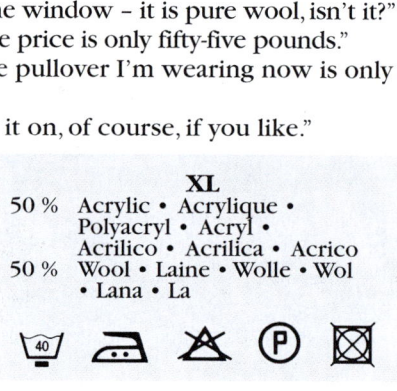

This large department store has got almost everything you need. Here you can buy sweaters, cardigans, blouses, skirts, coats, suits and many other things. Let's watch Mark and Laura:

Shop assistant: "Good morning, madam. Good morning, sir. Can I help you?"
Mark: "Good morning. That pullover you have in the window – it is pure wool, isn't it?"
Shop assistant: "No, it isn't. But it is very good quality, and the price is only fifty-five pounds."
Mark: "Well, it is size XXL – a little big, I think. The pullover I'm wearing now is only size XL. Have you got a smaller size?"
Shop assistant: "Yes, sir. Here you are – size XL. You can try it on, of course, if you like."
Mark: "Yes, thank you."
Laura: "May I see the care label, please? You know, Mark, your old pullover is too small now, because you probably washed it too hot."

      Laura looks at the label.

XL	
50 %	Acrylic • Acrylique • Polyacryl • Acryl • Acrilico • Acrilica • Acrico
50 %	Wool • Laine • Wolle • Wol • Lana • La

Laura: "Oh, dear! I don't understand all the signs on this label."
Shop assistant: "Well, may I explain it to you? On top of this label you see the size of the pullover – XL. Then you have the information for example what kind of material the pullover is made of. At the bottom there are five signs. The left sign tells you how to wash the pullover. The other signs give you information about the ironing, the bleaching, the dry-cleaning and the drying."
Mark: "Laura, do you think that I can wash this pullover properly in our washing machine?"
Laura: "Yes, I think so."
Mark: "Alright. I will buy this pullover."
Shop assistant: "Fine. Anything else?"
Mark: "No, thank you, that is all."

      Mark writes out a cheque for sixty pounds and gives it to the shop assistant.

Shop assistant: "Here is your change – five pounds. Shall I wrap the pullover up for you?"
Mark: "No, thanks. I'll put it into this bag with the other clothes I have bought."

A   Read the text and the dialogue and answer these questions.
1. When are Mark and Laura getting married?
2. What is Mark's profession?
3. Why are Mark and Laura in the department store?
4. How does Mark pay for the new pullover?

B Do you know the names of these clothes? Look at the pictures and match the numbers of the items with the words in the box.

belt – blouse – bra – dress – hat – jacket – pants – scarf – shirt – shorts – skirt – socks – tie – trousers – T-shirt

C Mark and Laura are leaving the department store. At the exit they meet Mr Kelly. He is working for a market research institute.
Read the following survey and complete the sentences. Use the words in the box.

symbols on the labels – a pullover – twenty–two – nineteen – social worker – blouses – skirts – coats – suits – in the evenings – domestic science

Mr Kelly: "Excuse me, please. I'm interviewing the customers to get more information for the management of this department store. May I ask you a few questions?"
Mark and Laura agree.

Mr Kelly: "What did you buy?"
Mark: "I bought ... ."
Mr Kelly: "How old are you?"
Mark: "I'm ... ."
Laura: "I'm ... ."
Mr Kelly: "Do you remember what items you can buy in this store?"
Mark: "You can buy ... ."
Mr Kelly: "What do you think about the information you get in this department store?"
Laura: "The shop assistant in the men's wear department knows a lot about the ... ."
Mr Kelly "Good. It's three o'clock in the afternoon - you are not working. May I ask for the reason?"
Laura: "I'm on holiday."
Mark: "I'm a ... . I work ... ."
Mr Kelly: "Now I understand that you are relaxing at this time of the day. Thank you very much for the interview!"

 How about a role play? Form groups. One of you could be the interviewer, and the others are the customers. You can ask each other different questions on textiles and shopping. On page 133 there is more information about role plays.

Present Progressive or Simple Present?

When do you use present progressive and when do you use simple present?
The progressive form of the present tense is used to express an activity which is happening *at the time of speaking*.

> • **Signal words:** at the moment – now – today – just – these days – Look!

The simple form of the present tense is used to express what *always* occurs or to express what happens *again and again*.

> • **Signal words:** always – never – normally – regularly – sometimes – usually – every day – every month – every year – on Saturdays/on Sundays/on …

Put the verb in brackets in the *present progressive* or the simple present.

▸ For rules see page 153

Examples:
At the moment I (look) for some bargains.
– At the moment **I'm looking** for some bargains.

Mark usually (work) in the evening.
– Mark usually **works** in the evening.

1. At the moment I (shop) in a department store.
2. Mark (help) students with their personal problems.
3. The pullover I (wear) now is only size L.
4. The signs on the label (give) you some information about the cleaning and the drying of the pullover.
5. Look! Mark and Laura (leave) the department store.
6. Mr Kelly, what are you doing this afternoon? – I (interview) the customers.
7. Laura (have) a shower every morning.
8. Mark: "I (work) every day from 4 o'clock in the afternoon to 10:30 p. m."

3.2   Care Labels

Look at Mr Brown in this picture. Why is he unhappy?

It may be that Mr Brown doesn't know enough about washing. Washing is a very complicated business because of many improvements in fabrics, washing machines and washing powders.

To give more information about the necessary care of clothes most textile articles have a care label. It contains instructions about the right care of a textile. It is very useful, but only when you are able to understand the instructions. Otherwise you may be as unhappy as Mr Brown.

Mark and Laura are studying a care label:

Mark: "Laura, I'm going to wash the pullover that I bought at C & A. But I don't understand every symbol on the care label. Can you help me, please?"

Laura: "Of course. Which symbols do you mean?"

Mark: "Well, I understand the first instruction – it informs about the size of the pullover. The XL means EXTRA LARGE. The next information is quite clear as well – the pullover is made of acrylic and wool. But I don't understand the tub with the broken bar underneath it."

Laura: "Oh, you always leave the difficult questions for me to answer! I know that the number inside the wash tub stands for the temperature of the washing water. And the bar underneath the tub means, … let me think, oh yes: The machine action should be reduced when you wash this pullover."

Mark: "I think I understand the next symbol. It has something to do with ironing."

Laura: "That's right. An iron with two dots means 'warm' and an iron with three dots means 'hot'. But I don't know the next symbol. I'll look it up in my book about domestic science. Wait a minute. … There it is: 'Do not use chlorine bleach.'"

Mark: "The next symbol looks funny. Let me look in your book, please: The 'P' means that the pullover may be dry cleaned. The 'P' stands for the solvent[1], which is used by the drycleaner."

Laura: "I know the last symbol: 'The pullover may not be tumble dried.'"

Mark: "That's not a problem for me, because I don't have a tumble dryer."

A Look at the symbols on the right – something is wrong with the descriptions. In two cases the meaning of the care label does not match the symbol. Can you find them?

1	⊠	a Do not tumble dry
2	Ⓟ	b Use a warm iron
3	95	c Do not use chlorine bleach
4	△	d Maximum temperature of the washing water 95 °C
5	iron	e May be dry-cleaned

---
[1] Perclorethylene

29

B Laura and Mark do the housework in their apartment.
Here is what they usually do, but right now they are doing something else. Put the words
in brackets into the *simple present* or the *present progressive*.

Example:
Mark usually (hang) up the laundry, but at the moment he (iron) a shirt.
*- Mark usually **hangs** up the laundry, but at the moment he **is ironing** a shirt.*

1. Laura mostly (wash) the clothes, but at the moment she (tidy) the wardrobe.
2. Mark normally (hoover) the carpets, but now he (empty) the dustbin.
3. Laura (unload) the dishwasher every day, but today she (water) the flowers.
4. Mark usually (clean) the bathroom, but just now he (sweep) the kitchen.

C Which part of the housework do members of your family regularly do? Tell the class what
the other members and you yourself usually do. Form sentences like this:

Examples:
My mother normally prepares the meals.
On Sunday my father makes the beds.

The Present Progressive Is Used for the Future

There is another case where you can use the present progressive: It is also used for the *future*
and for expressing *plans*.

Examples:
Laura: *Mark and I **are getting** married next month.* → They have agreed to marry next
month. It is going to happen in the future.

Mr Brown: *I**'m going** to learn more about washing.* → It is Mr Brown's plan.

A The following sentences tell you something about the future or about certain plans. Put
the words in brackets into the *present progressive* tense or use *going to*.

Examples:
Laura asks Mark: "What you (do) on Monday evening?"
Mark: "I (work). I'm on duty."
*- "What **are** you **doing** on Monday evening?"*
*"**I'm working** I'm on duty."*

Jim: "There's a football match tomorrow, but I (not go). I (meet) Laura and Mark."
*- "There's a football match tomorrow but **I'm not going** I'm meeting Laura and Mark."*

1. Mark:"My parents (go) on holiday next week. They have already booked the flight."
2. Laura:"Oh, that's nice. Where they (go)? What are their plans?"
3. Gina asks Fiona:"I (go) out with some friends tonight. Why don't you come too? We (meet) at Mark's house at 8 o'clock. That's what Mark suggested."
4. Mark asks Laura:"How you (get) home after the party tomorrow? By taxi?"
5. Laura:"No, I can go by bus."
6. Gina and Jim (have) supper with Ken and Fiona on Friday. They have invited them.
7. Mr Brown (buy) a new washing machine. It is his plan.

B What are you doing in the next few days? Form questions and answers. Don't forget to use the *present progressive*.

Example:
Question:"What are you doing tonight"?
Answer:"I/stay/at home."
If you plan to stay at home, you may say:
*"**I'm staying** at home tonight."*

Question: What are you doing on …
(Monday, Tuesday, etc.)?
Answers: 1. I/go/to a disco
2. I/play/football
3. …

3.3 Mr Brown – The Washing Expert

Laura: "Mr Brown, everybody knows that clean, well-cared for clothes look better and last longer. You know a lot about the care of clothes. May I ask you for some guidelines about washing?"

Mr Brown: "Stained or dirty clothes should be cleaned as soon as possible. Most clothes can be washed in **automatic** washing machines.
Before you wash the clothes you should check whether there are **stains** on them. Sometimes it is advisable to **soak** the clothes in soapy water before you wash them. If you want to wash silk which needs a gentle handling, a **handwash** may be the right method.
The washing powder normally contains **perfume** and sometimes **bleach**. In case you want the clothes very soft, you may finish the washing by using a fabric **conditioner**."

Test your knowledge about washing. What are the right answers to the following questions? You may use the underlined words in Mr Browns guidelines on page 31.
In case you don't know the answer, the number in the brackets may be of some help.

Example:
What kind of washing-machines can most clothes be washed in? (9)
*– Most clothes can be washed in **automatic** washing machines. (The word "automatic" has nine letters.)*

1. What is added to washing powder to make it smell nice? (7)
2. What do you call dirty marks on clothes? (6)
3. What is a wash without using a machine? (8)
4. What is added to washing powder to make clothes whiter? (6)
5. What kind of textile needs a gentle wash? (4)
6. What do you do when you leave clothes in soapy water? (4)
7. What do you use when you want clothes to be very soft? (11)

3.4   Protect the Environment

Here are five rules how to save money and protect the environment:

1 Read the amount of washing powder needed for washing which is printed on the packing.
In order to decide the correct quantity, you have to know two things:
- the degree of hardness of the water and
- how dirty your laundry is.
You can get information about the degree of hardness of the water from your local waterworks. Soft water may need less washing powder. If the clothes are not very dirty, you may use less water.

2 Always make full use of your washing machine.
Otherwise it means waste of water, waste of energy, and waste of washing powder. This is true even for an economy programme.

3 Wash without prewash.
You can clean normal dirty laundry without prewash. The main wash course then needs only 75 to 80 percent of the washing powder which is necessary for both washing programs!

4 Wash without fabric conditioner!
The fabric conditioner lowers the absorbency of textiles and can eventually cause skin problems.

5 Wash your boiling laundry with the 60 °C wash programme.
By doing so you save 40 percent energy in comparison to the 95 °C wash programme!
A hygienic clean washing is still ensured. Only in special cases (for example with clothes of ill people or baby laundry) a 95 °C wash programme is necessary.

One way to check all the things you learned about textiles is to prepare a quiz with your classmates. On page 141 you will find information about "Preparing a Quiz". Ask your teacher.

3.5   Mark and Laura and the Five 'Green Guidelines'

Mark: "Mr Brown told me that it is important to know the degree of … of the water and how dirty the laundry is."

Laura: "Well, it's easy to see how dirty the laundry is. But what about the degree of hardness of the water?"

Mark: "That is easy to find out. You can ring the … and they will tell you."

Laura: "I think we use quite a lot of water for washing. Is there a possibility to reduce the amount of water?"

Mark: "Mr Brown told me that we should always make … of our washing machine."

Laura: "Well, that is a silly 'guideline'. Everybody knows that!"

Mark: "That's right. But he advised as well to clean normal dirty … without prewash."

Laura: "That's a good idea, if the clothes become really clean. How much washing powder can you save?"

Mark: "About … to … %. By the way, if you wash without … you save money and you protect your health because –"

Laura: "I know, Mark, because fabric conditioners eventually cause … . Well, I see that most things Mr Brown told you are known by everybody. I guess he also told you something about saving … by using the 60 °C washing programme."

Mark: "Well, if you know everything anyway, I won't talk to you about this anymore."

Laura: "You don't have to. Let me put it like this: When you save your money, you protect the … at the same time."

A Fill in the gaps in the dialogue with the correct vocabulary. Use the guidelines and rules on the pages 31 and 32 for help.

Look at the packet label in the picture on the left.

B This packet contains 1.05 kg washing powder, and it costs 108 p. Calculate – how much money does a kilo of this washing powder cost in euros?

C Compare the price of this washing powder with the price of other washing powders. What do you find out?

D Try to find a washing powder which is less harmful for the environment. Are you successful?

On TV you can see a lot of commercials for washing powder – but can you believe all the information they tell you? If you want to learn more about 'reading' an advertisement or a commercial correctly, look on page 139. It will offer you some exercises on that.

Vocabulary

3.1 Laura and Mark Are Buying a Pullover		
(to) separate ['sepəreɪt]	when married people stop living together	sich trennen, scheiden
bargain ['bɑːgɪn]	something that costs much less than usual	Gelegenheitskauf
sales [seɪlz]	when things are sold at low prices	Schlussverkauf
sweater ['swetə]	a woollen piece of clothing worn on the top half of the body	Pullover
cardigan ['kɑːdɪgən]	a woollen piece of clothing worn on the top half of the body with buttons	Strickjacke
suit [suːt]	a jacket and trousers worn together	Anzug
(to) care [keə] for	to look after	pflegen
(to) iron ['aɪən]	to press clothes flat	bügeln
(to) bleach [bliːtʃ]	to make something white	bleichen
change [tʃeɪndʒ]	any money you get back after you pay for something	Wechselgeld
(to) wrap [ræp]	to put package around something	einpacken
survey [sə'veɪ]	a study of something	Untersuchung, Umfrage
(to) employ [ɪm'plɔɪ]	to pay someone to work for you	beschäftigen
customer ['kʌstəmə]	someone who buys something in a shop	Kunde
(to) agree [ə'griː]	to think the same as someone else	(jemandem) zustimmen
an item ['aɪtəm]	any one thing on a list	Sache, Gegenstand
reason ['riːzn]	anything that explains why something has happened	Grund, Ursache
rule [ruːl]	something that everyone must do; rules have to be followed	Regel

3.2 Care Labels		
an improvement [ɪm'pruːvmənt]	much better than it was	Verbesserung
fabric ['fæbrɪk]	material or cloth	Gewebe
(to) contain [kən'teɪn]	to have something inside	enthalten, aufweisen
tub [tʌb]	a container, for example for water	Wanne
bar [bɑː]	a thick short line	Strich, Balken
(to) reduce [rɪ'djuːs]	to lower or to make small or less	reduzieren
chlorine ['klɔːriːn]	a certain gas	Chlor, auch: chlorhaltig
(to) dry-clean [draɪ kliːn]	to clean clothes with solvent	chemisch reinigen
solvent [sɒlvənt]	a liquid that dissolves	Lösungsmittel
tumble dryer (also: tumble drier) ['tʌmbl 'draɪə]	a machine that dries clothes	Wäschetrockner
laundry ['lɔːndrɪ]	dirty clothes that need to be washed	(Schmutz-) Wäsche
wardrobe ['wɔːdrəʊb]	a tall cupboard in which you keep your clothes	Kleiderschrank

3.3 Mr Brown – The Washing Expert		
guideline [gaɪd laɪn]	information to help you do something	Richtlinie
stain [steɪn]	a dirty mark	Fleck
(to) soak [səʊk]	to leave something in water	einweichen
gentle ['dʒentl]	mild, soft	sanft
(to) handle something ['hændl]	to treat something	behandeln
fabric conditioner ['fæbrɪk kən'dɪʃnə]	liquid used to make clothes soft	Weichspülmittel

3.4 Protect the Environment!		
(to) protect [prə'tekt]	to look after	schützen
environment [ɪn'vaɪərənmənt]	everything around you	Umwelt
degree [dɪ'griː]	the amount of something	Grad
waste [weɪst]	to use more of something than is needed	Verschwendung
prewash [priːwɒʃ]	a wash done before the main wash	Vorwäsche
(to) lower ['ləʊə]	here: to make something smaller	hier: herabsetzen, verringern
absorbency [əb'sɔːbənsɪ]	how much liquid something can hold	Aufnahmefähigkeit

3.5 Mark and Laura and the Five 'Green Guidelines'		
(to) cause [kɔːz]	to make something happen	verursachen
(to) ensure [ɪn'ʃʊə]	to make certain	sichern
harmful [hɑːmfʊl]	not good for you	schädlich

Revision I (Units 1 – 3)

Are College Students Working Too Hard?

More and more older school students are working part time for extra pocket money. They work many hours and have no time for homework. So their tests are often very poor and they do not pass their exams.

Why do they work in part-time jobs? Well, young people want to buy smart clothes, they want to go on holidays, and the cinema and the disco cost money, too. It is also very expensive when they learn how to drive a car. Many students do not get enough pocket money from their parents, so they cannot pay for everything they want. For many teenagers a part-time job is the answer to their money problem.

And there is a lot of part-time work for teenagers in Britain today. Shops and restaurants are open longer now. Many places are also open on Sundays. So a lot of older students earn extra money after school and at weekends. They help in supermarkets, or they work at fast-food restaurants. Others do jobs like baby-sitting, or they deliver newspapers.

In 1988 50 per cent had part-time jobs. This number is getting bigger and bigger. A newer survey shows that 70 per cent of older students work, and some schools say that as many as 90 per cent of their students earn money after school.

Most teachers believe that it is okay if their students do a few hours of work a week. They say that it is quite good if their students learn how much they must work to earn a little money. If students work too much besides school, however, they often get bad marks at school.

Helen Penny, the head teacher of a girls' school in Brentwood, Essex, reports: "Some girls fall asleep at their desks because they're so tired." So these students have problems with their school tests, and if their certificates are not so good they can only get those jobs which others do not want.

Helen Penny's school has already got one unfortunate example. One talented girl says: "At the moment I am doing two jobs besides school. I am getting bad marks now, but I do not have enough time for studying, and when I come home I am often too tired for learning."

Another good student is also risking her chances. She works between 10 and 15 hours in a fast-food restaurant for £3.30 an hour. "I really only want to work at the weekend, but then the boss rings up and tells me that someone is lying in bed because she is ill. He says he needs my help. It is so hard to say 'no' then," she says. "It's hot in the kitchen and pretty hard work," she goes on. "We often have no break because there is so much work. When I get home at 10 p.m., I am very tired and want to sleep. I cannot do my homework when I am tired. I know I am risking my future, but what can I do? Life is so expensive!"

Now teachers are publishing a leaflet for students. They say that you must learn to wait if you want to make big money – and the key to your future wealth is good exams. So do not sacrifice your future in order to enjoy the present!

(based on: Read On)

A Answer these questions on the text.
1. Why do so many older students look for part-time jobs in their free time? Name some reasons.
2. How are the chances to find a part-time job in Britain today? Have they become better or worse?
3. Try to find facts from the text which support your answer to question 2.
4. Besides the money, why can a few hours of work per week be quite good for a student?
5. What can happen if students work too much besides school?
6. Why is it so hard for many students to say 'no' when their boss asks them to work more? (afraid of losing … job?, temptation of getting some extra money?)
7. What is really important for you if you want to earn enough money when you are older?

B Read the following definitions and find the matching words in the text.
(In the brackets you can find the number of the letters the word has/the words have. 'A' counts as one letter.)

1. A job for a few hours is a … job (9)
2. The teacher writes this under your test to show you how good or how bad your test was (4)
3. The regular money parents give their children (11)
4. Someone between 13 and 19 (8)
5. You look after small children while the parents are out (11)
6. It's a period of time which has sixty minutes. (4)
7. Not cheap (9)
8. To give away something because you want something which is more attractive to you at the moment (9)

C Now it's your turn. Try to explain the following words in English.

1. money
2. restaurant
3. pound
4. exams
5. tired
6. day
7. future

D Prepositions –
Fill in the right prepositions. Read the text again; this will help you to find the right preposition.

Well, with money you can…

Example: Many students are working … extra pocket money.
*– Many students are working **for** extra pocket money.*

1. Many young people want to go … the cinema.
2. Some kids say they do not get enough pocket money … their parents.
3. You can for example work … the afternoon.
4. Some college students just work … weekends.
5. At the moment, my friend is only working …Sundays.

> Remember: You work … a period of time, … a point of time and … a certain day!

E Pronouns – Fill in the right pronoun for the underlined word. Watch out, they can be in the subject case (e.g. *I,*) or in the object case (e.g. *me*), or in the possessive case (e.g. *my*).

*Example: Tom says: "**Tom** earns **Tom's** money by delivering newspapers. This brings **Tom** £10 a week."*
*– Tom says: "**I** earn my money by delivering newspapers. This brings **me** £10 a week."*

1. Teachers are worried that the teachers' students get bad marks in the students' exams.
2. Sheila is a girl who works in a fast food restaurant. Sheila's pay is not really good. Shcila's pay is just £1.50 an hour.
3. Maggy, another college student, says: "At the moment Maggy is doing two jobs besides school. Maggy's time for learning is simply too short. Something tells Maggy that it can't go on like this."
4. Two other girls, Cathleen and Jackie, say: "Cathleen and Jackie often have no break. Cathleen's and Jackie's boss shouts at Cathleen and Jackie that we must never stand around and do nothing."

F Simple Present or Present Progressive? Read the following text and fill in *present simple* or *present progressive*. Look for signal words.

> Remember: If you **smoke**, that's a (bad) habit which you often do.
> If you say, "I **am smoking**," you have a cigarette in your hand and inhale that dangerous stuff right now.

At the moment, many students (*work*) [1] part time. They (*work, usually*) [2] in fast-food restaurants or (*fill*) [3] shelves in supermarkets. What (*today's kids, do*) [4] with this extra money? In an interview a boy says, "I (*take*) [5] my driving test next week. This is why I (*work*) [6] every Monday and every Friday." A teacher says: "Sometimes, the part-time workers (*not have*) [7] enough time for doing their homework. When they (*work*) [8] in the night, they often (*fall*) [9] asleep in the lessons. Just look at that boy there in the back. He (*sleep*) [10] with open eyes." He calls the boy: "Hey, Chas, (*you, dream*) [11] again?"

Unit 4
Emotions

Make love – not war
(Hippies, 1968)

All you need is love
(Beatles)

Diamonds are a girl's best friend
(MARILYN MONROE)

The first cut is the deepest
(Ike & Tina Turner)

Love fool
(Cardigans)

You're not alone
(Michael Jackson)

How deep is your love?
(Take That)

A Which of these expressions do you like best?

B Do you know other songs or sayings about love? Which ones?

4.1 A Night at the Disco

A Combine the pictures with the texts. Start like this:
Picture A belongs to text number four.

1 Mary is in love with John. They have known each other for three months now.

2 John is an attractive, tall guy with brown eyes and blond hair. Mary has got blue eyes and is a bit overweight.

3 They usually meet each other at the ice café in the city once or twice a week.

4 Mary goes to a vocational school, and John has got a job as a carpenter.

5 They always go to a disco together at the weekends.

6 The last time they went to the disco, Mary brought her classmate Cathy with her.

7 Cathy looked good, and she danced perfectly.

8 John only had eyes for Cathy, and he danced with her all night long. He didn't care about Mary anymore.

9 Mary was very disappointed. When she arrived at her mother's house that night, she cried.

B Look at the pictures and repeat the story of Mary, John and Cathy.

C Has anything like that ever happened to you or to a friend of yours?

4.2   The Night after the Disco

Mary was still very upset. She hated John and Cathy for what had happened. She simply hated everybody.

She and John had such a good time with each other. They had so much fun. She loved him so much and he meant everything to her. All the kisses he had given her and all the promises he had made!

She could not wait to see him last night but then he only had eyes for Cathy. Nobody seemed to love her. John didn't, Cathy didn't, and her Mum was always working. Mary hadn't seen her Dad for ages. Her parents got divorced when she was eight years old.

She finally got up and went to school with hanging shoulders and full of sorrow. Her eyes were still red from all the crying in the night. She didn't know what to do. Life seemed to be so senseless without John. "John", she sighed, "oh, John."

A   Read the two texts. Which of these answers is correct – **A**, **B** or **C**?

1. Mary and John went to the disco
    A once a month.   **B** at the weekends.   **C** on Wednesdays and Saturdays.

2. They used to meet each other
    A in the park.   **B** at the bus station.   **C** in an ice café.

3. Mary
    A has got normal weight. **B** is underweight.   **C** is a bit overweight.

4. John
    A goes to school.   **B** works as a carpenter.   **C** has got no job.

5. Mary has got
    A brown eyes.   **B** blue eyes.   **C** green eyes.

6. Mary's parents
    A got divorced.   **B** married eight years ago. **C** were never married.

7. Mary lives
    A in her father's house. **B** on her own.   **C** together with her mother.

8. Cathy
    A works in a restaurant. **B** doesn't go to school.   **C** is in the same class as Mary.

You have a lot of ideas about the theme 'love'? You could create a mind map to collect them all. For help on creating a mind map, see page 136.

B   Find the right word in the texts.
If you need help – the numbers in brackets tell you how many letters the word has.
1. A place where many young people go to on Friday or Saturday night is a … (5)
2. People who are not married any longer are … (8)
3. When somebody hurts your feelings you are very … (12)
4. The opposite of hatred is … (4)
5. A person who makes wooden objects is a … (9)
6. A good-looking person is very … (10)

C   Start a discussion in class and talk about these aspects:
1. Which disco do you like to go to and why? Give reasons.
2. What do you think Mary should do – should she forget John or should she fight for her love?
3. What is the opinion of your classmates?

D   Activity – Probably not all of you are allowed to go to a disco at night.
Imagine that you desperately want to go to a disco next Saturday and your parents are against it.

Form two teams. One team has to find arguments you might have and the other team has to find arguments *your parents* might use.
Start with arguments from the list below.

In Favour of (Pro)	Against (Contra)
- all friends go	- too expensive
- help in the household	- too young
- late night bus	- no transport

You can find more information about discussions on page 140.

If you want to, you could play this situation in a role play. Do you want to know how to do that? Look on page 133 for details.

Simple Past

Statement Clause			
I You He She It We You They	walk**ed**	to the disco	last night.

Negative Clause			
I You He She It We You They	**didn't walk** **(did not walk)**	to the disco	last night.

Questions				
Why When How	**did**	I you he she it we you they	**walk** to the disco	last night?

How do you form the simple past?

● When you have *regular verbs* you add either *-d* or *-ed* to the verb.
love → love**d**
walk → walk**ed**

● When you have *irregular verbs* you use *the second form* of the verb.
go → **went**
see → **saw**

→ There is a list of the irregular verbs on page 151/152

● You form negative sentences with *didn't (or did not) + the infinitive*

didn't go
didn't see

● You form questions with *did or didn't + the infinitive*

Did you **go** there?
Didn't you **see** me?

● You can also form questions with a *question word + did* or *didn't + infinitive*

Why did you **go** there?

When do you use the simple past?
You use the simple past when something is *definitely over*.
Signal words: Last month – last year – yesterday – two weeks ago – in 2005 – …

A You already know some signal words which tell you that you have to use the simple past. Can you think of some more signal words? Try to find ten others for this tense.

B Combine the words from the box and form sentences.
Start like this:
She played in the garden an hour ago.
How many sentences can you find?

→ For rules see page154

I	**played**	the train	yesterday.
You	ran	home	last month.
He/**She**/It	missed	**in the garden**	**an hour ago.**
We	went	to the bus	last night.
You	came	here	in May 2004.
They	came	home at 4 o'clock	two days ago.

C   Put the verbs from the box below into the *simple past*. Then look at the statement clauses and find the correct place for the verb in the sentences.
Do the same with the negative clauses.

love – like – dance – get divorced – find – look – think – meet – be	not look – not believe – not like – not care – not want – not want – not sleep – not love

Statement Clauses

1. Mary … John, and … Cathy very much.
2. They … each other once a week when they were friends.
3. During the night at the disco John … with Cathy all the time.
4. He only … at Cathy, and Mary stood aside.
5. She … very disappointed.
6. Her parents … some time ago.
7. Mary … a lot about her problems.
8. She … another girlfriend.

Negative Clauses

9. Mary … John, and … Cathy anymore.
10. John … at her during the whole night.
11. She … in love anymore.
12. Her father … for Mary either.
13. The night after the disco she … well.
14. She … to go to school the next day.
15. She promised herself that she …. to give up hope.

D   Mary's new friend Sheila had a date with a nice young guy last weekend. When the girls met at school on Monday morning, Mary was very curious and asked Sheila a lot of questions.
Form questions which Mary might have asked. Use the *simple past*.

… he come in time?

What …

Where …

When …

…

Yes, he was in time.

He wore a green shirt and black trousers.

We went to a disco downtown.

I came home at 11 p.m.

Yes, I really enjoyed it.

4.3   What Happened to Mary?

Let us have a look at Mary's situation again. She is still sad but she also knows that life goes on. In the first days she always compared herself to Cathy. Was Cathy better than she was? Was Cathy prettier?
Yes, Cathy was prettier. But was Cathy also better? Last year Cathy was as good at school as she was, but this year Mary seems to be better. Cathy's marks in maths and religion were worse than hers, but Cathy was the best of her class in sports.

Mary decided to forget John - he just didn't deserve her. He was the worst guy she had ever looked at.
In the meantime she has found a new friend, who is as nice as Cathy was when they were friends. The new girl is fairer to Mary. What about the boys? Well, at the moment Mary is not interested in a new relationship.

Comparison I

Sentences with Comparison

● When we compare things which are the same we can use **as … as ….** with an adjective.

Example: *I'm* <u>as</u> *tall* <u>as</u> *my mother.*

● In negative sentences we can use **not as … as …** with an adjective.

Example: *I'm* <u>not as</u> *good at school* <u>as</u> *my brother.*

A   Now it's your turn. Choose eight words from the box below and form sentences like this one:
I'm as tall as Georg, but I'm not as tall as Phillip.

> tall – loud – quiet – nice – old – good – happy – rich –young – thirsty – brave – bad

→ For rules see pages 158/159

The Comparison of Adjectives

● You compare adjectives with one syllable and adjectives with two syllables and **-y,-er, -le, -ure** or **-ow** at the end like this:

clean	clean**er**	(the) clean**est**	One syllable
hot	hot**ter**	(the) hot**test**	
lucky	luck**ier**	(the) luck**iest**	Two syllables and -y at the end

B   Write down the comparison of the following adjectives.

> simple – clever – silly – narrow – happy – gentle – cheap – tidy – secure

Be careful! There is always an exception to every rule:
Good and *bad* have also got only one syllable. However, here you say:

good	better	(the) best
bad	worse	(the) worst

There are some more exceptions:

much, many	more	(the) most
little	less	(the) least
far	further	(the) furthest

C   Make a list of all the adjectives you find in the text "What Happened to Mary?" and compare them.

Example:
sad *(in the text)*	sadder	*(the) saddest*
good	**better** *(in the text)*	*(the) best*

D   Do the same with the adjectives in the box of exercise A – compare them.

4.4   Old Enough to Have a Baby?

Karen, Lisa and Hannah are very good friends. One weekend they had a pyjama party. The party was at Lisa's house because her parents went on a trip to London.

Their party started at 8 p.m. and they ate pizzas and drank coke. After the dinner they sat down in Lisa's bedroom with plenty of crisps and talked about their boyfriends.

Karen: "Lisa, how long have you been going out with Bob now?"

Lisa: "It's five months next Friday."

Karen: "What about you, Hannah, how long have you and Tim been going out now?"

Hannah: "For half a year now. What about you and Ray, Karen?"

Karen: "I broke up with Ray yesterday after three months."

Hannah: "Oh, no!! Why did you do that?"

Karen: "He didn't stop asking me to sleep with him – and I think I'm too young to have sex. I told him that I don't want to take the pill but that I don't want to become pregnant."

Lisa: "I had the same problem with Bob but we talked about it. Now we want to wait until it is the right time for both of us."

Hannah: "How do you plan to avoid pregnancy in the future?"

Lisa: "As I've told you, I don't want to take the pill. So we bought condoms."

Karen: "But – how safe are they? And I have no idea how to use them."

Hannah: "Are you kidding?"

Karen: "Sorry, but at home we don't talk about those things."

Lisa: "Ok, wait a minute – I'll go and get one for you out of my handbag. It is very important not to put it into your purse because it might get damaged there."

Lisa walks down the stairs to get her handbag and comes back.

A   Read the dialogue between the three girls. Are these statements right or wrong?

1.   The pyjama party is at Karen's house
2.   Lisa sleeps with Bob.
3.   A condom is made out of thick rubber.
4.   Karen doesn't know how to use a condom.
5.   Lisa wants to become pregnant.
6.   A condom is usually very dry.

B   There are more ways to avoid pregnancy than condoms. Here are some of them. Combine the pictures with the words in the box.

1

Lisa: "Here is one. You can open the package if you want to."
Karen: "Alright, I want to know what they – what they look like."
Hannah: "Be careful, don't damage it with your fingernails. A condom is made of thin rubber."

Karen opens the package and takes out the condom very carefully.

Karen: "It feels very funny. It's slippery."
Lisa: "Yes, that's true. It will give you an almost natural feeling."
Hannah: "I heard that a condom is also very useful to protect you from veneral diseases as
          from the AIDS-virus, right?"

At the age of 16
45 % female and
36 % male teenagers
have had sexual
experiences. Most of
them didn't plan to
have it.

C Make a list and write down everything
you know about contraception.

D Have a discussion in your class about
these topics:
1. Do you think it was right that Karen
broke up with Ray?
2. Look at the newspaper article above. Do
you think that people should wait longer?
Give reasons.
3. At what age are people old enough to
have a baby?

E Activity – Go to a gynaecologist or to 'Pro
Famila' with the class. There you could
have an interview and ask for more
information on contraception.

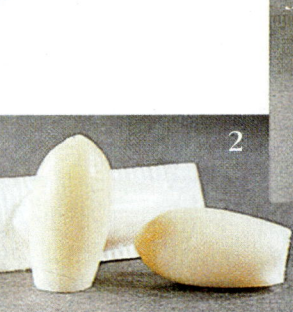

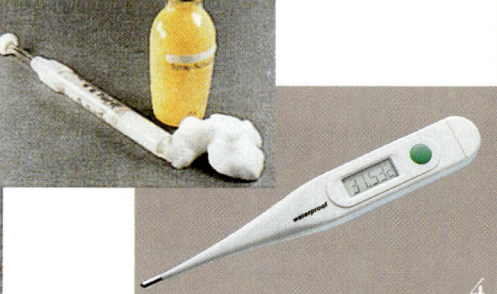

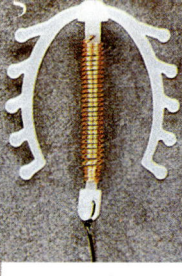

foam – suppository – pessary –
spiral – control of temperature –
pill

45

Vocabulary

cut [kʌt]	something you can do with a knife	Einschnitt, Schnitt
fool [fuːl]	someone who is stupid	Dummkopf
4.1 A Night at the Disco		
(to) be overweight [bɪ ˈəʊvəweɪt]	to weigh more than normal	übergewichtig sein
once [wʌns]	one time	einmal
twice [twaɪs]	two times	zweimal
vocational school [vəʊˈkeɪʃənl skuːl]	a school where your are trained for a job	berufsbildende Schule
carpenter [ˈkɑːpəntə]	someone who works with wood	Zimmermann
classmate [klɑːs meɪt]	a pupil who goes in the same class as you	Klassenkamerad
not to care about [nɒt tu keə əˈbaʊt]	to ignore	sich nicht kümmern um
(to) be disappointed [bɪ ˌdɪsəˈpɔɪntɪd]	not be able to fulfill hopes	enttäuscht sein
4.2 The Night after the Disco		
(to) be upset [bɪ ʌpset]	to be angry and disappointed	bestürzt sein
(to) make a promise [meɪk ə ˈprɒmɪs]	to say that something will be done	ein Versprechen machen
for ages [fɔː eɪdʒɪz]	since a long time	seit Ewigkeiten
(to) get a divorce [get ə dɪˈvɔːs]	to end a marriage	sich scheiden lassen
finally [ˈfaɪnəlɪ]	at last	schließlich, endlich
sorrow [ˈsɒrəʊ]	unhappiness, sadness	Traurigkeit
senseless [senslɪs]	without sense, without meaning	sinnlos
(to) sigh [saɪ]		seufzen
probably [ˈprɒbəblɪ]	almost sure	wahrscheinlich
definitely [ˈdefɪnɪtlɪ]	without doubt, clearly	ganz bestimmt
gap [gæp]	an empty space	Lücke
(to) be curious [bɪ ˈkjʊərɪəs]	to want to know everything	neugierig sein
4.3 What Happened to Mary?		
maths [mæθs]	a subject in school	Mathematik
(to) deserve something/someone [dɪˈzɜːv]		jemand oder etwas verdienen
brave [breɪv]	a brave soldier	tapfer (nicht: brav)
narrow [ˈnærəʊ]	a small street is very narrow	eng
secure [sɪˈkjʊə]	safe	sicher
4.4 Old Enough to Have a Baby?		
plenty of [ˈplentɪ əv]	enough	genügend viele
(to) break up with someone [breɪk ʌp wɪð]	to end a relationship	Freundschaft beenden
not to stop asking [nɒt tu stɒp ɑːskɪŋ]	to ask again and again	immer wieder fragen
(to) be pregnant [bɪ ˈpregnənt]	to carry an unborn child in the body	schwanger sein
(to) avoid [əˈvɔɪd]	to make sure something does not happen	verhindern
pregnancy [ˈpregnənsɪ]	the state of being an expectant mother	Schwangerschaft
Are you kidding? [ɑː juː kɪdɪŋ]	Are you making a joke?	Machst du dich lustig? Machst du Scherze?
purse [pɜːs]	a small bag to carry money	Portemonnaie
contraceptives [ˌkɒntrəˈseptɪv]	you use them to avoid to become pregnant	Empfängnisverhütungsmittel
(to) damage something [ˈdæmɪdʒ]	the hurricane damaged the houses	etwas beschädigen
fingernail [ˈfɪŋgə neɪl]		Fingernagel
rubber [ˈrʌbə]	to keep safe	Gummi
slippery [ˈslɪpərɪ]	something that slips out of your hand easily	rutschig, glatt
veneral disease [vəˈnɪərɪəl dɪˈziːz]	an illness because of sexual activity	Geschlechtskrankheit
foam [fəʊm]	a form of contraception	Schaum (Spermizid)
suppository [səˈpɒzɪtərɪ]	a form of contraception	Zäpfchen (Spermizid)
pessary [pesərɪ]	a form of contraception	Pessar/Diaphragma
control of temperature [kənˈtrəʊl ɒv ˈtemprətʃə]	a form of contraception	Temperaturmethode
pill [pɪl]	a form of contraception	(Anti-Baby-) Pille

Unit 5
Trouble on the Job

The Majestic Hotel

is looking for an
ambitious young man
to help in our hotel kitchen.
Send applications to

The Majestic Hotel
7 Ipswich Road
Bristol

Whew... sixty applications... that's too much!!!

Dear Sirs, m-y n-a-m-e

Dear Sirs,

My ... is Ryan Shanks, and I am 17 years .... At present, I go to a College of Further Education and I will ... my exams in housekeeping this summer. I would very much like to ... for the job you offered in today's ... I have always wanted to be a .., and my teacher says that I am quite good ...

I am ... and hard-working and I promise I will do my best if you give me a ....

You can find my last ... and my curriculum vitae in the ....

Yours ...,

Ryan Shanks

A   Complete Ryan's letter with the words from the list below.
Be careful – they are not in the correct order.

> to apply – certificate – cook – old – sincerely – chance – local newspaper – envelope –
> at cooking – name – to pass – reliable

B   You want a job, don't you? Try to answer these questions.
1. How and where can you get information? Make a list.
2. What must you do to get a job?
Form sentences and write them down.
Here are some words to help you:

> write/application – ask for/interview – phone/manager – go to/firm and speak to ... –
> employment office – Internet

3. If you write an application, what do you have to write?
4. What must you enclose in your envelope?

5.1   Ryan's Dreams

Ryan Shanks was very happy when school was over. He sat down, wrote some applications and sent them to hotels, factory canteens and hospital kitchens. He wanted a good training, because his Mum and Dad always said that "a good training is really important, Ryan". They often said so, until Ryan really believed it. He had learned domestic science at school, but his marks were not very good. He had spent too much time doing odd jobs. "Money is more important than school", he used to say.

He was very optimistic when he started writing applications, but he often got answers which said that they did not need someone like him.

Some employers did not even send an answer.

After sixty applications he was ready to take any training place. Ryan was listening to his Heavy Metal records when his mother came in and showed him a letter from *The Majestic Hotel*, that was what it said on the envelope. "Another refusal", he moaned and opened the letter with indifference. He felt frustrated by the many negative answers, but then he could hardly believe his eyes. They wrote that they were hoping to get "an ambitious young man" for their hotel kitchen. That was exactly what Ryan wanted!

While he was lying on the bed he was dreaming: Ryan – the cook, the chef, designer of culinary art.

A There are some key words in the text which you must know to understand the text. Here they are in German. Can you find the English words in the text?
Copy the words into your vocabulary notebook and complete them with the English words.

English	German
	Noten, Zensuren
	maulen
	Bewerbung
	Gleichgültigkeit
	Berufsausbildung
	ehrgeizig
	Kochkunst
	Briefumschlag
	Chefkoch
	schicken
	wichtiger als
	bereit sein
	Arbeitgeber

B Answer the following questions on the text.
1. How did Ryan feel when school was over?
2. What did he do to get a job?
3. Where did Ryan want to work?
4. What job was he dreaming of?
5. Why did Ryan want a training?
6. What is the reason that Ryan's marks were not very good?
7. What job does *The Majestic Hotel* offer Ryan?
8. Do you think *The Majestic Hotel* wants to make Ryan a chef?

C Read the headline of text 5.2. What does it mean? These two explanations can help you:
a rookie – someone who is new and has no experience of an activity
a booby – a stupid, foolish person; an idiot

D How did everybody treat Ryan? What do you think?

5.2   Rookie Ryan – Everybody's Booby?

Ryan was sitting in the hotel lounge. He was wearing a white pair of jeans and a white T-shirt. He wanted to be punctual. In the letter they had told him to be there by 6 o'clock. And now he was waiting for someone to come out of the kitchen and tell him what to do. It was ten to six already. But nobody came. So he tried to go through the kitchen door which said "OUT". He was slowly trying to open it, when there was a loud bang and a terrible clatter of plates with porridge flying through the air. The porridge felt pretty hot on Ryan's new white trousers and T-shirt, and the plates soon turned into bits and pieces on the tiled floor. The pretty waitress who had carried the tray was full of white porridge on her black costume. She screamed and ran away.

Ryan could not – he was standing there and thought he was in a nightmare.

"Who the hell are you?", a huge man with a chef's hat thundered.

"I ... am ... Ryan Shanks, the new man," Ryan stuttered.

"And what does an idiot like you want here?", the man questioned.

"I want to be a cook. My teacher at school said I can cook quite well", Ryan hurried to say.

"Booby", the cook started. He was looking like the devil himself. "The first thing you want is new clean clothes. Then you want to sweep up the bits and pieces, and wipe and polish the floor until it is as shining as a mirror!"

It was horrible. From the very beginning on, Ryan had his nickname: "Hey Booby", everybody shouted, and after that they always had something to do for him. He had to peel mountains of onions till there was no water left in his eyes, or he had to scrub pots and pans until they shone like mirrors. Whenever he was looking out of the window and dreaming of better times, someone always came and had a job for him.

"Hey Booby, you are not paid for dreaming. Move it!", everybody used to say.

When he had to get potatoes from the cellar to peel them, someone else said:

"Why do you walk around with empty hands? Here is a brush. Scrub the chopping block. And you hurry, Booby!"

While he was cleaning the chopping block, there was a scream: "Where the hell are my potatoes? I did not tell you to grow them but to get them from the cellar!"

Ryan was already thinking of quitting the job when Dora Mae, a friendly woman of around forty, said, "Ryan, why don't you have a talk with the chef? You want to learn something. You have to change, but the others must, too."

A Write down all the words in the text 5.2 which you don't know. Then form groups and share the job to look the words up in a dictionary. Ask the others for words you don't know, complete your list and help the others with the words you looked up.

There is more information about working with a dictionary on page 142.
You could use Ryan's story for a role-play. Interested? Look on page 133.

Example:
You can ask like this: *"What is the meaning of ..."* or
"Can you tell me what ... means?"

B Are the following statements right or wrong? Say why.
1. Ryan was unpunctual on his first day.
2. Ryan did not find the entrance for the hotel staff.
3. The accident which happened at the kitchen door was Ryan's fault.
4. Ryan was very busy in the kitchen.
5. The colleagues were happy to have Ryan around.

C What did Ryan do wrong? What did his colleagues do wrong? Try to complete the following sentences. Use the *simple past*. → For rules see page 154
1. not tell the receptionist he had arrived
2. Not ask for the staff entrance
3. Not read the writing on the kitchen door
4. Not ask what job Ryan was doing at the moment
5. Call him "Booby"
6. Not teach Ryan anything
7. Only shout at him

Past Progressive

You already know the *simple past*.

Example: *Nobody came.*

Here the *event* is important – that nobody came at all.

There is another aspect:

Example: Ryan **was** sitt**ing** in the hotel lounge.

Here the *period of time* is important – sitting in the hotel lounge took some time.
If you refer to a past period of time, you use this past tense: *the past progressive.*

How do you form the past progressive? Look at the next table:

→ For rules see page 155

Ryan was peeling mountains of onions

Statement Clause			
I	**was**	wear**ing**	a white shirt.
You	**were**	wait**ing**	for a letter.
He		dream**ing**	about his job.
She	**was**	ly**ing**	on her bed.
It		rain**ing**	heavily.
We		mak**ing**	cake.
You	**were**	peel**ing**	potatoes.
They		chopp**ing**	carrots.
Ryan	**was**	scrubb**ing**	pots and pans.
Plates	**were**	ly**ing**	on the floor.

A Now form sentences and use the *past progressive*.
What were the kitchen staff doing from 8 to 12 o'clock yesterday?
And what were you doing?
→ *See spelling rules on page 4.*
1. Ryan/peel/mountains of onions.
2. The chef/plan/next week's menu.
3. Two girls/peel potatoes.
4. They/chat/about their friends.
5. Dora Mae/make some salad.
6. She/clean/carrots.
7. Two waiters/lay/the tables.

Questions and Negative Clauses
Forming questions is quite easy. Just look: **He was** dreaming. – **Was he** dreaming?
                                             I was sleeping. – **Were you** sleeping?

Negative clauses are easy as well: No, he was**n't** (= was **not**) dreaming.
                                          No, they were**n't** (= were **not**) working.

B Form tables like the table "Statement Clause"
on page 50 for questions and negative
clauses in the past progressive.

Was	I	wearing	a white shirt?
Were	you	waiting	for a letter?
Go on!			
…			

C The chef is furious. Today there is a big
party at the hotel. So yesterday evening the
staff had to work from 8 to 10 o'clock. The
chef was not there – and now the food is
not ready.
He wants to know what they were doing in
those two hours …

Form two groups, ask questions and give
answers.

Example:
What/you/do/yesterday evening?
You/chat/about your friends again?
*– What **were you doing** yesterday evening?*
***Were you chatting** about your friends
again?*

*No, we/not chat/about them. We/peel/pota-
toes.*
*– No, we **weren't chatting** about our friends,
we **were peeling** potatoes.*

1. You/dream again, Booby? – No, I/not dream – I/peel/onions.
2. The waiters/lay/the tables? – No, they/not lay/the tables – They/help/in the bar.
3. Dora Mae/make/the soup? – No, she/not make/the soup – She sweep/the kitchen.
4. The girls/peel/potatoes? – No, they/not peel potatoes – They/wipe/the hotel lounge.
5. Most of the staff/work in the kitchen? – No, they/not work in the kitchen – Some
   people/watch/the football match on TV.

G Fill in the right preposition or conjunction.
● Prepositions are words that are used with a noun, pronoun or an –ing-form: *in, on, at.*
● Conjunctions are words that connect parts of sentences: *and, but, or, while, when.*
 Choose them from the box below.

> while – when (2x) – for – from – of – where – but

1. Ryan got a letter ... *The Majestic Hotel.*
2. He was very happy ... he read that they wanted him.
3. He wanted to be a cook, ... his marks at school were not very good.
4. He was waiting ... the chef.
5. ... he was lying on his bed, he was dreaming ... being the chef.
6. ... he was cleaning the chopping block, somebody shouted, "... are my potatoes?"

5.3 A Man-to-Man Talk

Ryan was pretty nervous. It was five to nine.
He was waiting in front of the chef's office. Today he wanted to talk with his boss. When the
long hand of the hotel clock had reached the
twelve, he knocked at the wooden door.

Chef: "Come in! Ah, it's you Booby. What
 can I do for you?"
Ryan: "Oh, quite a lot, sir. First, please
 don't call me 'Booby'. My name is
 Ryan. Did you know that? It hurts
 me if everybody calls me 'Booby',
 and it makes me angry."
Chef: "Okay, Ryan, sorry. And when you are angry, you start
 dreaming?"
Ryan: "Yes, I know, I was dreaming several times. But it is not easy when everybody treats you
 like a fool. And then I escape in dreams."
Chef: "But your dreams make things even worse. The staff think a dreamer must be a booby."
Ryan: "I am not a booby and I am not a dreamer. I really want to learn something, but I can't
 if everybody sends me around and never shows me anything."
Chef: "So you want to change yourself?"
Ryan: "Yes, and I want to change the situation here. I cannot stand it much longer."
Chef: "And how can I help you?"
Ryan: "Well, sir, why don't you give me more responsibility? I really know when the chopping
 block needs cleaning, and I know what we need for the breakfast buffet."
Chef: "Okay, young man – more responsibility. And let me give you a hint: Do not look so
 furious when people try to send you around. Tell them with a smile that you are busy
 at the moment. And another bit of advice: When the others notice that you *see* work
 and *do* it, they will see that they can rely on you, and you will no longer be 'Booby'."

A Are the following statements true or false? Say why.
1. Ryan had an appointment with his boss at 9 o'clock.
2. The chef wanted to help Ryan.
3. The staff did not rely on Ryan.

B Answer the following questions in full sentences. Use the words in brackets for your answers.
1. Why was Ryan pretty nervous when he was waiting in front of the chef's office? (he/not know/what the boss would say)
2. Why did Ryan wait for five minutes before he knocked on the door? (he/want to be/ punctual)
3. How did Ryan feel about his nickname? (he/get angry; it/hurt/him; he/not like it)
4. Ryan was often dreaming. Why? (he/want to escape/from the bad situation)
5. What did Ryan want the chef to do for him? (should not call/Booby; more responsibility; teach/something)
6. What bit of advice did the chef give Ryan? Name three points (see text 5.3).
7. What does it mean that someone "sees" work? Explain in your own words.

> Some verbs do not usually take the *progressive*.
> For further information look at page 156.

Simple Past or Past Progressive?

Remember:
You take *simple past* for events, *past progressive* for a period of time.
Look at the following sentence:

> *When* Ryan **was dreaming**, someone **shouted** at him.
> The dreaming took a *period of time*, and in this time *the event* happened, that someone shouted at him.

> There can also be **two parallel actions**, which occurred *at the same time*:
> *While* Ryan **was peeling** onions, the girls **were peeling** potatoes.
> Both actions were periods of time – so you take the *past progressive* for both.

Now do the following exercise, and use the *past progressive and the simple past*.
1. When Dora Mae (make) salad, the telephone (ring).
2. When Ryan (chop) carrots, he suddenly (cut) his finger.
3. While the waiters (lay) the table, the cooks (prepare) the porridge.
4. When Ryan (scrub) pots and pans, a girl (drop) a plate.
5. When she (sweep) the bits and pieces away, Ryan (go) to her and (ask) if he could help her.

When Ryan was dreaming, somebody shouted at him.

C Word quiz – Do you know these words? Write them down in your exercise book. (The numbers in brackets show the number of letters in the word.)
1. A vegetable which makes you cry when you peel it is **an** … (5)
2. **An** orange coloured vegetable is **a** … (6)
3. Someone who works in a household is **a** … (8, 6)
4. A verb for "cleaning with a brush" is **to** … (5)
5. An underground room for storing food etc. is **a** … (6)
6. A pot in which you fry something is **a** … (3)

Vocabulary

5.1 Ryan's Dreams		
(to) be over [bɪ 'əʊvə]	to have ended	vorbei sein
an application [ˌæplɪ'keɪʃn]	a letter to ask for a job	Bewerbungsschreiben
training ['treɪnɪŋ]	education on the job	Ausbildung
housekeeping [haʊs 'ki:pɪŋ]	working in a household	Hauswirtschaft
(to) spend; spent; spent (time) [spend; spent; spent]	to do something for some time	(Zeit) verbringen (auch: ausgeben)
employer [ɒm'plɔɪə]	someone who gives you a job	Arbeitgeber
(to) be ready for something [bɪ 'redɪ fɔ:]	to accept something	bereit sein
(to) force one's way [fɔːs wʌnz weɪ]	to try to get through	seinen Weg bahnen
noise [nɔɪz]	something very loud	Lärm
envelope ['envələʊp]	You put a letter in it.	Briefumschlag
refusal [rɪ'fju:zl]	act of saying "No"	Ablehnung
(to) moan [məʊn]	to complain	maulen
indifference [ɪn'dɪfrəns]	no interest	Gleichgültigkeit
(to) be ambitious [bɪ æm'bɪʃəs]	to be ready to work well	ehrgeizig sein
culinary art ['kʌlɪnərɪ ɑ:t]	skill of cooking	Kochkunst
key word [ki: wɜ:d]	very important word	Schlüsselwort

5.2 Rookie Ryan – Everybody's Booby?		
hotel lounge [həʊ'tel laʊndʒ]	place where hotel guests can sit	Hotelsalon
by six o'clock [baɪ sɪks ə'klɒk]	not later than six o'clock	bis spätestens sechs Uhr
clatter ['klætə]	A noise that breaking plates make	Geklirr
porridge ['pɒrɪdʒ]	a soup with milk and oatmeal	Haferflockensuppe
bits and pieces [bɪts ænd pɪ:sɪz]	broken parts of plates	Scherben
nightmare ['naɪtmeə]	a very bad dream	Alptraum
(to) thunder ['θʌndə]	to speak very loud and harsh	donnern
(to) sweep [swi:p]	to clean a floor by using a brush	fegen
(to) polish ['pɒlɪʃ]	make something shine	polieren
(to) scrub [skrʌb]	to clean something by using a brush	schrubben
chopping block [tʃɒpɪŋ blɒk]	a table where you cut meat	Hackklotz
(to) quit [kwɪt]	to stop working	kündigen
receptionist [rɪ'sepʃənɪst]	someone who welcomes guests	Empfangsdame, Portier
staff entrance [stɑːf 'entrəns]	a door through which people go who work in the hotel	Personaleingang
furious ['fjʊərɪəs]	very angry	wütend
(to) lay the table [leɪ ðə 'teɪbl]	to put things on the table	den Tisch decken

5.3 A Man-to-Man Talk		
hand of a clock [hænd əv ə klɒk]	a clock has two of them	Zeiger einer Uhr
wooden ['wʊdn]	made of wood	hölzern
(to) hurt someone [hɜ:t]	to make someone feel pain	jemanden verletzen
(to) treat [tri:t]	to behave towards someone	(jemanden) behandeln
hint [hɪnt]	a small suggestion	ein Tipp
responsibility [rɪˌspɒnsə'bɪlətɪ]	if you decide what to do on your own	Verantwortung
in brackets [ɪn 'brækɪts]	These are brackets: (...)	in Klammern
an advice [əd'vaɪz]	a hint	Rat

Unit 6
Somewhere to Live

6.1 Home or Hell?

A Why do so many young people leave their parents' home?
Look at the following words and match the verbs with the ideas. Form complete sentences.

Many young people **want to** leave home because ...		Many young people **have to** leave home because ...	
avoid	more freedom	be	in another town
dream of	conflicts with parents this way	have to work	when learning
want to live	more privacy, no control in their ...	must concentrate	trouble with parents
enjoy	with a friend	have	not enough place in their parents' flat

Do it like this:
Many young people want to leave home because they want to avoid conflicts with their parents this way.
Can you think of more reasons?

B Do you remember how to form the *simple past*? (If not, see page 41)
Why **did** many young people leave their parents' home? Do exercise A again and say why
young people want**ed** or **had** to leave home.

C Out of the saucepan into the fire?
Some kids begin to see what a good time they had when they still lived in "Hotel Mama".
They feel that their life has become worse than it was at their parents' home. But what are
the reasons for that?
Living on your own can be a **dream** – but it can also be a **NIGHTMARE**.
Look at what the four young people say. Living on their
own is a nightmare for them, but why?

> *My flat is both a sauna and a fridge. It's too cold in winter and too hot in summer …*

> *I used to love techno music – but how would you feel with "ouff-ouff-ouff" all night long …*

> *But Mum, you never told me …*

> *If I don't catch my bus, I will be two hours late!*

**Match the following facts to the young
people in the picture:**
1. … lives in the middle of nowhere.
2. … has a flat above a rave disco.
3. … is always short of money.
4. … has a home with a poor insulation.

6.2 Flat-Hunting in Bristol

Chas Banks was very optimistic. He got a job
in a factory where they produce fish fingers.
There was only one problem – he was from
Ipswich. That's on the east coast. Bristol,
that's where the fish finger factory is, lies on
the west coast of
England.
So he needed a flat
somewhere in
Bristol. He earned
£500 a month.
"That's enough mon-
ey for renting a nice
little flat", his father
said.

When Chas arrived in Bristol, he decided to
live in a youth hostel for a few days until he
could find a flat, a room or a bedsitter. He soon
found that flat-hunting was very expensive:
First he had to buy newspapers and read the
advertisements, then he had to phone the
landlords or landladies and finally he had to
buy bus tickets and look at the flats.
Very often the flats, rooms or maisonettes
were too noisy, too far away from

> Cold water, lavatory on the landing, no toilet use after 10 p.m.

> And no breathing either? Thank you, Mad… Madam.

his workplace or they were
real "dumps" with just cold
water – and one of them
even had just a lavatory on
the landing.

6.3   Property Hunter in the Internet

Later Chas read in the *Evening Post* that there was a web site in the Internet. He went into an Internet café and looked for the *Evening Post Property Search*. Its address was http://www.epost.co.uk/ (Look for 'Property')

You can find all sorts of information in the Internet, you just have to know where to look. On page 138 in this book it is explained how you can search in the Internet easily.

What kind of home *are you looking for?*

Enter details into some or all of the following search boxes. Those boxes with a RED triangle next to them are the minimum criteria that must be entered for a quick search. For a more precise match, complete as many search fields as possible.

Property *Type*	*** SALE and RENTAL OPTIONS *** ▾ ▶
No.of *Bedrooms*	At least one ▾ ▶
Reception *Rooms*	Any ▾
No.of *Bathrooms*	Any ▾

For Sale or *For Rent?*

Homes for *Sale*	⦿ ▶	Homes for *Rent*	○ ▶
Minimum *Price* £		Minimum *Price* £	100
Maximum *Price* £		Maximum *Price* £	500
All or new *Homes?*	All Homes ▾	Rental *Period?*	Monthly ▾
		Furni*shed?*	○
		Unfurni*shed?*	○

Choose a *Location*

Choose *County*	○ Gloucestershire
	○ Somerset
	○ Bristol, Bath & South Gloucestershire (AVON)
	○ Wiltshire
	○ Dorset

Choose *Distance From*

Use this search facility if you would like to search within a specific radius from a location. This feature requires City/Town, Village or Postcode to be filled in.

Choose *City/Town*	Bristol
Choose *Village*	
Street *Name*	
Name */Number*	
Post*code*	
Distance *in Miles*	

Search		Clear Details

A Chas' Mum could be a little (diplomatic) <u>more diplomatic</u> with her son. It is often (easy) <u>easier</u> to tell someone indirectly what he has to do ...
Use the comparative form of the adjectives in brackets.

> How do you do use comparison? Look at the grammar boxes Comparison I (in unit 4, page 43) and Comparison II (below).

Now, what does Chas' Mum want? Are you a good psychologist? Look at the text "Home Or Hell?".
Do it like this: *The air in your room could be (good).*
You say: *The air in your room could be **better**.*
What does Chas' Mum want? You say:
> *She wants **him to** open the window. (= that **he** opens the window.)*

1. "It is (dangerous) for your girlfriend to go home after 10 p.m."
2. "It would be (nice) if I could not write 'pig' on your desk – just with my finger."
3. "There could be (little) confetti on your floor."
4. "It would be (hygienic) if there was not so much dust on the floor."
5. "Chas, your washing gets (dirty) when it is lying on the floor."
6. "Couldn't your school marks be (good)?"
7. "Chas, wouldn't it be (intelligent) to learn vocabulary than to read that youth magazine?"
8. "Your window panes could be (clean)."
9. "Sorry, Chas, could you speak a little (loud)?"
10. "Chas, couldn't you be a little (understanding)?"

B Answer the following comprehension questions. Use the words in brackets.
1. What does Chas mean when he says he wants his own four walls? (own flat)
2. Why do you think does he say so? (no control, no orders)

C Chas and his Mum have a problem. Form two groups and look for solutions to their problem.
1. What can Chas' Mum do?
2. What can Chas do?

Comparison II

With comparison you can
for example say that:
Peter's box is large,
but Chas' box is larg**er** than Peter's.
Lucy's box is the larg**est** of the three.

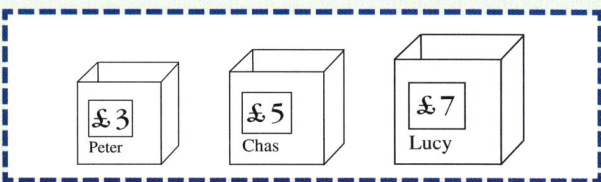

The comparison of longer adjectives is even easier to do – you don't do anything with the adjective.
● You just have to put ***more*** before the adjective in the comparative,
● and you put ***most*** before the adjective in the superlative.
Peter's box was expensive.
Chas' box was **more** expensive than Peter's.
Lucy's box was the **most** expensive of the three.   → For rules see pages 158/159

Look, comparing longer adjectives is quite easy:

	Adjective	Comparative	Superlative
longer adjectives with two or more syllables	charming	more charming	the most charming
	beautiful	more beautiful	the most beautiful
	interesting	more interesting	the most interesting
	independent	more independent	the most independent

D Here are some questions to text "Flat-Hunting in Bristol". Do you know the answers?
1. Why was Chas Banks very optimistic when he went to Bristol?
2. Why could he no longer live at his parents' home?
3. Why did Chas stay in a youth hostel for a few days?
4. What do you understand by the term "flat-hunting"?
5. What makes flat-hunting so expensive?
6. How did Chas want to save money?

E On page 57 you find the *Property Hunter Search Form* from the
Evening Post. Here are some questions about it.
For finding out the answers you could go to your school's computer room and surf the
Internet.

1. Why do you have to fill in something in all of the red triangle boxes?
2. Why don't you have to fill in the other search boxes?
3. Help Chas to fill in the search form. (If you have no access to the computer room, you
   might put this book on a photocopier and answer the exercise on paper.)
4. When Chas was looking for the property type, he got a little confused. There were so
   many terms he did not understand. Can you try to find out what the terms in the first picture stand for? Has your school got some
   dictionaries?

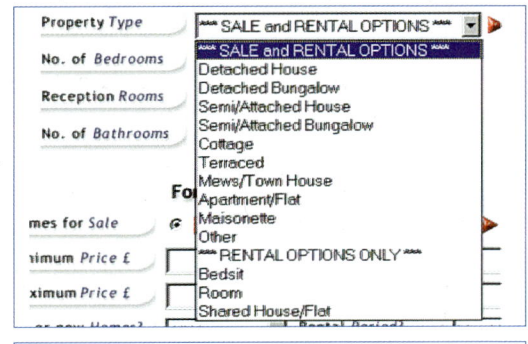

What is the term for …
   a) a house with two entrances for two
      families
   b) a former shed for horses which was
      rebuilt so that people can live there now
   c) a room for both living and sleeping in
   d) a row of houses linked to each other
   e) a house for a single family
   f) a flat in a smaller house, usually under
      the roof
   g) a small country house
   h) a set of rooms including kitchen and
      bathroom

5. How many bedrooms, reception rooms,
   bathrooms does Chas need?
6. What does the computer do if you click "At
   least one"?

7. Does Chas need a home for sale or for rent?
8. Chas earns £500 a month. Get together in
   groups and discuss the minimum and the
   maximum price of his flat. How much is
   £1?
9. What is the difference between a furnished
   and an unfurnished room?

10. Chas wants a flat not too far away from his
    workplace. He wants to go there by bike.
    The fishfinger factory is in Fishponds/
    Bristol.
    a) What is the use of the Distance Form?
    b) What would you fill in here?

6.4 Power Search Results

Here are some examples of Chas' findings.

Power Search Results   **? Your Matches Explained**

Power Search Results

The following properties have been returned matching your criteria. To create a list ready for printing or saving, select the properties you are interested in, and click the button at the bottom of the page.

Showing matches 1 to 5

1. Brislington, Bristol   **£40 per week**

☐ BRISLINGTON near HTV studios. On bus route to City Centre. Garden, parking, Gas c.h. furnished. Present bedsits from £40 p.w. plus bills. Deposit required. Employed only. Tel. 0117 9834509.
Match: ˅ ˅ ˅

Showing the matches

1. Downend, Bristol   **£26 per week**

☐ Room in shared house. £115 pcm. Twelve Trees Accommodation 0117 9328895
Match: ˅ ˅

2. Redfield, Bristol   **£30 per week**

☐ 4/5 House, perfect for sharers, unfurnished, garage and gardens, £30 per person per week. Accommodation unlimited 0117 9257474
Match: ˅ ˅

3. Fishponds, Bristol   **£23 per week**

☐ FISHPONDS Nicely dec, room to let in Victorian house. £100 pcm Tel. 0117 9863137 or 0976 673563 m.
Match: ˅ ˅

A What do the terms and the abbreviations in the advertisements on page 60 mean?
1. Match them to the explanations. The terms are not in the correct order.

	Terms and Abbreviations	Explanation	
1	a match	a home you can rent	R
2	on bus route	there is no furniture there	T
3	Gas central heating	the bus stop is quite near	R
4	£40 per week	this is the rent you have to pay per month	H
5	plus bills	a sum of money paid into an account as a guarantee if repairs are necessary	R
6	deposit required	these are additional costs, for example for heating, gas, water, electricity, sewage	E
7	employed only	a house in which several tenants live	Y
8	shared house	this is only for people who have a job	T
9	£115 pcm	the rent you have to pay per week	P
10	4/5 house	this matches what you are looking for	P
11	furnished	central heating which is run by gas	O
12	unfurnished	it means that there are already tables, cupboards, bed etc. in the home	N
13	nicely dec.	four other tenants are wanted, one is already there	U
14	room to let	a flat which looks good	E

2. If you match the letters to the right numbers, you will find a helpful Internet homepage which you can use to find a home quickly.

1	2	3	4	5
P (10)				

B Making phone calls …
Sure, you want to find the best flat for yourself. You need more information on the Power Search Results. The best way to get more information is to call the landlords or landladies. It is a good idea to make a checklist to compare the homes. You can do it like this:

> Bedsit in Brislington: Tel. 0117 98345096
> agency's/landlady's/landlord's name: _____

Now form complete questions which you want to ask the landlord.

Example:
address? (what)
– What is the address of the home, please?

1. nearest bus stops, bus lines (where, which)?
2. neighbours (how many)?
3. ground plan (can send)?
4. living space (how large)?
5. equipment of the home (what kind of)?
6. bills, extra costs (how high)?
7. deposit required (how much)?
8. kind of heating (what)?
9. insulation (how good)?
10. furniture (what)?
11. see the home (when)?

There is a disco below, but you can hardly hear anything of it!

ouff   ouff   OUFF

On Saturday Chas saw many homes – flats for sharers, maisonnettes, bedsits, rooms, mews and garden cottages.

Chas is glad that he has a checklist, so he can compare all the homes. Of course, he has to look at the money, too. He thinks he can pay £150 per month, perhaps plus £50 bills. He and his new friend George, who also works at the fishfinger factory, compare Chas' favourite three homes.

Brislington Drive – flat   Hopeless Walk – bedsit   Garden Street – maisonette

	Brislington Drive flat	**Hopeless Walk bedsit**	**Garden Street maisonette**
1. rooms (many)	1 bedroom, 1 living room, shower, wc, kitchenette	1 bedsit, shower and wc shared with landlady,	1 bedroom, 1 living room, 1 study, corridor, bathroom, kitchen
2. living space (large)	45 square metres	20 square metres	52 square metres
3. noise (noisy)	a disco below	50 metres near a railway line	near a large park
4. insulation (good)	brickwork is 25 cm thick	there is 8 cm glass wool under the roof	there is 15 cm new glass wool under the roof
5. shops (close)	1 minute's walk to the next supermarket	next shopping centre: 15 minutes by bike	20 minutes' walk to a large shopping mall
6. extra costs (high)	£30 per month	£15 per month	£50 per month
7. rent (expensive)	£100 pcm	£20 per week	£175 pcm
8. age (old)	built in 1959	built in 1920	built in 1965
9. home (comfortable)	linoleum floor, gas central heating, 1959 furniture	stripped floor, bulk rubbish furniture, coal heating	carpets or tiles, gas central heating, furniture bought in 1985
10. distance from work-place (far)	15 miles	10 miles	7 1/2 miles

C Form sentences in order to compare the three homes. Use the comparison. The adjectives in brackets in the table above can help you to form the sentences.

Example:
1. rooms (many) 2. living space (large)
- 1. The Brislington Drive flat has more rooms than the Hopeless Walk bedsit. The Garden Street maisonette has the most rooms of the three.
- 2. The flat is … than the … The … is … of the three.

If you don't understand an English word, and it is not in the vocabulary in this book, then you can look it up in an English-English dictionary. See page 142.

6.5 A Nice Elderly Landlady

1 Chas and George were sitting in a café. They were discussing the last three homes which they had looked at that morning. If only the maisonnette in Garden Street
5 was not so expensive! It was the nicest home of the three, much quieter than the flat above the rave disco in Brislington Drive. The bedsitter in Hopeless Walk was the worst of the three: It was a real dump.

10 "Do you *get* £20 per week or do you have to *pay* that if you want to live there?", his friend George asked ironically and laughed.
No, it was true, Chas did not want to live in
15 a dump like that, even if it was the cheapest home. On the other hand, it was quite expensive if you considered the money was just for one bedsit.
"I think I have to take the flat in Brislington
20 Drive. £175 per month are simply too much for me." Chas said.
"Well, why don't you go back to the landlady in Garden Street and try to beat the rent down a little?" George suggested.
25 "Hm, I could try at least", Chas replied.

The old lady was doing the lovely garden in front of the house when the boys arrived there.
"Hello, Mrs Underwood, here we are
30 again", Chas started the conversation.
The landlady got up and tried to straighten out her back.
"Ouch", she said. "I am getting old, the garden work is getting too much for me. – So,

35 Mr Banks, do you want to take the maisonette?"
"Well, Mrs Underwood, to be honest, it's a little too expensive for me", Chas began.
"Is there any chance to talk the rent over?"
40 Mrs Underwood gave Chas a sad look. "I am a widow", she replied. "My husband died two years ago. I decided to let the maisonette to someone because I need the money. With my back full of pain I will
45 need a gardener, too. Someone offered me to do my garden for £30 per month. So I am afraid I need all my money and I cannot reduce the rent."
"We had a garden at home in Ipswich,"
50 Chas answered. Suddenly he had an idea: "Couldn't I do your garden, Mrs Underwood? And if something needs repairing, I could do that, too."
"Really? I would be happy to have a gar-
55 dener and craftsman in my home", Mrs Underwood smiled. "Give me £115 pcm plus bills. Is that okay?"
Chas was enthusiastic.
"You have a new lodger, a top gardener and
60 a craftsman in one," Chas said, and shook her hand.

A Comprehension – Read the text again for yourself. Look up the words you do not understand and write them down.
Then answer the following questions in full sentences.

1. What did Chas and his friend George do that morning?
2. What were Chas and his friend doing before they decided on one of the homes?
3. Which of the homes was Chas' favourite?
4. Why did George say that you possibly get £20 if you want to live in Hopeless Walk?
5. Why was Hopeless Walk quite expensive, although the price was the lowest?
6. Chas wanted to take the flat in Brislington Drive although he liked the maisonette in Garden Street better. Why was this?
7. George suggested going back to the house in Garden Street again. What did he want Chas to do?
8. Why was Mrs Underwood ready to lower the rent in the end?
9. Is her suggestion a fair offer? What do you think?

B Look for all the information you can get about
Mrs Underwood and draw a mind map.
Then form sentences. Do it like this:
Mrs Underwood has problems with her back.

 Do you know how to draw a mind map? If you need
more information, look on page 136 –
"Mind Mapping".

C Vocabulary – Look at the following definitions. Can you find the right words from the text
"A Nice Elderly Landlady"? The words in brackets will help you.
1. To compare the good and the bad sides of a home (verb)
2. A flat in a detached house, usually under the roof (noun)
3. Costing quite a lot of money (adjective)
4. The opposite of 'the best' (superlative form of an adjective)
5. A dirty, ugly and uncomfortable home (noun)
6. Telling something in a way that you say the opposite of what you mean (adverb)
7. A woman who offers a home to let (noun)
8. A single house (noun)
9. The opposite of 'to bend' (verb + preposition)
10. Someone who can do repairs (noun)

D Getting ready for a housewarming party …
Chas had asked Mrs Underwood if she would allow him to arrange a housewarming party.
She suggested a garden party. Now Chas is sitting down and is making a list of who to
invite. Why should or shouldn't he invite the following people?
Use the words in brackets to give reasons.
1. Mrs Underwood (the landlady, her garden, noise)
2. some of his new colleagues (to make friends)
3. his old friends from Ipswich (enough accomoda-
tion?)
4. his new neighbours (to make friends, music,
noise)

E Writing an invitation …
Chas wants to write an invitation on his
computer, but he doesn't know how to put the words.
1. Would you like to go to the computer room and design a
nice invitation card with cliparts and texts? Ask your teacher.
2. You can write the invitation on simple paper as well. Your invitation card
should give answers to the following questions:
● What do you want to do?
● Why do you want to celebrate?
● For whom is the invitation?
● When is the party?
● Where is it?
● Shall the guests bring anything?
● Till when do you need an answer?

F Helping hands …
Everybody was delighted when they got the invitation. His colleagues, his friends and the
neighbours knew how much work a garden party would mean for a young man, and many
people offered to help him. In the afternoon they were working hard to have a nice party.
Form sentences and use either *past progressive* or *simple past*.

It's quite easy if you remember the rules. Here is a small revision:

While Chas (suspend) Chinese lanterns from the trees/two girls (prepare) the potato salad.	
__While__ Chas __was__ suspend__ing__ Chinese lanterns from the trees, two girls __were__ prepar__ing__ the potato salad.	These are two actions happening at the same time (2x past progressive).
When Chas (come) into his kitchen, George (fry) meatballs.	
George __was__ fry__ing__ meatballs, when Chas __came__ into the kitchen.	Entering a room is an event (simple past), frying meatballs takes a period of time (past progressive).

1. When Chas and two friends (put up) a large tent, Mr Miller (bring) two crates of beer.
2. While Lucy and Sara (lay) the garden tables, Sue Ellen (clean) the garden chairs.
3. Jack (make) sandwiches when a Chinese lantern (fall) on his head.
4. Mrs Smith (squeeze out) some oranges while the Millers (wash up) beer glasses.
5. Mrs Underwood (make) a party soup while Mary (cut) cheese cubes for a cheese platter.
6. When Chas (play) on his guitar, the guests suddenly (applaud).

In this unit there are a lot of words and vocabulary that you don't know. If you can't find the words in the following vocabulary, you can look them up in an English-English dictionary. Do you know how to use a dictionary like that? You will find all the information you need on page 142 – "How to Work with an English-English Dictionary".

Vocabulary

6.1 Home or Hell?		
hell [hel]	the place where the devil lives	Hölle
laundry basket [ˈlɔːndrɪ ˈbɑːskɪt]	you collect dirty washing in it	Wäschekorb
(to) hoover [ˈhuːvə]	British word for (to) vacuumclean	staubsaugen
(to) dust [dʌst]	to wipe away dust with a cloth	staubwischen
by 10 p.m. [baɪ ten pɪem]	10 p.m. is the latest point of time	bis (spätestens) 22 Uhr
(to) turn down [tɜːn daʊn]	to reduce the noise	leiser drehen
freedom [ˈfriːdəm]	the state of being free	Freiheit
privacy [ˈprɪvəsɪ]	the state that you can do something without being watched by others	Ungestörtheit
(to) concentrate [ˈkɒnsəntreɪt]	to direct one's attention to something	sich konzentrieren
"out of the saucepan into the fire" [aʊt əv ðə sɔːspan ˈɪntə ðe ˈfaɪə]	to get into something that is worse than before	"vom Regen in die Traufe kommen"
fridge [frɪdʒ]	refrigerator, for keeping something cool	Kühlschrank
cleansing agents [klenzɪŋ ˈeɪdʒənt]	anything used for cleaning	Reinigungsmittel
insulation [ˌɪnsjʊˈleɪʃn]	it prevents the heat from escaping	Isolation
fish fingers [fɪʃ ˈfɪŋgəz]	fish pressed in a rectangular form	Fischstäbchen
youth hostel [juːθ ˈhɒstl]	a simple hotel for young people	Jugendherberge
bedsitter or bedsit [ˈbed ˈsɪtə] [ˈbedsɪt]	a room for both living and sleeping in	Wohnschlafzimmer, Einzimmerapartment
6.2 Flat-Hunting in Bristol		
flat-hunting [flæt hʌntɪŋ]	trying to find a good flat	Wohnungssuche
landlord [ˈlænlɔːd]	man who offers a flat	Vermieter
landlady [ˈlænleɪdɪ]	woman who offers a flat	Vermieterin
maisonette [ˌmeɪzəˈnet]		Einliegerwohnung
hole [həʊl]	a bad place to live in	Bruchbude
lavatory [ˈlævətərɪ]	the room with wc and washing facility	Toilette, Waschraum

| landing ['lændıŋ] | small platform between two flights of stairs | Trepppenabsatz |
| web site [web saıd] | an Internet page | Internetseite |

6.3 Property Hunter in the Internet		
minimum criteria ['mınıməm kraı'tıərıə]		Mindestkriterien, -eingabedaten
location [ləʊ'keıʃn]	place where to live	Wohnort
rental period ['rentl 'pıərıəd]	the time for which you pay rent	Mietzeitraum
furnished ['fɜːnıʃt]	with furniture	möbliert
distance ['dıstəns]	how far it is from A to B	Entfernung
window pane ['wındəʊ]	the glassy part of the window	Fensterscheibe
property ['prɒpətı]	something you own	Eigentum, Besitz
property type ['prɒpətı taıp]	the kind of home	Wohnungstyp
detached house [dı'tætʃt haʊs]	a single house	Einzelhaus
semi-detached house [semıdı'tætʃt haʊs]	one of two houses that are linked to each other	Doppelhaushälfte
cottage ['kɒtıdʒ]	a small house, often in the country	kleines Landhaus
(to) be confused [bı kən'fjuːzt]	no longer able to think clearly	verwirrt sein
terraced houses ['terəst haʊs]	several houses in a row	Reihenhäuser
mews [mjuːz]	a flat in a former shed	zur Wohnung umgebauter Stall
apartment (AmE); flat (BrE) [ə'pɑːtmənt] [flæt]	a set of rooms in a house	Wohnung
(to) include [ın'kluːd]	to have as a part, to contain	einschließen

6.4 Power Search Results		
(to) return [rı'tɜːn]	here: to give back	hier: wiedergeben, anzeigen
deposit required [dı'pɒzıt rı'kwaıət]	if the landlord wants a sum of money as a safety	Mietkaution/Hinterlegung erforderlich
abbreviation [ə,briːvı'eıʃn]	'pcm' is an abbreviation for ?	Abkürzung
table ['teıbl]	vocabularies are often written in a table	Tabelle
ground plan [graʊnd plæn]	a plan of the flat showing the rooms	Grundrisszeichnung einer Wohnung
living space ['lıvıŋ speıs]	the size of the home	Wohnraum
equipment [ı'kwıpmənt]	things like stove, heating, wc	Ausstattung
bills, extra costs, extras [bılz] ['ekstrə kɒst] ['ekstrəz]	money needed for heating, gas, water etc.	Nebenkosten
kitchenette [,kıtʃı'net]	a small kitchen	Kochnische
stripped floor [strıpt flɔː]	there is no carpet or linoleum on the floor	Fußboden ohne Auslegeware
bulk rubbish furniture [bʌlk 'rʌbıʃ 'fɜːnıtʃə]	old furniture which others threw away	Möbel vom Sperrmüll
carpet ['kɑːpıt]	cloth put on the floor	Teppich
tiles [taılz]	they usually cover bathroom walls	Fliesen, Kacheln

6.5 A Nice Elderly Landlady		
elderly ['eldəlı]	looking somewhat old	ältlich
(to) beat the rent down [biːt ðe rent daʊn]	to get a lower price	die Miete herunterhandeln
at least [ət liːst]		wenigstens
ouch! [aʊtʃ]	that's what you say when you feel pain	Aua!
(to) talk over [tɔːk 'əʊvə]	to speak about it in order to solve a problem	darüber reden, durchsprechen
widow ['wıdəʊ]	a wife whose husband has died	Witwe
craftsman ['krɑːftsmən]	someone who works with hands and tools	Handwerker
enthusiastic [ın,θjuːzı'æstık]	very happy	begeistert
lodger ['lɒdʒə]	someone who pays rent	Mieter
housewarming party [haʊs'wɔːmıŋ 'pɑːtı]	a party you give after you moved in	Kistenparty, Einzugsparty
accommodation [ə,kɒmə'deıʃn]	a place where you can stay and sleep	Unterkunft
meatballs [miːt bɔːl]	minced meat that is fried	Frikadellen
(to) squeeze out [skwiːz aʊt]	to get the juice out of it	auspressen
cheese platter [tʃiːz 'plætə]	a plate with various sorts of cheese	Käseplatte

Revision II (Unit 4 – 6)

A Simple Past
This text on the right is what Mary wrote in her diary when she was twelve years old.
Now she is sixteen, and she tells her friend what she thought at that age.
She starts telling: "When I **was** twelve, I **was** deeply in love with …"

Now it's your turn. Look at the diary and go on telling.

Some girls even dream of marrying a prince. Look at this newspaper report:

I am deeply in love with Dave. Only he doesn't know. How can I show him my love? Will he ever go out with me? I don't know what to do. I can't even do my homework without thinking of him.
Why am I so shy?

Prince William – Cute, Hot and So Sexy!

Everyone agrees. Prince William, tall, with blond hair and blue eyes, is extremely good-looking. He clearly takes after his mother rather than his father, who was teased at school for his sticky-out ears.

During a four-day holiday in British Columbia/Canada, together with his father and his young brother Harry in March, Wills was greeted by groups of screaming young girls everywhere he went. The media spoke of "Wills mania".

"He's so cute," Clarissa told a reporter from The Guardian. "He looks really nice. He's really hot."

Clarissa and her two friends, Jessica and Leah, were watching the young prince skiing. "He's so sexy," cried Leah. There were also girls standing outside his hotel in Vancouver. One held a banner which read: "William, it's me you have been looking for." Fourteen-year-old Shannon, stopped by police as she jumped over a crash barrier to get closer to William when he arrived at Vancouver's Pacific Space Centre, declared:

"I love Prince William and I just wanted to see him for a second.

Of course I'm disappointed. He should have met his future wife."

One 15-year-old Canadian, Erin Hochstein, had an explanation for the mass hysteria over the handsome young prince: "Every little girl dreams of marrying a prince," Erin commented to the press.

(from: Read On)

Hey, Dad, you just wear your cap this way and the girls go crazy for you!

B Infer the meaning of words
Sometimes you can infer unknown words if you understand the context. Can you get the German meaning of the following words?
1. cute (sweet, good-looking)
2. hot (chilli pepper is hot)
3. he takes after his mother rather than his father (he looks more like Diana than like Charles)

4. sticky-out ears (look at Prince Charles)
5. crash barrier (a fence to protect the prince against his fans)

C Comprehension Questions
1. What do many girls think about Prince William?
2. Where was he with his father and brother?
3. What did they want to do there?
4. Why did 14-year-old Shannon jump over a crash barrier?
5. What does she mean with her sentence "He should have met his future wife"?

D Simple Past or Past Progressive
Fill in the gaps in the sentences.

> Remember: You take *simple past* for one or more past events, *past progressive* for a period of time.

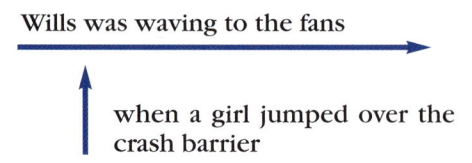

Wills was waving to the fans

when a girl jumped over the crash barrier

1. When Wills … (leave) the plane, all the girls (scream).
2. Wills (smile) when a 14-year-old girl (give) him a red rose.
3. When Wills (wake) up at 6 a.m., girls (already, wait) in front of the hotel.
4. While the girls (wait), Wills and his family (have) breakfast.
5. A reporter wanted to know: "(you, come) here from England?"
6. The girl (say) that she and her parents (spend) the holidays in British Columbia at the same time.

E Comparison – Is it so important to be the nicest girl in town?
Compare the two young ladies and you will see that everybody has his sunny and his shady sides!
Use the following adjectives from the box:

> short – fat – heavy – excellent – intelligent – old

Example: *Linda is more intelligent than Sheila.*
Look at the personal data, and decide where you have to use
● *-er than* or
● *more … than* or
● *as … as*

Personal Data		
	Linda	**Sheila**
School	marginal	excellent
Weight	120 lbs	160 lbs
IQ	70	100
Age	16	16
Behaviour	conceited, unhelpful	friendly, helpful

F Personal Pronouns – Fill in the right personal pronouns.

> mine – theirs – ours – his – hers – our – yours

> Remember the rules: She is **my** girl, in other words, she is **mine**.
> What is the difference between **my** and **mine**?
> **my** stands before a noun (my girl), **mine** stands alone.

Did the girl really think Prince William was (1)? She told the reporter, "Prince William is (2), only, he doesn't know yet." Another girl laughed: "You are a dreamer. He will never be (3) alone." The other girl replied: "You may be right, but he will be (4) King, one day. He will be (5), for all of us. The future is (6), he will make it."
When a Canadian boy was asked what he thought about those girls who were lovesick, he said:
"There are so many other nice boys. If those crazy girls love the wrong boy, that problem is (7)."

Unit 7
Going Abroad

FRANCE

GREECE

UNITED STATES
OF AMERICA

Which of the named countries would you like to go to?

GREAT BRITAIN

TURKEY

7.1   Sarah and Michael Are Going Abroad

Sarah and Michael go to a vocational school in Papenburg, which is a small town near the Dutch border. They are in a class for domestic and social science. Sarah wants to become a nurse in a hospital and Michael wants to become a geriatric nurse. They've already had a lot of practical experience in their future job this year. They have both worked full time for eight weeks: Michael in an old people's home and Sarah in a hospital.

In many lessons, their class has worked on an international project about traditional home remedies. Another school in Groningen/ Netherlands and one in Ballymahon/Ireland are also taking part in this project.

Sarah and Michael are now on their way to the partner school in Ireland. They are going to prepare a presentation of the project with students from the partner schools.

Michael and Sarah went by train to an airport near Amsterdam. They are now waiting to be checked in. The plane to Dublin is delayed.

A   Choose one of the alternatives (a – c) to complete the sentences.

1. Sarah wants to become
a) a doctor.
b) a nurse.
c) a pilot.

2. Michael got a lot of practical experience by
a) reading a book about caring for people.
b) working in an old people's home.
c) taking pictures of old people with his camera.

3. Sarah and Michael travel to their partner school
a) by car.
b) by bicycle.
c) by plane.

4. Sarah and Michael are travelling to Ballymahon because they
a) want to prepare a presentation of a project.
b) want to get married.
c) want to spend their holidays in Ballymahon.

5. With which plane are Sarah and Michael flying? Look at the picture.
a) With the delayed plane
b) With the plane which flies on time
c) With the cancelled plane

6. In which country has Michael been before?
a) Ireland
b) United States of America
c) Great Britain

It can be fun to work on a project – you can learn and make your own experience at the same time. Our friends Michael and Sarah are working on a project about traditional home remedies. You can work on other projects as well, for example planning an English breakfast for your class. Look on page 134 for more information and ask your teacher about it.

Present Perfect

When do you use the present perfect?
The present perfect expresses an action which began in the past and still continues.
It also expresses the effect of past actions on the present. → For rules see page 155

Examples:
- *The class **has worked** on an international project. (The results can be seen now.)*
- *Michael **has been** to the Netherlands and to Great Britain. (Michael has some knowledge about these countries now, it has an effect on him.)*
- *Sarah and Michael **have had** a lot of practical experience this year. (So they are better informed now.)*

How do you form the present perfect?
You form the present perfect with
a present tense form of *have* + the third verb form (past participle)

Past participle:
- Most verbs have a regular past participle: *verb + -ed*   (work**ed**)
- Some verbs have an irregular past participle.   (been, had, written, made, held etc.)
→ *There is a list of the irregular verbs and their verb forms on page 151.*

Statement Clause		
I We You They	**have**	work**ed**.
He She It	**has**	

Negative Clause			
I We You They	**have**	not	work**ed**.
He She It	**has**		

Questions		
Have	I we you they	work**ed**?
Has	he she it	

Put the words in brackets into the *present perfect* tense.

Examples:
- *Michael … on an international project (work).*
- *Michael **has worked** on an international project.*
- *It is Sarah's birthday tomorrow and Michael … her a present yet (not, buy).*
- *It is Sarah's birthday tomorrow and Michael **has not bought** her a present yet.*
- *Ken:"Can I take this newspaper? … you … with it (finish)?"*
- *Ken:"Can I take this newspaper? **Have** you **finished** with it?"*
- *Sarah:"Michael, this is Mary." Michael:"Yes, I know. We … already(meet)."*
- *Sarah:"Michael, this is Mary." Michael:"Yes, I know. We **have** already **met**."*

1. Ken and Gina … in the same house for six years (live).
2. Sarah … to Great Britain yet (not, be).
3. Ken:"Are Fiona and Jim here?" Gina:"Yes, they … just (arrive)."
4. Mark asks Laura:"When does Mr Kelly start his new job?" Laura:"He … already (start)".
5. Ken:"Where is the recipe for apple crumble?" Fiona:"I don't know. I … it (not, see)."
6. Mr Kelly … as an interviewer since January 2004 (work).
7. Jim:"Hmm, that's a lovely meal. Who … it (cook)?"
8. Gina:"I … plum pudding before (not try). It is very nice."

B Look at the pictures of the flags. Which flag goes with which text? Name the country.

1. This country has a population of 3.5 million. It is an island in the North Atlantic Ocean, west of Great Britain. The landscape is beautiful. The people are very fond of tea. Flag: three equal vertical bands of green, white, and orange.
2. This country has a population of 14.7 million. The people travel a lot, learn foreign languages and buy a lot of bicycles.
3. This country has a population of 55.5 million. It is an island off the North West coast of Europe. The people have small families and love their own national food. The people smoke and drink more than their European neighbours. The national colours are red, white and blue.
4. This country has a population of 82.2 million. There is no speed limit on the motorways. The people like to drink coffee.

C This is the flag of the European Union.
1. Which countries belong to the European Union?
2. What are the capitals of these countries?

 By the way: The Internet is a great place to find all sorts of information on foreign countries. Here you can find almost anything you want to know. If you want to learn how to use the Internet, look on page 138 – "Searching Information in the Internet".

7.2 The Meeting

When Sarah and Michael arrive in Ballymahon, they are welcomed heartily by those students from the Ballymahon Vocational School who take part in the project.
Juliana and Wim from the partner school in Groningen/Netherlands have arrived as well.

Soon they are talking about the kind of work they have been doing for the project, and are sharing their experiences. Look at their conversation:
Sarah: "This week we have learned how to put a compress on somebody."
Wim: …

A What else has been done for the project? Here are some words which give you ideas what has been done already. Use the *present perfect* of the verbs.

→ For rules see page 155

Examples:
Wim: we/already/produce/bath salts
*Wim: "We **have** already **produced** bath salts."*

William: our class/make/a herbal garden
*William: "Our class **has made** a herbal garden."*

1. Marian: a team in our class/collect/herbs for steam baths
2. John: this year/my mother/dry/herbs/for making tea
3. Patrick: I/buy/a guide book about home remedies

4. Juliana: our project team/make/a video for an exhibition in a pharmacy
5. Michael: we/write/an essay for the journal *Examples – Teaching in Lower Saxony*
6. Mary: Bernadette/design/a professional homepage about the project
7. Marian: Annie and I/recently/start/a survey about the use of natural cosmetics
8. Annie: I/press/plants for a herbarium …
9. Annie: … but/my three-year-old sister Ruth/tear/quite a lot of the pressed plants

7.3   In a Pub

It was a successful presentation and the students are all very happy. They have worked very well! Moreover, many of them have actually made friends with the students from another country.

Irish Pub

Juliana: "What are we going to do in the evening?"
Michael: "Well, we could just go to a pub!"
Geert: "I think that's a good idea. Does anybody know if there is live music in any pub?"
William: "On Thursdays there usually is music in *The Plough*."
Juliana: "Oh, that's nice. Shall we meet there at – let's say 9 o'clock?"

Later on the students meet in the pub. They are really disappointed because they don't see any musicians.
They order their drinks. Most of them have a coke. Some of the older students have a pint of lager or a glass of stout.

Sarah: "I think it is very funny that the Irish still keep to their traditional measurements."
John: "It is not only the measurements. The traffic regulations are another example. Unfortunately if you don't drive on the left, you are likely to have an accident. "
Geert: "But I think that they have changed their distances from miles to kilometres, haven't they?"
Tom: "That's right. But only in Ireland. In Great Britain the traffic signs are still showing the distances in miles."
Michael: "I think it is nice when a country keeps to its traditions. As far as I know, the British have the oldest monarchy in the world. And the majority of the people are still very fond of it. Is that right, Mary? You have worked in England for nearly a year, you must know."
Mary: "That is true. Many official events begin or end with the national anthem 'God Save The Queen'."

School uniforms

Juliana: "Oh, a few days ago I saw some students wearing a uniform. Is there a special reason for that?"
Mary: "Well, it is quite common here to wear uniforms at school. Most schools have their own special uniform."

73

In the meantime three musicians have arrived in the pub and have started to play. The Dutch and German students listen very carefully – they have never heard some of the instruments before, for example the harp. They all enjoy the music, and the musicians play very well.

Mary: "There are many things here in Ireland that are different, compared to your country, for example Christmas. It is a great, big festival here: We decorate the houses colourfully, for that we often use balloons, holly and mistletoe. We have a traditional dinner with turkey and plum pudding."

Michael: "When I listen to you talking, I think it would be lovely to stay here."

Mary: "Well, dear Michael – why don't you? You know, I will really miss you when you leave."

When the pub closes at 1 a.m., Michael and Mary go home silently.
The stay of the foreign students is almost over. Two days later Michael has to fly home.

A week later Mary gets a letter from Michael:

Mary Barrins
21 Parnell Street
Ballymahon
Co. Longford
Ireland

Dear Mary,
thank you so much for being so kind and hospitable to me last week. I really had a wonderful time and I especially enjoyed my stay with you. Thank you for the interesting tours and the entertaining evenings. And I will never forget the night in our pub "The Plough".
I will send you the tourist information on Germany that you asked for as soon as possible.
You are welcome to stay in our house anytime!
Best regards,

Michael

Plum pudding is a famous, traditional English dessert on Christmas Day.

A Read the text "In a Pub" again. Now look at these sentences. Each of the sentences has a mistake. Find it and correct it.

Examples:
In Great Britain the traffic signs show the distances in kilometres.
*- In Great Britain the traffic signs show the distances in **miles**.*

In Ireland the pubs can stay open all night.
*- In Ireland the pubs **close at 1 a.m.***

1. The Irish have the oldest monarchy in the world.
2. On Sundays there is usually music in *The Plough*.
3. Many official events begin with the song 'What shall we do with the drunken sailor'.
4. About 10 % of the people in Great Britain are fond of the monarchy.
5. At Christmas the Irish have a traditional dinner with turkey and plums.
6. The students want to go to a cinema.
7. When you buy a beer in a pub you order either half a litre or a litre.
8. The musicians started to play before 8:30 p. m.

 How much do you know about a foreign country, for example Great Britain? Do you want to compare your knowledge with your classmates? A good way to do that is to prepare a quiz. You will find a lot of information about preparing a quiz on page 141.

Adjectives and Adverbs

When do you use adjectives, and when do you use adverbs?
● Adjectives describe *nouns*.
Example: *It was a **successful presentation**. (a presentation = noun)*

● Adverbs describe *verbs*.
Example: *The students **worked successfully**. (to work = verb)*

How do you form an adverb?
● You form regular adverbs with
adjective + -ly

→ For rules see pages 158/159

Spelling rule: Adjectives that end in *-y* change to *-ily*.

Adjective	Adverb
quick	quickly
bad	badly
careful	carefully
easy	easily
successful	successfully

Be careful, because some adverbs are irregular:

Irregular	
good	well
hard	hard
early	early
fast	fast

A Do you know? Are the underlined words adjectives or adverbs?
1. Michael and Mary go home <u>silently</u>.
2. The Irish have a <u>traditional</u> dinner with turkey and plum pudding.
3. There is <u>live</u> music in *The Plough*.
4. Many <u>official</u> events begin or end with the national anthem.
5. Most schools have their own <u>special</u> uniform.
6. The Irish decorate the houses <u>colourfully</u>.
7. The Dutch and German students listen very <u>carefully</u> to the music.
8. That is a very <u>good</u> idea.
9. The musicians play very <u>well</u>.

B Fill in the gaps by using the following words.
They are not in the correct order. One word is used twice.

> quick – quickly – bad – badly – careful – carefully – easy – easily – good – well – hard

1. Lunch is a … meal for many people.
2. Many people eat their food in a fish and chip shop …
3. Manchester United played … and lost the match.
4. Smoking is a … habit.
5. Ken is a … driver.
6. The students work on their project …
7. Gina is very good at tennis. She won the game …
8. The homework is …
9. Gina and Ken know Jim …
10. Jim is a … cook.
11. For nurses it is a … life.
12. Nurses work … and don't earn much money.

Vocabulary

7.1 Sarah and Michael Are Going Abroad		
old people's nurse [əʊld ʹpiːplz nɜːs]	someone who looks after old people	Altenpflegerin, Altenpfleger
old people's home [əʊld ʹpiːplz həʊm]	a place where old people live	Altenheim
practical experience [ʹpræktɪkl ɪkʹspɪərɪəns]	learning by doing	praktische Erfahrung
home remedy [həʊm ʹremɪdɪ]	medicine which is produced at home	Hausmittel
presentation [ˌprezənʹteɪʃn]	to show your work	Darbietung, Vorstellung
destination [ˌdestɪʹneɪʃn]	the place to go to	Zielort
flight [flaɪt]	the plane you will fly in	Flug
remark [rɪʹmɑːk]	a short piece of information	Bemerkung
on time [ɒn taɪm]	not late	pünktlich
delay [dɪʹleɪ]	something is too late, not on time	Verspätung
knowledge [ʹnɒlɪdʒ]	to have information about something	Kenntnis
(to) express [ɪkʹspres]	to put an idea into words	ausdrücken
7.2 The Meeting		
heartily [ʹhɑːtɪli]	friendly, warm	herzlich
compress [kəmʹpres]	a cloth used to stop high temperature	Kompresse, Wickel
bath salts [bɑːθ sɔːlt]	herbal remedies used in bath water	Badezusatz, Badesalz
herb [hɜːb]	a plant used for flavouring or for medicines	Kraut, Kräuter
herbal garden [hɜːbl gɑːdn]	a garden with many herbs	Kräutergarten
steam bath [stiːm bɑːθ]	very hot bath	Dampfbad
an exhibition [ˌeksɪʹbɪʃn]	a show	Ausstellung
pharmacy [ʹfɑːməsɪ]	a medicine shop	Apotheke
an essay [ʹeseɪ]	a small piece of written work	Aufsatz, Zeitschriftenartikel
7.3 In a Pub		
pub [pʌb]	a place where alcohol is served	Gaststätte
successful [səkʹsesfʊl]	with success, a good result	erfolgreich
a pint [paɪnt]	a glass which contains 0,568 litre, a British measurement	0,568 Liter
lager [ʹlɑːgə]	beer with a golden colour	helles Bier
a glass (of stout etc.) [ə glɑːs (əv staʊt)]	the half of a pint	0,284 Liter
stout [staʊt]	strong dark beer	dunkles Starkbier
measurement [ʹmeʒəmənt]	unit which is used to find the quantity of a thing	Maßeinheit
unfortunately [ʌnʹfɔːtʃnətlɪ]	to have bad luck	unglücklicherweise
likely [laɪklɪ]	it may happen	wahrscheinlich
monarchy [ʹmɒnəkɪ]	a country which is ruled by a king or queen	Monarchie
majority [məʹdʒɒrətɪ]	the most	Mehrheit
event [ɪʹvent]	an activity or an action	Ereignis
national anthem [ʹnæʃənl ʹænθəm]	a piece of music belonging to a country and its people	Nationalhymne
holly [ʹhɒlɪ]	an evergreen plant with prickly leaves and red berries	Stechpalme
mistletoe [ʹmɪsltəʊ]	a plant with white berries	Mistel
turkey [ʹtɜːkɪ]	a large bird which is eaten	Truthahn
plum pudding [plʌm ʹpʊdɪŋ]	a kind of boiled cake with fruit	Plumpudding

Unit 8
People at Work

Which professions do the people on the pictures have?
These are their jobs …

> cook   male nurse   lady teacher (AmE) /nursery nurse (BrE)

… and these are their workplaces:

> kindergarten (AmE) /nursery school (BrE)   old people's home   kitchen of a hospital

Look at the pictures and combine them with the words. Who works where and what are their jobs?

8.1   A Day in Sheila's Life

Sheila works in a nursery school in Bristol. She lives close to her workplace, so she can walk.

> – get up at 6:30 a.m.
> – arrive at nursery school at 7:30 a.m.
> – prepare breakfast
> – help children to brush their teeth
> – help them go to toilet
> – go for a walk
> – put children in circle, study a new song
> – help them to draw pictures
> – mothers come/1 p.m./take their children home
> – go home/tired/take a nap

A   Describe her day in complete sentences.
Use the expressions from the box.
Use the *simple present* and start like this:
*Sheila **gets** up at 6:30 a.m.*

B   In the evening her mother wants to know what Sheila did during her working day. Give Sheila's mother a full report. Use the *simple past* and start like this:
*I **got** up at 6:30 a.m.*

C   Would you like to be in Sheila's place? Give reasons why or why not.
The words from the box below might help you. Discuss it with your classmates.

> interesting – boring – fascinating – like to work with children – useful job – monsters – good / bad working hours – work with people – colleagues – help children – hate children – low income – dangerous – mothers know everything better – responsible work – a lot of different activities – stay young myself – see world new

   You can find more information on having a discussion on page 140.

D Unfortunately one of Sheila's colleagues has lost her job and is now unemployed. She has made a big mistake. What could she have done wrong? Here are some explanations. Use the *present perfect* for your sentences.

Example:
*steal something – She probably has lost her job because she **has stolen** something.*

---

steal something – not be at work sometimes – be late too often – have arguments with colleagues – be ill too often – not inform a mother that her child walk home – drink alcohol at work – be too lazy – not see problems of children – not be hygienic enough

---

→ For rules, see page 155 ff.

E What tense do you have to use in these sentences? *Present perfect* or *simple past*?
1. I (read) this magazine last month.
2. There (be) an accident. You have to drive another way.
3. We (live) in London from 1995 to 2005.
4. Sorry, can you say that again? When … (you live) there?
5. I (never be) there, but my father (go) there last Christmas.
6. We (see) each other every day when we (be) small kids.
7. When Mary was young, she (be) a little overweight.
8. During the last three months she (lose) five kilos and looks pretty good.
9. … you … (go) to the party last night? No, I (do). I (go) to Melanie instead.
10. What … you … (wear)? My green shirt and my black trousers.

8.2 What about John's Working Life?

1 **How It Started**
John worked in an old people's home some time ago. He was a male nurse and he really liked his job. When he was 12 years old,
5 he used to go shopping for an old lady who was unable to leave her home because she couldn't walk anymore. This lady was always so grateful and every now and then she gave him a little pocket money.
10 She died when he was 16. He was just about to leave school, making plans for his future. He had a hard time getting over her death because John liked her so much, and she had been like a mother to him.

15 He knew from the statistics that the number of old people was increasing very fast. There were plenty of old people who needed help and support. Two years later he started an apprenticeship in an old peo-
20 ple's home in Winchester.
John finally took his exams after three years of training and he did very well. At present he works as a teacher for nurses and tells the pupils about the work of an old peo-
25 ple's nurse in an old people's home.

This is what he tells them:

Working Time

"I had to work on shifts. When I had the morning shift, I had to start at 8 a.m. and
30 worked for seven hours. Every other week I had to work the late shift and started work at 1 p.m. Every six weeks I had to do the night shift for seven days. After that I had one week off. I also had to work twice
35 a month at the weekends."

Residents

"At the time when I left the old people's home we had 38 residents. Most of them were in their eighties or nineties. One resi-
40 dent was 45 years old. She had tried to commit suicide and did not succeed. The woman had been paralysed and could not do anything on her own ever since. Most of the residents were female. We only had
45 three male residents.
    Some of the old people were confused and so I had to tell them again and again what I was going to do and where they were, because they couldn't remember. The ones
50 who were not confused liked to talk about their lives – and I had to listen very carefully. They also wanted to do something useful. Some of them liked to help the cook, so they peeled the potatoes or cleaned the
55 dishes."

Qualifications

"I had to be very patient and sensitive - and this is what I expect from you, too. You must put yourself into their situation and
60 treat them as you want to be treated when you are old yourselves. You have to find out as much as you can about their lives. For example, if somebody always gets up at 2 o'clock in the night, ask yourself why he
65 does so. He might have been a baker in his working life. You will only be able to understand them when you know them as well as you can. You need a lot of physical strength, too. Always be careful with
70 your back. Ask a colleague to give you a hand when you turn the residents to prevent bedsores."

A Answer the following questions on the text.
1. Why did John want to become a male nurse?
2. What does he do at present?
3. What do you know about the residents?
4. Which qualifications do you need in this job?

B Have a discussion in class about these topics:
1. You all know some old people. What do you think is good or bad about getting old?
2. Have you ever been or worked in an old people's home? What was it like?

For more information on discussions look up page 140.

C Activity – You can combine this activity with your class in "Lernfeld 10" and „Lernfeld 11".
    Ask your teacher about it.
1. Invite an old person and ask him about his life experiences. Before you do so, make a list of the questions you want to ask. It is also helpful to imagine what has happened in someone's life who is now 75 years old.
2. Do you have an old people's home in your area? If so, ask the manager of the home if you could come for a visit.

D

1. Compare the German life trees with each other. What do they tell you about your future?
2. Comment on the statement "Everybody wants to get old, but nobody wants to be old."

 You find some helpful information about reading statistics and graphs on page 137.

8.3   A Day in Ann's life

Ann works in the kitchen of a hospital. Today she is on the morning shift. They are very busy and the chef gave her a lot of work to do. He wanted everything to be ready by 10 o'clock.

A Look at the pictures. Form complete sentences – what did the chef tell Ann to do?
Start like this:
He told her to wash the cabbage.
He told her to …

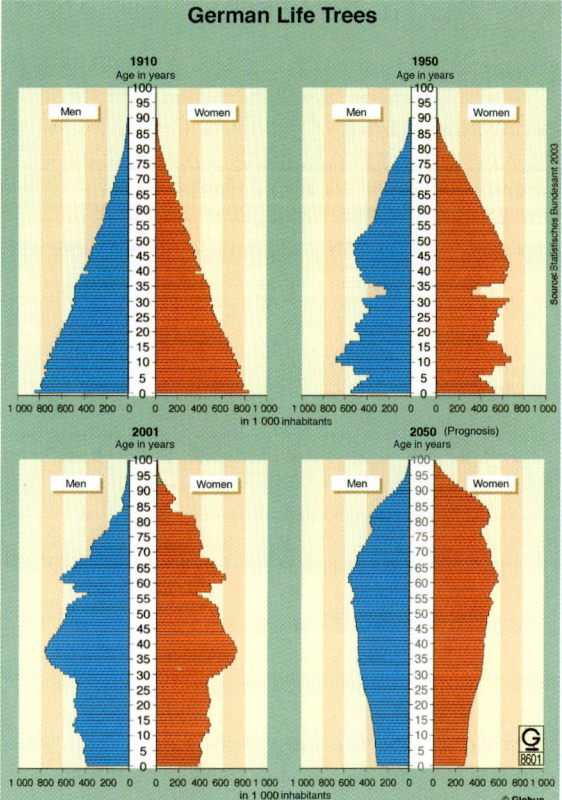

German Life Trees

| wash the cabbage | slice the bread | make salad dressing | cut the onions |

| prepare the sauce | peel the potatoes | cut the parsley | |

At 10 a.m. he wanted to know what Ann had already done.
Ann said:
*I **have** already **washed** the cabbage.*
I have …
I haven't … yet.

B Complete the sentences. Use the *present perfect* this time to show that there is a visible result of what you have done. → For rules see page 155

8.4   The Future Is Yours

What do you want to do when you leave school? Here are some ideas:

Professional Life

nurse – baker – cook – social worker – hang about – gardener –
odd jobs – further education – social assistant – doctor's assistant –
teacher – domestic science – nursery nurse – no idea – help disabled people
…

Private Life

sports (basketball/football/gym …) – have a lot of friends – go to pubs –
discos – computer – stay at home a lot – have children – get married –
build a house – go abroad – travel a lot – go to the church more often
…

A Choose two professions and two private
activities which come close to your
wishes for the future and form sentences
like this:
When I leave this class I am going to
qualify as a baker or a cook. In my private
life I plan to get married and I also want
to have some children.

B Activity – What is your classmate sitting
next to you going to do in his professional
and private future?
Interview him or her.
Tell the class what you have found out
about the other person's plans.

The Future

Going-To-Future

Statements and Negative Clauses			
I	**am**		
You	**are**		
He	**is**		
She		(not)	
It		**going to**	**play** football.
We			
You	**are**		
They			

Questions			
	am	I	
	are	you	
	is	he	
What		she	**going to do?**
		it	
		we	
	are	you	
		they	

How do you form the going-to-future?
You form the going-to-future with
am/is/are + going to + infinitive.

When do you use it?
- You use going to when you talk about
  concrete future plans and intentions.
- You use going to *when you can see* what
  is going to happen in the future.

Examples:
- *What **are** you **going to do** after school?
  Have you got any plans?*
- *I **am going to be** a nurse when I leave
  school. I have already applied at the hos-
  pital.*
- *It's **going to rain**, just look at the clouds!*
- *John **is going to be** quite fat. This is his
  fifth hamburger.*

→ For rules see page 156

Will-Future

Statements and Negative Clauses		
I		
You		
He	**will**	**help** you.
She	**will not**	
It	**(won't)**	
We		
You		
They		

How do you form the will-future?
You form the will-future with
will or will not (won't) + infinitive.

When do you use it?
- You use the will-future instead of the
  going-to-future when you do something
  spontaneously.
- You use the will-future *when you have no
  influence* on what is going to happen.

Examples:
- *Oh, dear! These bags are too heavy for
  you. I will carry one of them.*

- *What will the town look like in ten years?*
- *I think there will be many high-rise
  buildings.*

**If you are not sure which tense you have
to use – take the will-future.**

83

Vocabulary

8.1 A Day in Sheila's Life		
male nurse [meɪl nɜːs]		Krankenpfleger
lady teacher (AmE) [ˈleɪdɪ tiːtʃə], auch: nursery nurse (BrE) [ˈnɜːsrɪ nɜːs]	a woman who works with small children	Kinderpflegerin, Erzieherin
Kindergarten (AmE) [ˈkɪndə‚gɑːtn], auch: nursery school (BrE) [ˈnɜːsrɪ skuːl]	a place for children aged 0 – 6	Kindergarten
tooth (singular), teeth (plural) [tʊːθ, tiːθ]	You show them when you smile.	Zahn, Zähne
exactly [ɪgˈzæktlɪ]	very precise	genau
low income [ləʊ ˈɪŋkʌm]	not enough money for your work	geringes Einkommen
responsible [rɪˈspɒnsəbl]	When you do baby-sitting your are responsible for the baby.	verantwortlich, verantwortungsvoll
(to) have arguments [həv ˈɑːgjʊməntz]	to quarrel	Streit haben
(to) be hygienic [bɪ haɪˈdʒiːnɪk]	to be washed and dressed properly	hygienisch sein
8.2 What about John's Working Life?		
(to) be unable [bɪ ʌnˈeɪbl]	not to be able	unfähig sein
(to) be grateful [bɪ ˈgreɪtʊl]	feel thankful to another person	dankbar sein
statistics [stəˈtɪstɪkz]	a collection of numbers, often in a diagram	Statistik
(to) increase [ɪnˈkriːs]	to arise in number or degree	hier: zunehmen
(to) support [səˈpɔːt]	to help someone	jemanden unterstützen
apprenticeship [əˈprentɪʃɪp]	to do two or three years of training until someone is qualified in the job	Ausbildung
(to) take exams [teɪk ɪgˈzæmz]	You do that at the end of your apprenticeship.	Examen machen
(to) work on shifts [wɜːk ɒn ʃɪftz]	You work either in the morning shift, in the late shift or in the night shift.	im Schichtdienst arbeiten
(to) have a week off [həv ə wiːk ɒf]	not to work for a week	eine Woche dienstfrei haben
resident [ˈrezɪdənt]	a person who lives in an old people's home	Bewohner, Heiminsasse
(to) commit suicide [kəˈmɪt sjʊɪsaɪd]	to end your life willingly	Selbstmord begehen
(to) succeed [sakˈsiːd]	to have success	Erfolg haben, gewinnen
(to) be paralysed [bɪ ˈpærəlaɪzd]	to be unable to move your body	gelähmt sein
(to) be patient [bɪ ˈpeɪʃnt]	to be able to wait	geduldig sein
(to) be sensitive [bɪ ˈsənsɪtɪv]	to understand the feelings of others	sensibel sein
physical strength [ˈfɪzɪkl streŋθ]	the strength of your body	körperliche Stärke
(to) prevent [prɪˈvent]	to avoid	verhindern
bedsore [bedsɔː]		Druckgeschwür; Dekubitus
8.4 The Future is Yours		
(to) hang about [hæŋ əˈbaʊt]	not to know what to do	herumlümmeln
(to) be disabled [bɪ dɪsˈeɪbld]	to be handicapped	behindert sein
(to) go abroad [gəʊ əˈbrɔːd]	to go into another country	ins Ausland gehen
intention [ɪnˈtenʃn]		Absicht

Unit 9
Living with Computers

Describe the cartoons.
Would you like to be a person in the cartoons?

Do you know how to look for information on the Internet? Why don't you turn to page 138 and find some more about it.

9.1   Computers and Chores

A Many people have wrong ideas about what a computer can do and what it cannot do. How about you? Check the following jobs and say if you think a computer **can** or **cannot** do them.

Example: – Lay the table?
Say it like this:
– *A computer <u>cannot</u> be used <u>for laying</u> the table.*

1. Write letters?
2. Calculate nutritional values?
3. Cook?
4. Sweep the floor?
5. Tidy up your room?
6. Start and stop the washing machine?
7. Check and control the temperature of the heating?
8. Help you with budgeting?
9. Iron your trousers?

B Look at the picture on this page. Which number stands for which word? Write the words and their German meanings into your vocabulary notebook.

> keyboard – disks – disk drive – hard disk – CD-ROM drive – monitor – mouse

C What are these things used for? Use the words from Exercise B and form complete sentences. Use this help:

Example: *keyboard – A keyboard is used for wr<u>iting</u> texts.*

1. to store large programmes
2. to watch what you type on the keyboard
3. to load new software
4. to move the cursor quickly
5. to read disks
6. to store small files
7. to write texts

The Gerund I   → For rules see page 162

Sara is not quite sure if she should buy a computer for herself. She wants to work in the field of housekeeping, but she believes that cooking, washing, sewing and all the other household chores don't have a lot to do with computers. Joel, the son of their new next-door neighbours, a really handsome young man, is fond of working with computers. He tells her that she is absolutely wrong. Look at what Joel says and then help him to form sentences.

After prepositions (*by, instead of, for, …*) the following verb takes the ing-form. We call that the gerund.

Example: *A mouse is used **for (move + ing)** the cursor quickly.*
              *A mouse is used **for moving** the cursor quickly.*

The spelling rules for the verbs in the progressive and gerund are the same.
→ You can look them up on page 4.

Try using the gerund yourself. Form sentences with the help of the prepositions in the box. Choose the right one for each of the following sentences. The prepositions are not in the correct order.

> in – for – for – by – by – to - of – of – from – instead of – at – about

1. … (calculate) nutritional values per hand, you can use a computer programme. You'll be much faster.
2. … (write) nice invitation cards for a party, you can get CDs with clipart pictures on them.
3. … (use) spread-sheet programmes, you can do your budgeting much faster.
4. Modern dictionaries on CD-ROMs are very good … (translate) words from one language into another.
5. A computer can even be used … (design) a pattern for knitwear.
6. Some people are fond … (control) their knitting machines by a knitwear programme they wrote themselves.
7. More and more women are interested … (go) to computer courses at evening schools.
8. I am really looking forward … (see) a brand-new computer in your home.
9. Your friends will be happy … (get) letters with photos from you which you can infix in a text.
10. You can store your latest photos on your hard disk … (put) them on a flatbed scanner.
11. You don't know what to cook today? No problem. Many people are proud … (have) a modem and (surf) the Internet. There are lots of recipes out there!
12. If you suffer … (get) bored, you can have a chat on the Internet.
13. If you think … (go) on holiday or (buy) a new car, get one via Internet.

9.2   Writing an Invitation

Sara Miller was very excited. She would be eighteen next week! This had to be celebrated with a fantastic birthday party. Her parents had already told her that they would go to the theatre that evening, so Sara and her friends would have the house for themselves without getting disturbed. She was looking forward to dancing, and she was particularly keen on seeing this nice boy Joel from next door again. Joel – would she succeed in winning his heart? She had invited him to the party this morning, when he was leaning over the garden fence.
Sara had started writing invitation cards, but no – all the ideas she had had looked too childish – they were simply not good enough for such an important party. Joel had seen her problem, and said that he didn't want to disturb. He went into his house. Now she was in her room, with the problem of writing invitation cards again. While she was dreaming of dancing with Joel, cheek to cheek, there was suddenly a knock on her room door. Sara almost fainted. Her mother had let Joel in and now he was standing in front of her – he was hiding something behind his back.
Joel seemed to be a little embarrassed but Sara did not mind seeing him like this. Maybe he was as excited about meeting her as she was.

Joel: "I have got something for you, – well, it's just an idea, it's not finished yet."
Sara got curious.
"Show me, please!" she begged impatiently, and he gave her a sheet of paper with one of her best photos on it. It was the beginning of an invitation – to her birthday party. Mum must have given him that photo.
Joel stuttered: "You know, it's not finished yet. It's, it's … just an idea and I … I thought …"
Sara: "But that's fantastic!", she interrupted him. "How did you do that? Are you a magician? How did you get my photo onto the paper?" she wanted to know.

Joel: "Too many questions at the same time," Joel now laughed. "I did all of this with my computer. You just need a flatbed scanner, a good colour printer and the right software. It is really not too difficult."

Sara said admiringly: "You must have read many books – or been to many computer courses to learn that."

Joel: "No, not really. I can show you how to create your own invitation card. 'Learning by doing' is the motto. You will see, you can do that, too."

He was so fair, so friendly! Not as conceited as those other macho boys who thought they were the greatest, Sara thought. She went to his room, and they sat down in front of Joel's computer.

Joel: "Let me open your file, I called it 'Sara.doc'." …

Read the text "Writing an Invitation" and answer the following questions in full sentences.
1. Why was Sara Miller very excited?
2. What did Sara's parents offer her?
3. Who is Joel? Collect all the information you can find about him.
4. How did Sara invite Joel to her party?
5. What did Sara dream of?
6. What was Sara's problem on the morning when she met Joel?
7. What did Joel probably do after he said that he didn't want to disturb?
8. Why did Sara almost faint when there was a knock on her room door?
9. Why was Joel a little embarrassed? What do you think?
10. What did Sara think about what Joel had hidden behind his back?
11. Describe what Joel had produced and how he had done it.
12. What speaks for the fact that Sara had fallen in love with Joel? Collect some hints from the text.

Past Perfect or Simple Past?

Joel carried out several steps when he designed the invitation card for Sara. It all happened in the past. If you want to combine these actions in one sentence, then you use the past perfect. You combine the sentences like this:

Example:
Joel started his computer. He loaded his text processing programme.
*- **After** Joel **had** started his computer he loaded his text processing programme.*

         Past Perfect

How do you form the past perfect?   → For rules see pages 154/156

I, you, he, she, it, we, you, they	had (second form of have)	already, never, … (adverb)	started (regular verb) told (irregular verb) (third verb form)
Joel	*had*	*already*	*started …*

When do you use the past perfect and when do you use the simple past?
There were two events in the past: *Joel started his computer. He loaded his programme.*
Take past perfect for what happened **earlier**.   Take simple past for what happened **later**.

Past Perfect	Simple Past
earlier	later

Joel started his computer.   He loaded his programme.

*After Joel **had** **started** his computer he **loaded** his programme.*

Sara and Joel worked step by step, as you can see below. Now form combined sentences with 1. and 2., then with 2. and 3., then 3. and 4., and so on.
Remember: The earlier event always takes the tense ??? and the later one ???. See page 88.

(Note: On German keyboards *Ctrl = Strg*)
1. Joel switched on his flatbed scanner.
2. He loaded his scanner programme by clicking on the *Ipplus* icon.
3. He clicked on the word *Acquire* in the pull-down-menu (shortcut: *Ctrl + q*)
4. He clicked on *Preview*.
5. Sara pulled the frame around the part of the photo that she wanted to scan.
6. She clicked the *Scan* button.
7. She clicked the ✂ icon to cut out the photo.
8. She copied the photo with the copy instruction. *(Ctrl + c)*
9. She changed to the *WORD* programme.
10. She typed *Ctrl + v* and infixed the picture in the place where she wanted it.
11. Sara pulled the cursor onto one of the corner squares.
12. She pressed the left mouse button and pulled the cursor to change the size of the picture.
13. Joel changed the frame type to *Outline*.
14. Sara clicked on the *WordArt* button to have a fancier script type.
15. She typed in her text.
16. She infixed her text by clicking *OK*.

 Why don't you go to your computer room and try it yourself? What did Joel say?
Learning by doing! Ask your teacher about it.

The Gerund II

When you are in the computer room and try to make your own invitation card, it will be easy for you to answer the following questions. Do that by using the words and prepositions in brackets and a gerund construction.
Study page 86 and you will know how to use the gerund.

Example: *How do you start a programme? (click its icon/by)*
– You start a programme **by** *double clicking its icon.*

1. What must you do before you load the scanner programme?
   (load programme/switch on the scanner/before)
2. What is the *Preview* function for?
   (frame the part of the photo you want/for)
3. How can you get your photo from the scanner programme into the text processing programme?
   a) use the copy function/by;
   b) switch to the other programme: click the multitasking bar at the bottom of the monitor screen/by
   c) use the shortcut *Ctrl+ v*/hold the *Ctrl* key and strike the *v* key/by
4. How can you make your photo larger or smaller?
   a) pull the cursor to a square/press the left mouse button and move the cursor/after
   b) watch the changing size of the photo on the screen/you will get the size you want/by
   c) release the mouse button/the size will no longer change/after
5. How can you make your text flow around the photo?
   a) You can make your text flow around your photo/format the frame/by
   b) the text will flow around your photo/you choose *Outline*/after

Don't worry, your computer won't turn into a monster – unless you speak German!

9.3   A Morning in Caren's Life in the Year 2008

It is 6 o'clock in the morning. The alarm clock rings, the bedroom curtains open, the computer screen turns itself on. "Good morning, Caren, you have to get up now," a voice says. Caren opens her eyes.

"Music," Caren says and at once the radio programme is started. Caren is a nineteen-year-old woman who lives in a flat in York.

Suddenly the radio programme is interrupted by a voice: "It is 6:15 a.m. – you are late, Caren." Caren finally gets up and presses a few keys on the bedroom terminal to end the wake-up-programme. Then she keys in orders to open the window for three hours. "The only thing I still need is a robot to turn back the bed clothes in the morning," she thinks.

In the bathroom the temperature has already been increased to 23 °C.

"Light," Caren says as she enters the room – and the light is switched on by invisible hands. Caren has to hurry up because the water in the shower is started at 6:30 a.m. She works as a cook in a hospital, so she always has to be in time.

At exactly 6:30 a.m. the shower is started and five minutes later the water is stopped. "I must change the showering time to ten minutes," Caren thinks as she leaves the shower.

It is 7 o'clock now and Caren enters the kitchen. The coffee is ready, and the toaster has just been started. A look into the fridge tells Caren that she has to order some food. So she turns on the kitchen computer and goes online. First she compares the prices of the three grocers in town, and finally she orders things like milk, bread, cereals, a cucumber, tomatoes, a cabbage, potatoes, onions, a dressing and ham.

While Caren is having breakfast, the computer tells Caren that she has got mail: "You've got a message". Caren starts the programme to exchange messages, and immediately her friend's face appears on the screen. "I'm sorry, Caren," her friend Maggie says, "I can't come over this evening. My mother is ill and I want to visit her. I'll call you later to make a new appointment." In the meantime it's 7:30 a.m. Before Caren leaves, she programmes the washing machine to start itself in the afternoon. Then she runs to her car whose engine has already been started.

A Read the text on the left carefully and answer the following questions in complete sentences.
1. Which information do you get about Caren?
2. What does Caren do in the morning?
3. What does the computer network do
   – in the bedroom,
   – in the bathroom,
   – in the kitchen?
4. Would you like to have a morning like this? Give reasons for your answer.

B Look for words in the text that fit these definitions:
1. A piece of cloth which hangs from the top of a window.
2. A set of rooms for living in.
3. To stop an action from continuing.
4. You press a control for an electrical device such as light or a radio.
5. A device used for washing your full body.
6. A shopkeeper who sells regular food such as flour, sugar and tinned food.

C Look for definitions for the following words.
1. alarm clock   4. hospital
2. bathroom   5. fridge
3. invisible   6. milk

D Find out the nouns of the following verbs.
1. to enter   3. to live
2. to visit   4. to open

E What are the verbs of the following words?
1. comparison   3. interruption
2. appearance   4. thoughts

F A puzzle – Here you have nine pictures and eighteen words. Look at the pictures and match each drawing with two words from the list.

Example: *picture number 6 + screen + window*

computer
e-mail
floppy disk
hard disk
input unit
keyboard
key
mouse
modem
network
paper
printer
return key
screen
space bar
stored data
telecommunication
window

Passive Voice

Caren's dreams have become true – she has got a robot. Now she can be lazy …
The housework is done by the robot: The meals are cooked, the rooms are cleaned, and much more.

Active sentence: *The robot cooks the meal*.

We show that someone/something does something.
  (subject)

Passive sentence: *The meal is cooked by the robot*.

We tell what has happened to the subject.
It is not so important to know who does it.
→ For rules see page 160

How do you form sentences in the passive voice?
Have a look at what happens to the different parts of the sentence when you put it in the passive voice:

1. <u>Active:</u>   The robot cooks **the meal**.

   <u>Passive:</u> **The meal** is cooked by the robot

   ⇨ The **object** of the active sentence is now the subject.

2. <u>Active:</u> The robot **cooks** the meal.

   <u>Passive:</u> The meal is **cooked** by the robot.

   ⇨ The **verb** of the active sentence is put into the third form (past participle, see page 151) You also need a **form of** *to be* in front of the verb. The tense of the sentence stays the same. (*to be* + past participle)

3. <u>Active:</u> **The robot** cooks the meal.
   <u>Passive:</u> The meal is cooked **by the robot**.

   ⇨ The former **subject** is now the object, and you add the preposition *by*.

When we use the passive voice, who or what causes the action is often unknown or unimportant:
A lot of money was stolen. The window was broken.

A Simple present sentences – The verbs in brackets have to be put in the simple present. Then you have a correct passive sentence in the simple present.

Example:
clean/cleans (active) – is cleaned (passive)
see/sees (active) – is seen (passive)

1. The coffee (cook) at 7 o'clock.
2. The kitchen (clean) after breakfast.
3. The laundry (wash) every Monday.
4. The flowers (water) very often.
5. The windows (polish) once a week.
6. The carpets (hoover) when it is necessary.

B Simple past sentences – The verbs in brackets have to be put in the simple past.

Example:
painted (active) – was/were painted (passive)
wrote (active) – was/were written (passive)

1. This house (build) in 1985.
2. The trees (plant) in 1987.
3. The bathroom (paint) last year.
4. The roof (repair) two weeks ago.
5. The neighbour house (sell) some weeks ago.
6. The cars (damage) last night.

C Rewrite the following sentences. However, instead of using somebody/they/people, form a passive sentence.

Example:
active: Somebody cut my flowers yesterday.
passive: My flowers were cut yesterday.

1. Somebody stole my bike yesterday.
2. Someone repaired my computer screen last week.
3. People use computers for a lot of things.
4. They bought 50 personal computers to improve education.
5. Someone invented the scanner.
6. They took my article to be a part of the homepage of our school.

D Put these active sentences into the passive voice. Use simple present or simple past.

Example:
active: Caren prepares breakfast.
passive: Breakfast is prepared by Caren.

1. The computer network controls all electrical devices.
2. The software made the mistake.
3. Peter copied all files.
4. The virus destroyed the hard disk.
5. Caren uses the Internet regularly.
6. The programmer made a backup.

E This is the hospital where Caren works. When you are in a hospital as a patient, a lot of things happen to you.
Some weeks ago Caren's boyfriend Bob had a bad accident. He lost consciousness.

Hospital

Write a story about the things that happened after Bob had lost consciousness. The following list of expressions will help you. Use the passive as often as possible. Use the simple past.

to call an ambulance
to take someone to the hospital
to take someone to the emergency room
to examine
to control blood pressure
to take the temperature
to make a blood test
to give an injection
to lift someone onto the operating table
to operate on someone
to take someone to the patients' room

9.4   How to Work with a Nutritive Programme

Now we are back in reality. Caren really works as a cook in a hospital. Her task is to prepare the meals for those patients who need a special diet because of their illness or because they have to lose weight. Before Caren can start to prepare the meals she has to choose the right food and the amount of food. In order to do this quickly and correctly Caren uses the computer. Now have a look at one part of Caren's work:

First Step

Caren needs information about the patient like age, weight, height, illness. When she keys these data in, the nutritive programme tells her at once how many kilojoules and nutrients this patient needs a day.

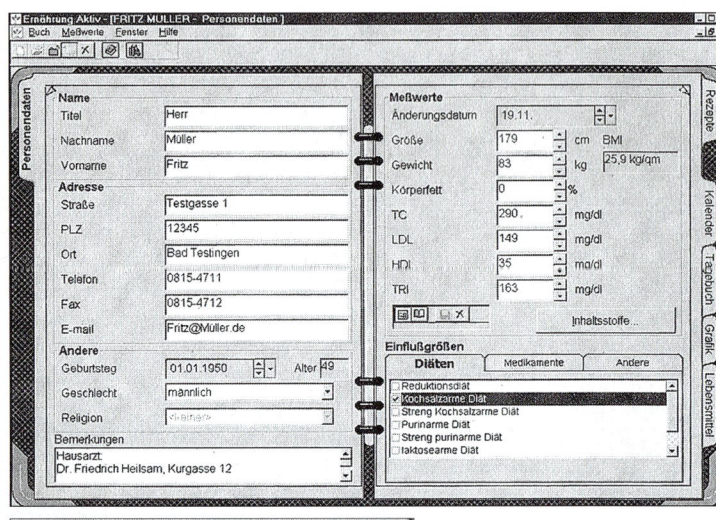

Second Step

After that Caren keys in all the meals with all the food the patient gets a day. Therefore she has to know the exact amounts of all food the patient gets a day, divided into five meals. The programme then calculates the exact amount of kilojoules and nutrients the meals contain.

	Kücheneinh.	Bezeichnung	Menge	
	1 Portion	Rührei (4)	200	g
	1 Portion	Schwein Speck	30	g
	4 Portionen	Weißbrot-Toastbrot	120	g
	1 Portion	Markenbutter	20	g
	1 Portion	Marmelade	25	g
	2 Portionen	Kaffee (Getränk)	300	g

Inhaltsstoffe des Lebensmittels

Third Step

When Caren wants to know if her planned meals guarantee the correct supply of energy and nutrients, she activates the file which compares the nominal value with the actual value.
The programme shows the results for the indicated person on the screen.
Now Caren knows if the suggested meals are alright or if she has to improve something.

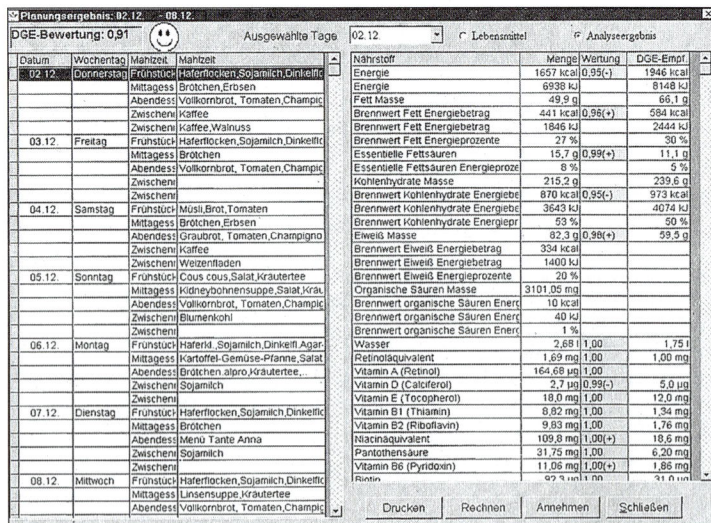

Past Perfect or Simple Past?

This evening Caren is very late. Her boyfriend is already waiting for her at home. He sees at once that Caren had a bad day, and asks Caren what had happened. Caren says:
"In the morning I wanted to make the necessary calculations for a few new patients but the computer didn't start the programme. After the technician ***had repaired*** the computer, I keyed in the data of the patients and the meals I wanted to cook, but I was already late now. After the computer ***had done*** the necessary calculations I prepared lunch in only one hour …

When do you use the past perfect?
Sometimes there is more than one thing that happened in the past. In that case we use the *past perfect* to tell about things that had happened *before* other things in the past.

past perfect in the morning 8:30 a.m.	past in the morning 9:00 a.m.	present in the evening 8:00 p.m.
The technician repaired the computer.	Caren keyed in the data.	Caren tells about it.

*After the technician **had repaired** the computer, Caren **keyed** in the data.*
→ For rules see pages 154/156

A Caren has had some terrible days before …Look at these sentences. Put in the right tense: *past perfect* or *simple past*.

Example: *When Caren (finish) work she (drive) home. – When Caren **had finished** work she **drove** home.*

1. Caren (feel) tired because she (work) a lot.
2. When she (eat) something she (go) to bed.
3. She (just go) to bed when the phone (ring).
4. When Caren (wake up) the following morning she (see) that she (forget) to switch off the lights.
5. When she (arrive) at the station the train (already leave).
6. So she (call) a taxi, and in the taxi she (notice) that she (forget) her money.
7. In the hospital her colleagues (tell) her that her boss (ask) for her twice.

B A nice weekend for Caren – Rewrite these sentences. Use the *past perfect* and connect the sentences with 'after'.

Example: *Caren had breakfast. Then she went shopping. – **After** Caren **had had** breakfast she went shopping.*

1. Caren bought new shoes, and then she drank coffee with a girlfriend.
2. She drank coffee with a girlfriend, and then she visited her mother.
3. She drove home and took a bath.
4. She dressed, and then she waited for her boyfriend.
5. Bob arrived, and they went to a party.
6. She woke up late on Sunday and prepared for the meeting with her uncle.
7. They had an excellent meal in a good restaurant, and then they went for a walk.

95

Vocabulary

chore [tʃɔː]	a job which you have to do in the household	Hausarbeit
nutritional value [njuː'trʃənl 'væljuː]	a figure which says how good/healthy the food is	Nährwert
(to) budget ['bʌdʒɪt]	to plan the household money wisely	haushalten, mit Haushaltsgeld umgehen
(to) iron ['aɪən]	to smooth a wrinkled cloth	bügeln
disk drive [dɪsk draɪv]	here you insert the disks	Diskettenlaufwerk
hard disk [haːd dɪsk]	the part of the computer where everything is stored, it can have 10 gigabytes or more	Festplatte
(to) store [stɔː]	to put onto a hard disk or disk	speichern
(to) process ['prəʊses]	to change something into binary digits	aufbereiten
file [faɪl]	here: a letter, a picture, a table	Datei
in the field of [fiːld]		im Bereich
(to) sew [səʊ]	to use needle and thread	nähen
handsome ['hænsəm]	good-looking (used for boys or men)	gutaussehend, prächtig
(to) be fond of something [fɒnd]	to love doing it	etwas mögen, gern haben
spread-sheet programme [spred ʃiːt 'prəʊgræm]	a programme for calculating numbers	Tabellenkalkulationsprogramm
knitwear [nɪtweə]	clothes made of wool like pullovers	Strickwaren
(to) infix [ɪn'fɪkз]	to put into	einfügen
flatbed scanner [flætbed 'skænə]	a machine for getting photos into the computer	Flachbettscanner, Bildabtaster

9.2 Writing an Invitation		
(to) disturb [dɪstɜːb]	to stop s.o. doing s.th.	stören
(to) be keen on something [kiːn]	to really want s.th.	scharf sein auf
(to) succeed in doing something [sək'siːd]	to reach what you want	Erfolg haben
childish [tʃaɪldɪʃ]	like done by a child	kindisch
cheek [tʃiːk]	part of the face	Wange
(to) faint [feɪnt]	to lose one's consciousness	in Ohnmacht fallen
(to) be embarrassed [ɪm'bærəst]	to feel a little uneasy	verlegen sein
magician [mə'dʒɪʃn]	someone who says 'Abracadabra'...	Zauberer
(to) admire [əd'maɪə]	to say how good, pretty, clever someone is	jemanden bewundern
(to) be conceited [kən'siːtəd]	thinking of oneself to be better than others	eingebildet sein
corner square ['kɔːnə skweə]	a black or white box	Eckquadrat
fancy ['fænsɪ]	nice, luxurious	fantasievoll, kunstvoll
an icon ['aɪkɒn]	a small picture/symbol for a computer programme	Piktogramm, Zeichen für ein Computerprogramm
preview ['priːvjuː]	what you see before	Vorschau
(to) release [rɪ'liːs]	not to press/hold any longer	loslassen
frame [freɪm]	pictures are often put in a frame	Rahmen

9.3 A Morning in Caren's Life in the Year 2008		
(to) interrupt [ˌɪntə'rʌpt]	to stop someone in doing something	unterbrechen
invisible [ɪn'vɪzəbl]	something or someone you can't see	unsichtbar
an appointment [ə'pɔɪntmənt]	you arrange to see a person at a particular time	Verabredung
(to) invent [ɪn'vent]	you are the first person to build or make it	erfinden
consciousness ['kɒnʃəsnɪs]	if you lose consciousness you are no longer awake	Bewusstsein
blood pressure [blʌd 'preʃə]	a measure of the amount of force with which your blood flows inside your body	Blutdruck
an injection [ɪn'dʒekʃn]	someone puts a liquid into blood with it	Spritze
patients' room ['peɪʃnts ruːm]	a room in which a sick person is lying	Krankenzimmer

9.4 How to Work with a Nutritive Programme		
nutritive ['njuːtrətɪv]	relating to the food you eat and the proteins, vitamins e.g. in your food which help you to remain healthy	Ernährungs-
weight [weɪt]	your heaviness, measured in kilos/pounds	Gewicht
height [haɪt]	the measurement from bottom to top	Größe
nutrients ['njuːtrɪəntz]	substances that help humans, animals, plants to grow and to live	Nährstoffe
(to) guarantee [ˌgærən'tɪ]	you are certain that something will happen	garantieren
nominal value ['nɒmɪnl 'væljuː]	the amount of nutrients you should eat	Bedarfszahl, Sollwert
actual value ['æktʊəl 'væljuː]	the amount of nutrients you actually eat	Zufuhr, Istwert

Revision III (Unit 7 – 9)

A Improve your knowledge of words.

1. Describe these words in one sentence:

> vocational school – colleague – competition – appearance

2. Find a noun to these verbs and adjectives.

> to prepare – successful – to arrive – to calculate – to translate – to compare – busy – to expect

3. Find the opposite word of …

> to be disappointed – majority – boring – hate – to be late – to be ill – to laugh – to increase

B Translate the postcard from Ann to her boyfriend Bill into German.

Hi Bill,
Sorry I couldn't come last night. I have been ever so busy till now. We have very much work to do, you know. I like working in the kitchen – but sometimes it is just a strain.
Maybe we can manage to go out with each other on the next weekend. I've got a weekend off then. Hope to see you.
Waiting for your call.
Love, Ann

Mr. Bill Stone
28 Clinford Road
Winchester WE 10 2SA

C Tenses – Look at the sentences. What tense are they written in?

1. Ann works in a kitchen.
2. The chef gave her a lot of work to do.
3. He wanted to know what she had done.
4. I'm going to get some tea.
5. Where are you ringing from?
6. He was looking like the devil himself.
7. I will give you a hand.
8. Ryan was listening to Heavy Metal.
9. Why did many young people leave their parents' home?
10. Look, they have just arrived.

D Look at the pictures. Can you find the missing words in the text?
The words in the box might help you.

Some years ago John worked as a … Most of the … were female. At present he works as a …
and tells the pupils about his work. Some people liked to help the cook and … the potatoes or
did the … When you want to work in this profession yourself you must always … It is also very
important that you take care of your … Ask a … for help if something is too heavy for you.

> male nurse – teacher for nurses – listen very carefully – back – residents –
> washing up – colleague – peel

E Questions – Ask for the underlined part of the sentences.
1. Sara Miller was very excited.
2. She would be eighteen next week
3. Her parents had already told her that they would go to the theatre.
4. She had invited Joel this morning.
5. She had written invitation cards.
6. Sara interrupted him.
7. "I can show you how to write your invitation card."
8. 'Learning by doing' is the motto.
9. He was so fair, so friendly.
10. She went with him and they sat down on two chairs.

Unit 10
Dangerous Model of Beauty?

A Mark three aspects that are important for you when someone wants to be your friend:

honest	humorous	tastefully dressed	good-looking
generous	sportive	slim	well-educated
intelligent	wealthy		

B Which of the persons in the pictures would you like to meet? Give reasons for your answer (for example, which person is good-looking, which one seems to be strange).

C Think about what is important for you to like a person.

10.1   People Like Us

Susan

"My name is Susan. I'm sixteen and I live in a semi-detached house in a suburb of London. I still go to school. My girlfriends say that I am a lively girl. That may be true, although I very often feel sad. That's because I am over-weight. I don't dare to wear tight clothes, and I never go swimming. My best friend Pam always says that I'm a little crazy about my figure, but last year when I was on holiday in France with my parents the boys called me 'the plump girl from England'. I could go on a diet but my problem is that I can't stop eating, and I love sweets and fast food. The doctor told me to stop eating so much, and he also said I had to do some sports. I will try to and perhaps then I'll succeed in finding a boyfriend. All my girlfriends always talk about their boyfriends. Even Pam told me last week that she had met a boy named Mark. She said she had known him only a little while but she was already hopelessly in love with him. The only boy that is interested in me is my brother Christopher. He is six! He always asks me to play with him."

"I am Carol. I'm 18 years old and I'm a trainee instructress. My friends say that I'm a good-looking girl but because I'm not interested in clothes, parties and especially in boys they think I'm not quite normal."

"Okay, I prefer horses to parties, I mostly wear jeans and trainers, and I don't eat meat, but I like boys! I must admit that I haven't told them that I got to know a very nice student."

Carol

"I met him near my hometown Cambridge where he was doing biological studies. We soon noticed that we are both environmentalists and vegetarians because we love nature and animals."

"He told me that he condemned fast food and ready-to-serve-meals. So do I! I like to eat salad, vegetables and cereals, and even if I have a problem with chips (I love them). I don't have to care about my weight."

"Hallo, I'm Jason and I'm seventeen years old. I work as a trainee cook in a big hotel in Edinburgh. I've rented a furnished room near the hotel. My family lives in a small village near Inverness, and this is the first time that I'm my own master. I like Edinburgh because you can meet a lot of interesting people there. In summer this town is crowded with tourists, and you can meet a lot of nice girls. In my spare time I usually go to a leisure centre where I do body-building. My parents say that they don't like my hobby but I want to get a perfect-ly trained body. When I was at school the girls always laughed at me because I was very small, but now they look at me admiringly. Lately my boss asked me if I want-ed to become the 'Schwarzenegger of Scotland'. It's impor-tant for me to watch my diet. I need a high amount of protein so I have to buy special drinks and pills. Oh, next week I'll take part in a competition. If I win I'll be very proud."

Jason

On TV there are a lot of commercials with beautiful people. Do you think that has an ef-fect on us? If you are interested in commercials and advertisements, look on page 139. There you will find more information about the advertising business.

A Complete the information sheet about the three young people. Draw a chart like this:

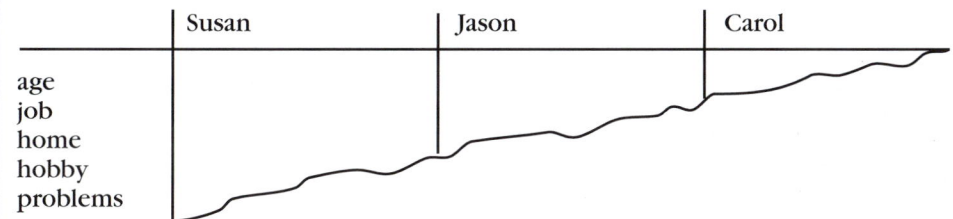

	Susan	Jason	Carol
age			
job			
home			
hobby			
problems			

B Now write a report about the three young people using the information above.

C Answer the following questions in complete sentences.
1. Why does Susan often feel sad?
2. What does she love to eat?
3. What does Susan think is the reason that boys aren't interested in her?
4. Why does Jason like Edinburgh?
5. What do you think – why does Jason want to win a competition in body-building?
6. Why do Carol's friends think that she is different from other people?
7. What do Carol and the student have in common?

D Find the opposites of these words in the text "People Like Us".

> happy – slim – town – winter – unfurnished – empty – boring – to cry –
> unimportant – low – ugly

E On the left side here you find some words from the text. On the right there are their dictionary definitions. However, they are not in the correct order. Can you find the matching pairs?

1. suburb	a) heaviness which can be measured in units such as kilos, pounds or tons
2. weight	b) full of people
3. crowded	c) special shoes that people wear for running or jogging
4. nutrition	d) an area of town which is not close to the centre
5. trainers	e) someone who doesn't eat meat
6. vegetarian	f) the process of providing and receiving food necessary for health and growth

F Which of these foods would Susan, Jason and Carol like to eat?
Name the foods. Look on page 105 for help.

Reported Speech

We use the reported speech to tell somebody else what someone said, asked, wrote or thought.

Changes in the Reported Speech – Personal Pronouns

Example:
direct: Jason says: "**I am** feeling ill."
reported: Jason says that **he is** feeling ill.

A Read what Susan, Pam and Christopher say and then write sentences starting with *She/He says that …* or *They say that …*
1. Susan: "I am sixteen and I live in London."
2. Pam: "I met a nice boy."
3. Christopher: "I like to play with the computer."
4. Susan: "I am overweight."
5. Susan/Pam: "We want to go to the cinema."
6. Christopher: "I want to come with you."

Changes in the Reported Speech – Possessive Pronouns

Example:
direct: Jason says: "**My** room is near the hotel."
reported: Jason says that **his** room is near the hotel.

B Report what Jason and the girl say and write sentences starting with *He/She says that …*
1. Jason: "My name is Jason."
2. Girl: "My name is Kate."
3. Jason: "I'm interested in your training programme."
4. Girl: "Your body looks perfect so your own programme must be very good."
5. Jason: "We can put our training programmes together."

Changes in the Reported Speech – Tenses

Tenses I
When the reporting verb is in the simple present, there is no change of tense in the words reported.

Example:
*direct: Carol says:"I **like** horses."*
*reported: Carol says that she **likes** horses.*

C   Read what Carol and Mark say and then write sentences starting with *She/He says that …*
1.   Carol:"I often eat salad."
2.   Mark:"I also prefer vegetarian food."
3.   Carol:"I will never eat meat."
4.   Mark:"I saw a transport of pigs yesterday."
5.   Carol:"I can't understand people who eat meat."
6.   Mark:"Most people don't think about the animals."

Tenses II
When the reporting verb is in the simple past or past perfect tense, the words reported are viewed in a different perspective and the tenses are changed accordingly.

● Present tense → past tense

Example:
*direct: Mark said:"I **study** biology."*
*reported: Mark said that he **studied** biology.*

D   Read what Carol and Mark said and then write sentences starting with *She/He said that …*
1.   Mark:"I'm cooking a vegetable soufflé."
2.   Carol:"It smells good."
3.   Mark:"I prefer to cook vegetarian meals."
4.   Carol:"I like that because I never eat meat."
5.   Mark:"The soufflé is ready."
6.   Carol:"I'm very hungry."

● Past Tense/Present Perfect → Past Perfect

Example:
*direct: Susan said:"I **bought** a pair of jeans."*
*reported: Susan said that she **had bought** a pair of jeans.*

E   Put the following sentences into the reported speech.
Use different reporting verbs like *answer, tell* and *remark*.
1.   Pam:"Mark and I went to a party."
2.   Susan:"I have never been to a party."
3.   Pam:"We met some interesting people."
4.   Susan:"I haven't met interesting people for ages."
5.   Pam:"We danced and chatted the whole night."
6.   Susan:"I have never been to such a nice party."

● Will Future → Conditional I (would)

Example:
*direct: Jason said, "I **will train** every day."*
*reported: Jason said that he **would train** every day.*

F   Put the following sentences into the reported speech.
1.   Jason:"I will train two hours every day."
2.   Trainer:"I will help you."
3.   Jason:"I will buy special drinks to get enough protein."
4.   Trainer:"I will give you some good pills."

G   Read what the people in the pictures below think and write sentences starting with *She thought that …/He said that …*

→ You can look on page 160 as well, there you will find some grammar information in German.

Everyone will look at me

I look ugly

My bathing suit has become too tight

I ate too much chocolate

I'm doing training every minute of the day

All the girls will love me

I look like Jason

I have improved my fitness very much

10.2   Eating Habits

We spend a lot of the daytime with eating, but usually we don't think much about it. We eat what our parents give us or what advertisements tell us to eat, or we eat together with friends. But do we think about our health and our appearance when we choose our food?

A   Now think about your eating habits and write down at most two answers to each of these questions.

1. The theme nutrition is …
    - boring
    - interesting
    - it doesn't matter to me

2. When I eat I care for …
    - the calories
    - the taste
    - the nutritional value
    - getting enough to eat

3. I eat what …
    - the others eat
    - I like
    - is healthy for me

4. Food should be …
    - cheap
    - healthy
    - tasty

5. I eat fast food …
    - often
    - seldom
    - never

6. I eat vegetables and salad …
    - daily
    - nearly daily
    - seldom

7. I mainly drink …
    - coke
    - juices
    - mineral water
    - coffee, tea

8. Which of the following statements is true?
    - I eat when feel bored.
    - I count the calories and I'm afraid of becoming fat.
    - I only eat because it's necessary.
    - I like to eat.
    - I eat when I feel sad.

B   Compare your result with that of your class neighbour.

C   Try to find out what eating habits the other members of your class have. Ask questions like this:
Who thinks that the theme nutrition is boring, interesting or doesn't matter to them?
Count the number of persons.

D   Write a report about your own eating habits. Start like this:
I'm not interested in nutrition. When I eat I only care for …

E   Work in pairs. Tell your partner about your eating habits. Then tell all the other pupils in your class what your partner has just told you.

Example:
Student A told me that she ate fast food very seldom.

Vocabulary Concerning Eating and Drinking

You should eat a lot of the following foods:

Vegetables

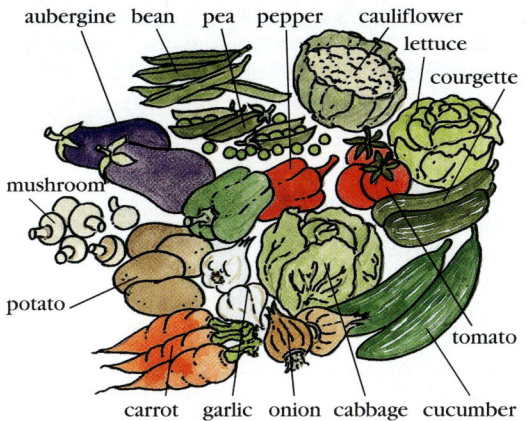

aubergine bean pea pepper cauliflower lettuce courgette mushroom potato tomato carrot garlic onion cabbage cucumber

Fruits

pineapple apple plum orange lemon banana peach pear strawberry cherry

Cereals

rice cereal noodles

roll bread

Drinks

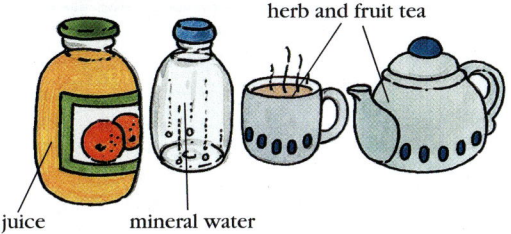

herb and fruit tea juice mineral water

Food you should eat regularly, but not too often:

Dairy Products

yoghurt cheese curd milk

Meat

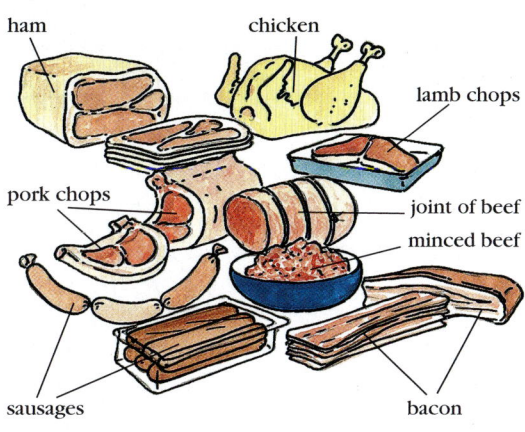

ham chicken lamb chops pork chops joint of beef minced beef sausages bacon

These foods you probably like to eat but you shouldn't:

Sweets

cake a bar of chocolate biscuits a bag of sweets ice cream

Fast Food

hamburger pizza chips

10.3   What to Eat

Last week Susan went to her doctor to talk to him about her weight problem. The doctor asked a lot of questions. He wanted to know if she ate regularly and if she ate at least five meals a day. He also wanted to know how often she ate meat, sweets, fruit and vegetables. He was even interested in getting to know how her meals were cooked.

After that he gave her a leaflet containing rules what to eat and what not to eat. In the leaflet there was also information about how to prepare meals.
In the end the doctor showed her the following picture:

Welcome to the Food Pyramid Guide
The Easy Way to Eat Right

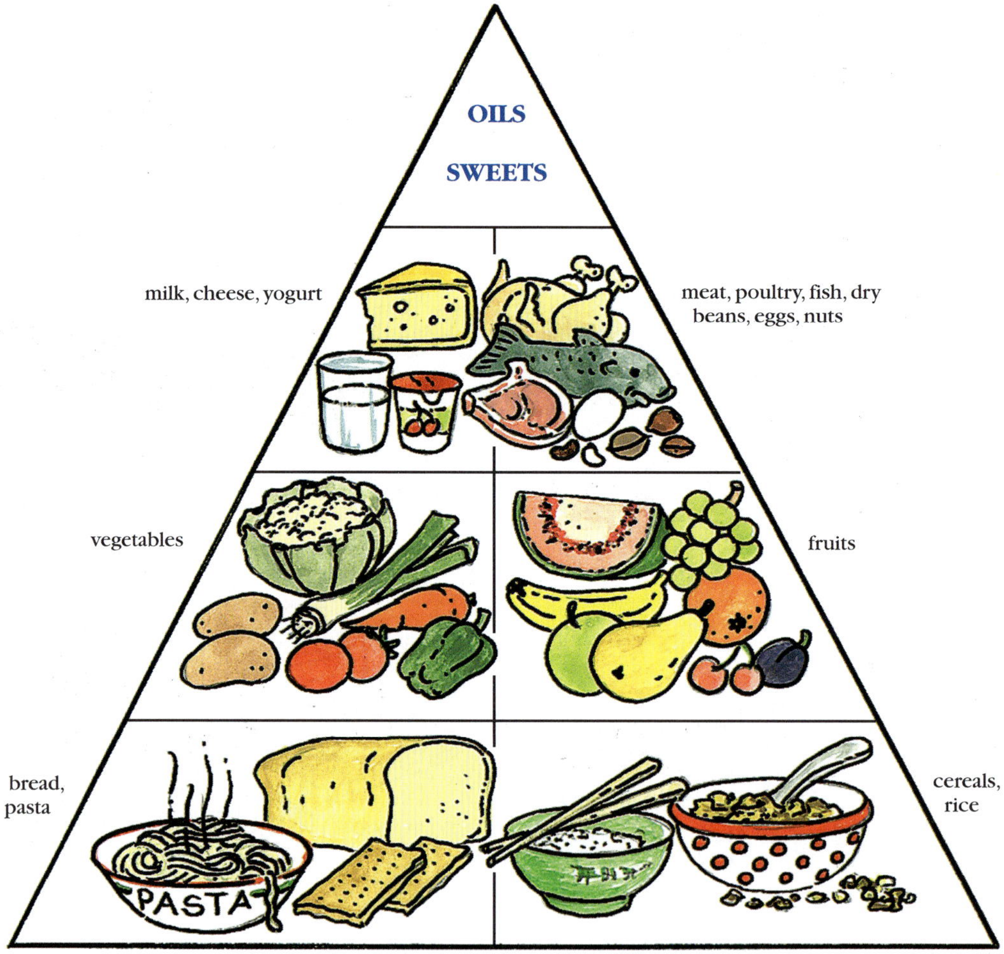

OILS

SWEETS

milk, cheese, yogurt

meat, poultry, fish, dry beans, eggs, nuts

vegetables

fruits

bread, pasta

PASTA

cereals, rice

It's easy to eat right. Just follow the guidelines of the Food Guide Pyramid to guarantee a healthy, balanced and tasty diet.

Here is a suggestion for a food project, maybe even in combination with your classes in „Lernfeld" 4, 5 and 6: Create a picture for your classroom walls where you combine the German words for food with the matching English vocabulary. It would look best if you included pictures of food as well. Ask your teacher about a project like that.

In the leaflet that the doctor gave to Susan she found the following explanations:

Bread, cereals, rice, and pasta:
6 – 11 servings per day

These foods provide complex carbohydrates, an important source of energy. They also provide B vitamins, minerals, and fibre. Starchy foods aren't fattening if you do not add butter, cheese, or cream sauces. Select whole-grain products to maximize fibre and other nutrients.

1 serving = 1 slice of bread; 1 ounce of ready-to-eat cereal; 1/2 cup cooked ceral, rice or pasta.

Vegetables: 3 – 5 servings per day

Vegetables provide vitamins (especially A and C), are excellent sources of fibre, and are naturally low in fat. For maximum nutrients, select dark leafy greens, deep-yellow orange vegetables, and starchy vegetables like potatoes.

1 serving = 1 cup raw leafy greens; 1/2 cup other vegetables chopped; 3/4 cup vegetable juice.

Fruits: 2 – 3 servings per day

Fruits are a rich source of vitamins, most notable vitamin C. They are low in fat and calories. Select fresh fruits and fruit juices, and frozen, canned, or dried fruits. Avoid fruits that are processed with heavy syrups and sugar-sweetened juices.

1 serving = 1 medium apple, banana, or orange; 1/2 cup of chopped fruit or berries; 3/4 cup fruit juice.

Weights to calculate meals: US/GB/D

US		GB		D	
		1 ounce	=	28.35	grams
16 ounces	=	1 pound	=	0.454	kilograms
14 pounds	=	1 stone	=	6.356	kilograms
112 pounds	=	1 hundred-			
		weight	=	50.8	kilograms

Meat, poultry, fish, dry beans, eggs, and nuts: 2 – 3 servings per day

Animal foods are excellent sources of protein, iron, zinc, and B vitamins, as are beans, nuts, and seeds. Tofu (made from soybeans) and white beans also supply calcium. Some seeds, like almonds, are good sources of vitamin E.

1 serving = 2 - 3 ounces of cooked lean meat, poultry, or fish; 1 egg; 1/2 cup cooked beans; 2 tablespoons seeds and nuts.

Milk, yoghurt and cheese:
2 – 4 servings per day

Milk products are the richest sources of calcium. They also provide protein and vitamin B12. Choose low-fat varieties to keep calories, cholesterol, and saturated fat at a minimum.

1 serving = 1 cup of milk or yoghurt, 1 - 1/2 ounces of cheese.

Fats, oils, and sweets: use sparingly

These foods provide calories, but little else nutrionally. Exceptions are vegetable oil, which is a source of vitamin E (one tablespoon is all you need), and molasses, an excellent source of iron.

A Describe the food pyramid on the left page.

B Make a list: What amounts of the suggested foods can a person eat a day?

Example: *You can eat 3 slices of bread, 2 ounces of ready-to-eat cereals, and a cup of rice to meet the first group.*

C Create a table containing the six groups of the food pyramid and write down the nutrients.

Group	Nutrients

D Write down as many rules about a healthy diet as you can think of.

There are a lot of new words and vocabulary in this unit. If you don't understand some of the words, and you don't find them in the vocabulary in the back of this book, then look them up in an English-English dictionary. Do you know how to use one? If not, see page 142 for information and exercises.

Vocabulary

10.1 People Like Us		
honest ['ɒnɪst]	telling the truth	ehrlich
generous ['dʒenərəs]	more than expected	großzügig
wealthy [welθɪ]	to have a lot of money	reich
slim [slɪm]	thin and well-shaped body	schlank
overweight ['əʊvəweɪt]	you are too fat	Übergewicht
tight clothes [taɪt]	clothes that fit close to your body	engsitzende Kleidung
plump [plʌmp]	rather fat	mollig
(to) watch	here: to be careful about	hier: aufpassen auf
environmentalist [ɪnˌvaɪərən'mentəlɪst]	someone who wants to protect nature and prevent pollution	Umweltschützer/-in
vegetarian ['vedʒɪ'teərɪən]	someone who doesn't eat meat	Vegetarier /-in
to condemn [kən'dem]	to say that something is very bad	verurteilen
ready-to-serve meals ['redɪ tʊ sɜːv miːlz]	meals that are already prepared when you buy them	Fertiggerichte
crowded [kraʊdɪd]	full of people	überfüllt
leisure centre ['leʒə 'səntə]	a large building where you can do different activities or sports	Freizeitzentrum
(to) chat [tʃæt]	to talk in a friendly way	plaudern

10.2 Eating Habits		
advertisement [əd'vɜːtɪsmənt]	an announcement in a newspaper, on TV etc. to encourage people to buy something	Werbung
appearance [ə'pɪərəns]	the way you look	Aussehen
nutritional value [njuː'trɪʃnl 'væljuː]	the quality of food, i.e. the amount of proteins, vitamins, minerals etc.	Nährwert
juice [dʒuːs]	a drink made out of fruit	Saft

10.3 What to Eat		
(to) provide [prə'vaɪd]	give something to someone	bereitstellen; hier: liefern
source [sɔːs]	the place or item from which you get something	Quelle
fibre ['faɪbə]		Ballaststoff
starch [stɑːtʃɪ]		Stärke
whole grain [həʊl ɡreɪn]	the complete grain	Vollkorn
(to) select [sɪ'lekt]	to choose	auswählen
leafy greens ['liːfɪ griːn]		grünes Blattgemüse
canned [kænd]	something is wrapped in a metal container	in Dosen
chopped [tʃɒpt]	cut into pieces with a knife	gehackt, zerkleinert
seeds [siːdz]	the small part from which a new plant grows	Samen
almonds ['ɑːməndz]	a nut	Mandeln
lean [liːn]	with only a little fat	mager
sparingly ['speərɪŋlɪ]	(to use something) in small amounts	sparsam
molasses [məʊ'læsɪz]		Melasse, Zuckersirup

Unit 11
Problems in Life

A Look at the pictures. What do you think are people afraid of?

B Is there anything you are afraid of? What do you do against your fear?

11.1   Being Ill

Mark is ill. He has had fever for two days and he has not eaten during the last two days either. Normally he can eat at least five slices of bread for breakfast – but at present he is not interested in anything. He neither cares about meals nor is he interested in TV or football. He only lies in bed and sleeps. His mother starts worrying about him. She has tried to get his temperature down with wet and cold towels wrapped around his calves, and she has also given him two pills against fever, but it wasn't very successful. The fever sank only a little bit. Mark has told her that something was wrong with his stomach.

The night was restless. Mark was tossing and turning in his bed. His mother was sitting at his bed during the night and was holding his hand. She was also very tired, and every now and then she had a little nap. Half sleeping, half awake she was thinking:

If I don't sleep myself, I won't manage to stay awake tomorrow.

If Mark feels better tomorrow, he will take part in his next football match.

If his temperature doesn't fall by midnight, I will call the doctor.

The doctor came at 1 a.m. He looked at Mark's tongue, looked into his eyes and asked about his temperature. When he finally pressed his thumb into the right side of Mark's stomach, the boy started to scream.

"Oops," the doctor said. "This is an emergency case. I'm pretty sure that you have got appendicitis.
You must to go to hospital at once. I'll call for the ambulance."

A Working with the text – Are these sentences right or wrong? Correct the wrong ones.
1. Mark has been ill for five days.
2. Mark complained about pain in his stomach.
3. While he was ill Mark ate a lot.
4. His mother wanted to call the doctor the next morning.
5. The doctor pressed his thumb into the left side of Mark's stomach.
6. The doctor said that Mark could stay at home.

B Can you complete these sentences with words from the text?
1. When your temperature is very high you have got … (5 letters)
2. When you only get bad marks at school you are beginning to … (5)
3. When you reach everything you want to you are very … (10)
4. When you go to school without breakfast you have got an empty … (7)
5. When you are unable to sleep you will spend a very … night. (8)
6. When you have a short sleep after school you take a … (3)
7. The short thick finger that is set apart from the other four of your hand is your … (5)

C Have you or one of your relatives ever been in hospital? If so, what was wrong with you or with them? Form complete sentences, the words from the box below and the pictures might help you.

> appendicitis – broken leg/arm/knee – hernia – heart attack – diabetes – tonsillitis
> birth of child – abuse of drugs – anorexia nervosa – infection – high temperature

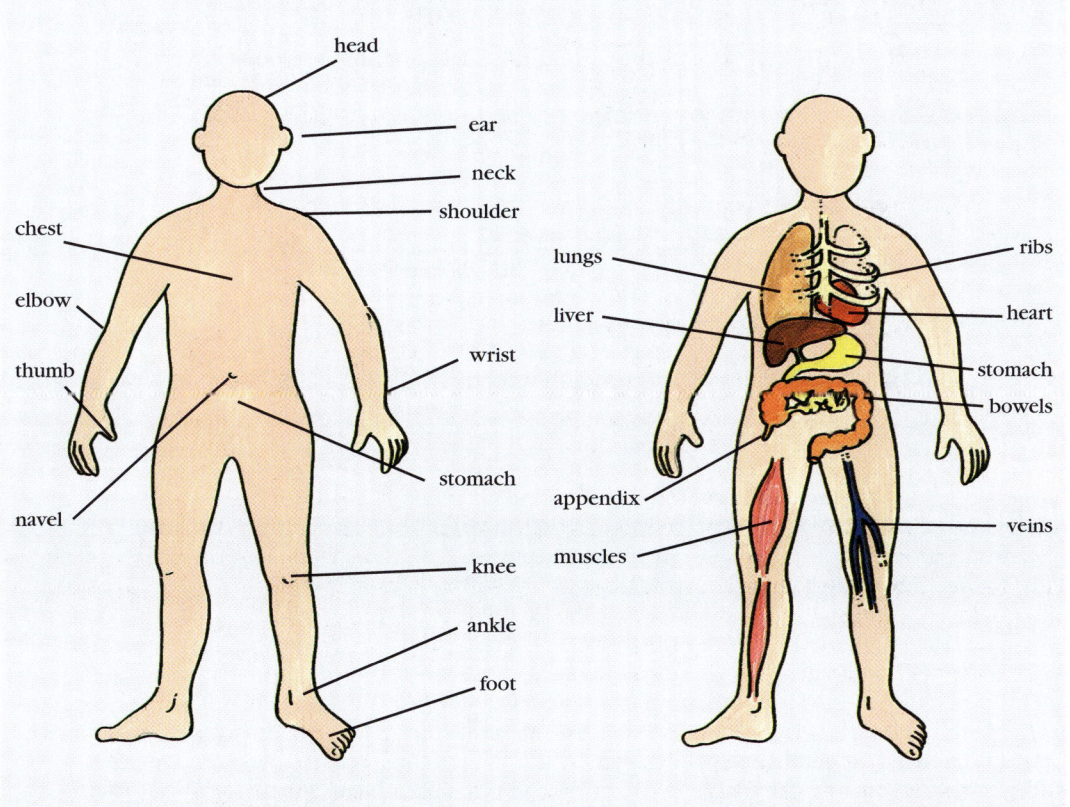

111

If-Clauses Type I

If-Clause	Main-Clause

Example 1: *If I __go__ to the hospital, I __will get__ help.*
Example 2: *If the temperature __doesn't fall__, I __will call__ the doctor.*

→ For rules see page 161

● If-clauses have got two parts: The if-clause and the main-clause.
● The if-clause can be placed before or after the main clause.

When do you use the if-clause type I?
You use it when you are sure that something is very likely to happen.
The possibility that it will happen (or not happen, if it is a negative sentence) is about
80 per cent.

How do you form an if-clause type I?
If-clause:
You use the *simple present*.

Main-clause:
You can use the *will-future + infinitive* or *won't (will not) + infinitive*.

A Now it's your turn. Use if-clauses type I to form the following sentences.

Example: *You not live healthier/will/become ill one day.*
– If you __don't live__ healthier, you __will become__ ill one day.

1. Susan/eat less/will/lose weight.
2. Peter/not do more sports/will/get less attractive.
3. You/will disturb the neighbours/not turn down the radio.
4. Ellen/will/break her leg/not wear proper shoes.
5. Mark/still lie in bed/won't come with us.

B Form some more sentences of your own in which you use the if-clause type I. Work with a partner.

C Do you want to stay healthy? Here are some ideas what you should do.
Match the two halves of these sentences that fit together. Careful, they are not in the correct order.

1. If I brush my teeth regularly …
2. If I stop smoking …
3. If I sit down a while ..
4. If I don't drink alcohol …
5. If I don't go out into the hot sun …
6. If I sleep regularly …
7. If I do a lot of swimming …
8. If I want to become pregnant …
9. If I don't drink so much coffee …

a) … I will be less nervous.
b) … I will avoid lung cancer.
c) … I will not have to see the dentist so often.
d) … I will stop smoking and drinking.
e) … I won't be so tired at school.
f) … I will strengthen my muscles.
g) … I will get my breath back.
h) … I will avoid a sun burn.
i) … I won't die of liver cirrhosis.

If-Clauses Type II

If-Clause	**Main-Clause**

Example 1: *If I __owned__ a house, I __would have__ a garden, too.*
Example 2: *If I __had__ € 2,000, I __could go__ to Spain for three months.*
Example 3: *If I __were__ you, I __would tell__ my parents.*

→ For rules see page 161

When do you use an if-clause type II?
You use an if-clause type II when you doubt that something is going to happen.
The possibility that it is going to happen is about 20 per cent.

How do you form an if-clause type II?
If-clause: You use the simple past in the if-clause.
(However, that does not mean that you talk about the past! It is only the tense you are using.)

Main-clause: You use   *would or*
                            could or
                            might + infinitve in the main-clause.

┌───┐
│   You never ever use *would* in the if-clause!   │
└───┘

A Now it's your turn. Use if-clauses type II to
   form the following sentences.

If I had a swimming pool, I would …

Example:
Sue/have swimming-pool/swim every day.
– If Sue __had__ a swimming-pool, she __would__
__swim__ every day. But she has none.

1. I /have driving licence /invite you to a nice
   trip in the car.
2. Bob finishes school/apply for a job.
3. I know her name/tell you. I forgot it.
4. I have longer holidays/be happier.
5. I like you better/you are not so loud.
6. Life be easier/not have to do so much homework.
7. Peter be better to live with/have more friends.

B Complete these first parts of if-sentences with your own examples.
1. If I left home, …
2. If I had enough money, …
3. I would eat a frog if …
4. If I were a teacher, …
5. If I lived in Spain, …
6. I would be happy if …
7. I would visit more countries if …
8. My parents would shout at me if …

11.2   Drugs

When you hear the word 'drugs' you might think of 'illegal' drugs, like heroin, pot or ecstasy. But there are a lot more things people can be addicted to.

A   Write down everything that comes to your mind about drugs.

B   Collect all the ideas of your classmates, and then decide which one you personally think is the most dangerous drug. Say why you think so.
These words from the box below might help you.

> make you lazy – make you aggressive – damage your brain – cause hallucinations – damage your liver – cause lung cancer – make you nervous – let you live in a dream world – isolation – death – loss of money

Samantha: "Alcohol makes people aggressive. Heroin and crack are dangerous. People who take ecstasy are often unnaturally friendly and want to talk to all sorts of people. They often kiss and hug everybody. On a good night the atmosphere is unbelievable."

John's father: "My son John drank himself to death when he used ecstasy. He didn't drink too much alcohol, he drank too much water! He was not used to ecstasy. However, he knew that when you dance all night and take this drug, you have to drink a lot. He drank 20 pints of water." (From a newspaper)

Doctor John Henry: "This year 52 patients died of heroin and 20 of ecstasy in our hospital in London. Ecstasy allows people to dance all night without feeling a need for rest or fluids.
Their temperature rises uncontrollably which leads to blood clotting. This affects every organ – especially heart, kidneys, muscles, and brain. 92 per cent of my patients who took ecstasy died of heatstroke. This can even happen if they take the drug for the first time. Long term effects can also be depression, panic attacks and mental breakdown."
(World and Press)

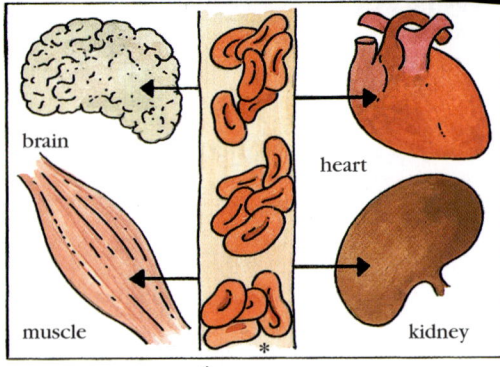

These organs are affected by ecstasy

brain

heart

muscle

kidney

* clotted blood cells

C Read what the people have to say about ecstasy. Which of these answers are correct – A, B or C?

1. Alcohol …
   A makes people aggressive   **B** raises your temperature   **C** has no effect
2. People who take ecstasy are …
   A very unfriendly   **B** extremely friendly   **C** tired
3. John died because …
   A he didn't drink enough   **B** he drank too much beer   **C** he drank too much water
4. Doctor John Henry works in …
   A Winchester   **B** London   **C** Dorset
5. People who take ecstasy …
   A want to sleep   **B** can dance all night   **C** get aggressive
6. Blood-clotting means …
   A your blood is too thick   **B** your blood is too thin   **C** your blood is too red
7. 92 per cent of the people who took ecstasy died of …
   A a heatstroke   **B** a heart attack   **C** depression
8. Long-term effects of ecstasy are …
   A happiness   **B** depression   **C** lung cancer

A junkie once said in a TV talk show:
"It is illogical if a society distinguishes between legal and illegal drugs. All drugs are dangerous – and we should either forbid or allow all of them. Unless alcohol and nicotine are forbidden, a society has no moral right to ban other drugs."

D Have a discussion in class about this statement, answering these three questions.
1. Do you agree or disagree with the statement of the junkie? Give reasons.
2. Why do people take drugs at all? Why can't they be happy just as they are?
3. Do you know some alternatives to taking drugs? Which ones?

Look on page 140 to refresh the rules of a good discussion.

Relative Pronouns

Relative pronouns are used to connect the two parts of a relative clause. Relative clauses are used to define an object more closely. → For rules see page 161

Examples:
*People **who** take ecstasy can die.*
*People **that** take ecstasy can die.*

Which pronoun do you use?
● You use *who* or *that* when you talk about persons.

*A lot of drugs **which** are used are dangerous.*
*A lot of drugs **that** are used are dangerous.*

● You use *which* or *that* when you talk about things and animals.

● If you are not sure which relative pronoun you have to take, you can always use **that**!

Complete the following sentences using *who* or *which*.
1. The girl … I saw last night was drunk.
2. There are a lot of things … are forbidden.
3. The drug … you take is dangerous.
4. The money … you spend on drugs is wasted.
5. Is this the boy … needs heroin?
6. People … are satisfied don't need any drugs.
7. Someone … smokes a lot might get lung cancer.
8. Is that the hospital in … they treat drug addicts?

Vocabulary

11.1 Being Ill		
fever ['fiːvə]	a body temperature above 39 degrees Celsius	Fieber
slice of bread [slaɪs əv bred]	bread cut into smaller pieces	Brotscheibe
(to) worry ['wʌrɪ]	to be anxious	sich Sorgen machen
towel ['taʊəl]	you dry your wet body with a towel	Handtuch
calf; calves (pl.) [kɑːf] [kɑːvz]	lower part of leg	Wade
stomach ['stʌmək]	When you haven't eaten anything you have got an empty stomach	Magen
restless ['restlɪs]	giving no rest	ruhelos; schlaflos
(to) toss and turn [tɒs ænd tɜːn]	move about continously	sich hin und herwälzen
(to) be awake [bɪ 'əweɪk]	the opposite of being asleep	wach sein
(to) stay awake [steɪ ə'weɪk]		wach bleiben
midnight [mɪdnaɪt]	12 o'clock at night	Mitternacht
tongue [tʌŋ]	the moveable organ in the mouth	Zunge
thumb [θʌm]	the short thick finger that is set apart from the other four of a hand	Daumen
(to) scream [skriːm]	to shout out loud	schreien
an emergency case [ɪ'mɜːdʒənsɪ keɪs]		Notfall
at once [ət wʌns]	immediately	sofort
an ambulance ['æmbjʊləns]	the car that takes you to hospital	Notarztwagen
(to) complain about something [kəm'pleɪn ə'baʊt]	to express feelings of unhappiness	über etwas klagen
relative ['relətɪv]	your uncle is your relative	Verwandter, Verwandte
appendicitis [ə,pendɪ'saɪtɪs]		Blinddarmentzündung
hernia ['hɜːnjə]		Leistenbruch
heart attack [hɑːt ə'tæk]		Herzinfarkt
tonsilitis [,tɒnsɪ'laɪtɪs]		Mandelentzündung
abuse [ə'bjuːz]	wrong use, to use badly	Missbrauch
anorexia nervosa [,ænə 'reksiə nɜːvoʊsɑː]		Magersucht
regularly ['regjʊlə]	if you do s. th. every day at the same time	regelmäßig
lung cancer [lʌŋ 'kænsə]	disease that comes from smoking	Lungenkrebs
(to) strengthen muscles [streŋθn 'mʌslz]	you can strengthen your muscles in a fitness centre	Muskeln stärken
breath [breθ]		Atem
liver cirrhosis ['lɪvə sɪ'rəʊsɪs]	disease of liver because of alcohol	Leberzirrhose
frog [frɒg]	an animal that lives in the water and on the land	Frosch
11.2 Drugs		
(to) be addicted to something [bɪ 'ædɪktɪd tuː]	to depend on something	abhängig sein von etwas
(to) collect ['kɒlekt]	some people collect stamps	sammeln
(to) hug [hʌg]	to hold someone in your arms	umarmen
unbelievable [ʌnbɪ'liːvəbl]	hard to believe	unglaublich
(to) allow [ə'laʊ]	your parents don't allow that you come home late	erlauben
fluid [fluːɪd]	water is a fluid	Flüssigkeit
uncontrollably [ʌnkən'trəʊləbl]	not under control	unkontrollierbar
blood clotting [blʌd klɒttɪŋ]	your blood gets thicker	Blutverdickung, -gerinnsel
kidneys ['kɪdnɪz]	you have a pair of these organs	Nieren
heatstroke [hiːtstrəʊk]		Hitzschlag
long-term effects [lɒŋtɜːm ɪ'fekt]		Langzeitwirkungen
mental breakdown ['mentl breɪkdaʊn]		Nervenzusammenbruch
illogical [ɪ'lɒdʒɪkl]	something that is not logical	unlogisch
(to) distinguish [dɪ'stɪŋgwɪʃ]	small children can't distinguish right from wrong	unterscheiden
(to) ban [bæn]		verbannen

Unit 12
The Way I Want to Live

Imagine you are ten years older than now. Where do you want to live by then?

Think about it and then answer the question. The following words may help you:

block of flats – terraced house – detached house – rented room – village – city – suburb – bungalow – semi-detached house – hotel – boarding-house

12.1   Different Ways of Life

7:00 a.m. – At the Hanks'

"Good morning Sue, darling," Peter says as he returns to the bedroom, "The shower is yours now." Sue stays in bed another five minutes because her work as a doctor's assistant starts later than Peter's. In the meantime Peter has already dressed. "Your new suit looks great," Sue murmurs out of bed, "your superior will be very pleased with your perfect styling."

"I hope so," Peter answers, "next week they'll make the decision about my promotion. Is there anything for breakfast in the house?" "I'm afraid not," Sue answers, "please stop at a coffee shop to have breakfast." "Okay, bye, darling." "Bye, Peter, and don't forget to get your old suit and your shirts from the cleaner's."

7:00 a.m. – At the Johnsons'

"Mum, where are my socks?" eight-year-old Brian asks. Caroline, who is just preparing breakfast, tells him and waits for the next question. "Mum, I can't find my maths book." Like nearly every morning Brian can't find his things, but because her husband Charles left home half an hour earlier, Brian is the only one she has to take care of at the moment. Caroline takes two cutlets out of the freezer and starts to peel the potatoes. She has to hurry up because she has to begin her work at the kindergarten earlier this morning. "Please Brian, hurry up, there are only ten minutes left for your breakfast," she shouts. "Hi, Mum. I'm not hungry," Brian answers as he comes into the kitchen. "No, Brian, I at least want you to eat some cereals."

1:00 p.m. – At the Hanks'

As Peter enters the canteen he remembers that it's his job to go shopping and to fetch the laundry from the cleaner's this evening. "I'll go to Quinnsworth," he says to himself, "my favourite pizza is on sale there." At the counter Peter chooses chicken, French fries and a salad. His colleagues have already finished their lunch, and so he looks for a quiet place to enjoy his chicken. "It's a pity that Sue doesn't like to cook," Peter thinks while eating, "all these ready-to-serve meals we buy cost a lot of money, and here I also have to pay a lot of money. But I'm glad to get such delicious meals here."

1:00 p.m. – At the Johnsons'

Caroline is cleaning the carrots she has bought on her way home. She is thinking about what to do in the afternoon. Because it's Monday she has to do the laundry but she wants to visit her mother afterwards. "When Charles returns at 4 o'clock he'll have time to check Brian's homework and to warm up his lunch," she thinks as she puts the potatoes and the carrots onto the cooker, "and I have to make an appointment with my hairdresser urgently," she says to herself. Ten minutes later Brian returns from school. "I'm the best long jumper in my class," he shouts proudly, "and now I'm as hungry as a wolf."

9:00 p.m. – At the Hanks'

Peter and Sue are sitting in the living-room now. Peter is watching TV, and Sue is chatting in the Internet. Their flat is very modern, especially their living-room. The last five years they've spent a lot of money on buying the newest computer, TV-set and so on. Both of them enjoy these modern forms of communication, and they are 'online' most of their evenings. Only at weekends they go out into the city to meet friends and have fun. Sometimes they drive to a nearby holiday park.

"If I get the promotion there won't be time to have a holiday this year," Peter says suddenly. "Oh Peter," Sue's reaction sounds angry, "but we are planning to travel to France with Roy and Tina." "I'm very sorry, but at the moment the job is more important . Think of the high costs we have every month. We urgently need the higher wage."

9:00 p.m. – At the Johnsons'

Caroline and Charles are sitting in the living-room. Charles works for a big motor company. His job is a hard one so he always comes home very tired in the evening. His wife Caroline is a little bit disappointed about this sometimes, because she wants to talk about lots of things with him. At the moment they are making plans for the weekend. "What about a cycling tour?" Caroline asks. "Yes, good idea," Charles answers, "but I've promised Brian to go to the football match with him." "Okay, but don't forget the invitation in the evening." They are invited to a big birthday party at one of their friends. Charles isn't too happy about this invitation because that certainly means dancing and chatting the whole evening.

A   Read the texts about the two families. You will then notice that all these following statements are false.

Rewrite them to turn them into true statements.

1. Peter has his breakfast at home.
2. Peter wears a new suit because he has got a promotion.
3. Charles and Caroline have got two children.
4. Bob gets a cutlet and potatoes for breakfast.
5. Peter returns home for lunch.
6. Peter and Sue only spend a small amount of their housekeeping money on foods.
7. Every Friday morning Caroline does the laundry.
8. Caroline has bought frozen carrots.
9. Peter's and Sue's flat is very modern and has got a lot of electrical appliances.
10. Susan doesn't mind staying at home during her holiday this year.
11. Charles likes chatting in the evening.
12. Caroline and Charles often use all modern means of electronical communication.

B   There are many differences in the lives of the Hanks and the Johnsons, especially in their way of household management. Write down the differences.

Example: *Caroline prepares the meals for her family herself.*
- Sue doesn't like to cook.

C   Think about the advantages and the disadvantages of these two ways of household management. Write them down in a chart like this:

	advantages	disadvantages
The Hanks		
The Johnsons		

D   Imagine you manage your own household. What do you spend your money on? Make a list of the possible costs a household of two persons has.

Different Tenses Training

A Put the verbs in brackets into the given tense.
1. Sue (to chat/present progressive) with a girl from Ireland.
2. Peter (to love/simple present) series like 'Star Trek'.
3. The prices for petrol (to increase/present perfect) enormously.
4. Last year Charles (to be/simple past) in the hospital for two weeks.
5. The doctor (to tell/simple past) him to do a lot of sports.
6. After Caroline (to iron/past perfect) the shirts she (to telephone/simple past) her girlfriend.
7. The weather (to be/will-future) nice next week.
8. Peter and Sue (to travel/going-to-future) to Spain.

B Form questions – Ask for the underlined words.
1. Peter buys a new suit each year.
2. Sue is having a shower at the moment.
3. Caroline has worked as a nursery nurse for ten years now.
4. The pizza Peter had bought tasted awful.
5. The children were playing outside when the accident happened.
6. Ryan and Sally will marry next year.
7. The students are going to write a test tomorrow.
8. Charles had danced with Caroline five times.

C Negatives – Form negative sentences with the words and the tenses given.
1. Sue/to dance last night → simple past
2. The dog/to chase/the cat → past perfect
3. Brian/to be good/at long jump/yesterday → simple past
4. The girls/to chat/when the teacher came in → past progressive
5. We/to get/a hot summer → will-future
6. The car/to be repaired/yet → present perfect
7. Peter/to get/his promotion → going-to-future
8. Caroline/to cook/a meal just now → present progressive
9. Charles/to go/to the cinema often → simple present

D A game – Choose a noun or pronoun and a verb out of the first two boxes and then a tense out of the third box. Tell this your neighbour or any other person in the class. He or she has to form a sentence with those words in the right tense.

noun/pronoun

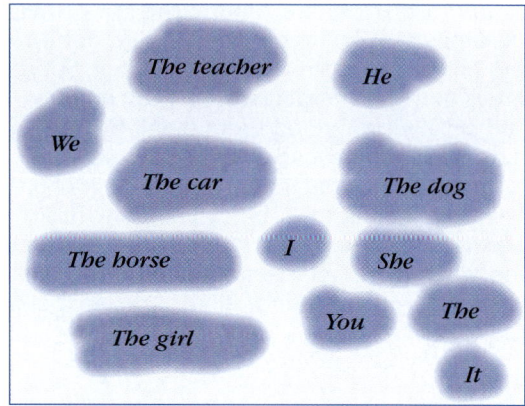

verb

tense

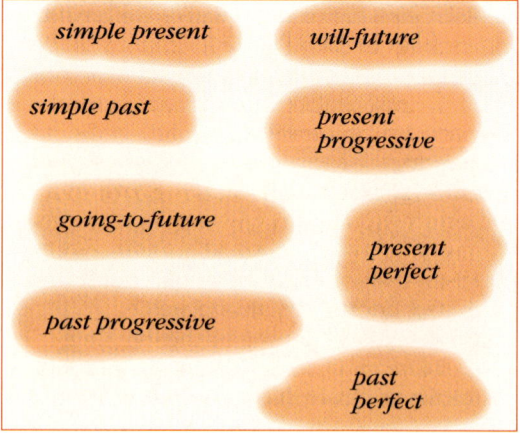

12.2   Are You an Environmentalist?

Test your knowledge and your behaviour concerning our environment. Answer the questions spontaneously and most important: Be honest. Write down your answers (example: 1 A). You can find the solutions on the next page.

1. How many litres of air does a human being breathe a day?
   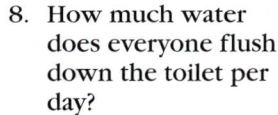
   - A   1.000 litres
   - B   15.000 litres
   - C   50.000 litres

2. At what time of the day is the most energy spent?
   - A   8 a.m. – 12 p.m.
   - B   13 p.m. – 5 p.m.
   - C   8 p.m. – 12 a.m.

3. You go by means of public transport or by bike …

   - A   as often as possible
   - B   only sometimes
   - C   never

4. The destruction of the tropical rain forests supports the greenhouse effect …
   - A   by around 40 per cent
   - B   by around 15 per cent
   - C   not at all

5. Suppose the bottle bank and the recycling containers are three kilometres away from your home. Then you would bring the waste there …
   - A   by bike
   - B   by car
   - C   You would put the waste into your regular dustbin.

6. CFCs destroy the ozone layer. When going shopping you prefer products without CFCs …
   - A   always
   - B   sometimes
   - C   You have never thought about that.

7. If each smoker in Berlin should throw away his non-return-able lighter, how many tons of rubbish would that amount to?

   - A   1 ton
   - B   3 tons
   - C   33 tons

8. How much water does everyone flush down the toilet per day?

   - A   10 litres
   - B   15 litres
   - C   50 litres

9. Which gas increases the greenhouse effect mostly?
   - A   carbondioxide
   - B   methan
   - C   CFC

10. You are in a traffic jam with your car. What do you do?
    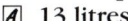
    - A   You stop the engine.
    - B   You let the engine run.
    - C   You let the engine run because when you start the engine again, more harmful gases will be released.

11. You write your letters on recycled paper …
    - A   always
    - B   sometimes
    - C   You always take completely white paper.

12. A car that needs 11 litres at a speed of 130 kmph needs how many litres at a speed of 170 kmph?

    - A   13 litres
    - B   15 litres
    - C   18 litres

13. There are a lot of films about environmental themes on TV. You …
    - A   watch those films regularly.
    - B   are not interested in such films.
    - C   try to get information about environ-mental themes by other media as well.

14. How much energy can you save if you lower your room tem-perature by 1 degree Celsius?

    - A   1 per cent
    - B   3 per cent
    - C   6 per cent

15. In inner city traffic bikers should breathe by nose because they absorb less harmful gases that way. How much less?
    - Ⓐ About 20 per cent less
    - Ⓑ About 50 per cent less
    - Ⓒ About 90 per cent less

16. You buy drinks in returnable bottles …
    - Ⓐ always
    - Ⓑ sometimes
    - Ⓒ seldom, because you don't like to bring them back

17. Because of the destruction of the rain forests a lot of species of plants and animals become extinct. How many per day?
    - Ⓐ 10 species
    - Ⓑ 50 species
    - Ⓒ 70 species

18. You can go to school by bike, by car, or by means of public transport. What do you do?
    - Ⓐ I prefer to go by car.
    - Ⓑ I surely go by means of public transport.
    - Ⓒ Whenever possible I go by bike.

19. A returnable bottle is used about 60 times. How many cans does it replace?
    - Ⓐ 77 cans
    - Ⓑ 136 cans
    - Ⓒ 195 cans

20. You use the full capacity of the washing machine …
    - Ⓐ sometimes
    - Ⓑ always, because you want to save energy and water
    - Ⓒ You have never thought about that.

	1	2	3	4	5	6	7	8	9	10	11	12	13	14	15	16	17	18	19	20
A	1	3	3	1	3	3	1	3	3	3	3	1	3	1	1	3	1	1	1	2
B	3	1	2	3	2	2	1	2	1	2	2	1	1	1	1	1	3	3	3	3
C	1	1	1	1	1	1	3	1	1	1	1	3	3	3	3	1	1	2	1	1

Have a look at the chart and add all of your points. The result will tell you how much you care about our environment.

20 – 30 Points

You must admit that you aren't interested in environmental things. You have never seriously thought about these things. You want to believe that all the so-called environmental problems are exaggerated. But sometimes you aren't quite sure because you notice the consequences of all the environmental sins. You are worried about algae in the oceans and the increasing number of allergies. But you don't take action. That is not the right way – get information about these themes and change your behaviour. Even little steps help.

31 – 45 Points

Your environmental consciousness is rather marked – you are aware of the problems. But you find it difficult to do without the beloved comfort. You excuse yourself with the lack of time, and you say that one person alone cannot change anything.

Try to be more consequent, even if that means spending more time selecting rubbish or going by bike. Understand that as a consumer you can influence retailers, producers and the products they sell.

46 – 60 Points

Congratulations. You are an expert in environmental themes. You are involved in environmental things and you do a lot in your daily life to protect the environment. Maybe you are even a member of an environmental organization.

Continue like this and try to improve the environment. Even if you sometimes feel a little discouraged because of all the disasters and the consequences they have, be sure that more and more people will think like you do.

On TV you can find a lot of commercials that deal with the environment and its protection. However, commercials and advertisements are sometimes difficult to understand.

On page 139 you can learn how to 'read' an advertisement correctly, if you are interested.

Mixed Tenses Training

A Present and Past

Put the verbs into the correct form: simple present, present progressive, simple past, or past progressive.

1. We can't go out now. It is _____ (to rain) cats and dogs.
2. Susan usually _____ (to do) the laundry on Monday but she _____ (not do) it last Monday.
3. Yesterday evening a lightning _____ (to strike) the neighbour's house while we _____ (to watch) TV.
4. What's that noise? Who _____ (to mow) the lawn?
5. Tom _____ (not go) to work yesterday. He didn't feel well.
6. Where _____ (come from)? Is he English?
7. Look, what _____ those boys_____ (play)?
8. "Charles has bought a new car." "Oh, has he? When _____ (to buy) it?"

B Present and Past

Choose the correct one of the two alternatives in each of the sentences and write it down.

Example: *Charles **has worked** for the motor company for ten years now.*

1. He earns/is earning a lot of money there.
2. Last year he has got/got a promotion.
3. Caroline has always worked/ had always worked as a kindergarten teacher.
4. Sometimes she hates/hated her job.
5. Some days ago while the children washed/were washing the dishes she saw that a boy hit a little girl with his fist.
6. The boy said that the girl doesn't want/didn't want to clean his plates.

C Past Tenses

Put the verbs into the correct form: simple past, past progressive, or past perfect.

1. Yesterday evening Sandy _____ (to go) to the cinema to meet Paul. When she _____ (to arrive) there, Paul _____ (already/wait) for her. His bus _____ (to arrive) early.

2. Last night when I _____ (lie) in bed and _____ (read) a book I suddenly _____ (hear) a noise. I _____ (get up) and _____ (to go) to the window to see what it was. Outside I _____ (to see) that a car _____ (damaged) our fence.

3. I _____ (to meet) Joyce and Ron yesterday as I _____ (to walk) through the city. They _____ (to be) at the job centre where they _____ (to ask) for an odd job. We _____ (to decide) to go to a café for a drink.

12.3   My Decisions as a Consumer

A magazine carried out an opinion poll about reasons for consumers' selection of foods. They interviewed a lot of people in a supermarket. Their question was:
"Can you tell us which aspects were decisive that you have put these foods into your trolley?" Here are some of the answers they got:

Jane: "Ron and I have invited friends for dinner. We want to sit outside and enjoy the evening. So we were looking for dishes which are tasteful and look nice, for example …"

Mark: "I only chose products that don't do any harm to the environment. I prefer foods with no or only little packaging, like fresh fruit and vegetables. I only bought vegetables today which were produced in an environmentally-friendly way, grown with no pesticides for example."

Gina: "Jim and I are vegetarians because we are against the mass production of animals. We hate the way they are transported and how they are treated. We think that meat makes us ill, and that is why we bought …"

Sue: "I've got a hard job and so I chose food that is easily and quickly prepared. I also have to look at the price. So I've chosen …"

George: "I'm convinced that a healthy diet keeps my body fit. Therefore I pay attention to the nutritive value of the food. It should contain a high amount of vitamins, minerals, fibres, and carbohydrates, and only a little fat. I've bought …"

A Write down all the reasons for the people's selection of food.
1. Jane and Ron chose food which …
2. Mark …
3. etc.

B The reasons for the decisions can be for example the following aspects:
ecological value
look
nutritive value
psychology (opinion, experience)
practical value
price
taste
Sort these terms to the shopping behaviour of the people above.
1. Jane and Ron …
2. Mark …
3. etc.

C Write down examples for food that you might find in the trolley of …
1. Mark
2. Sue
3. George

D Think of other reasons to prefer or reject food and write them down.

E Which of the aspects mentioned are important for your own buying of food? Talk about it with a classmate.

There are a lot of reasons for the selection of food and drinks. As a consumer you take influence on the offer of supermarkets and retailers. Remember for example the mad-cow-disease and the consequences this disease had on the sales of beef. Another example is organic foods. The consumers demand those products, and because of this the range of organic goods has increased enormously during the last years.

Here are some aspects you should think about when you go shopping:

Ecological Standard

Different aspects must be mentioned here. Firstly you should not buy products with a lot of packaging, and you should avoid non-returnable bottles or cans for drinks.

Secondly you should consider that organic products are less harmful to the environment and that they are usually safer and more nutritious than conventionally grown products.

The third aspect to be mentioned here is that you as a consumer should prefer products which were harvested or produced in an area close to you. This is one step to reduce the rush of traffic.

Nutritive Value

Healthy food contains only a little fat, sugar, energy, and salt. It contains a lot of vitamins, minerals, fibres, and complex carbohydrates instead. You should eat fresh food often and avoid things that have been manufactured intensively.

100 gm	energy kJ	fat gm	fibre gm	carbo-hydrate	water gm
boiled potatoes	290	+	2	15	79
chips	1 140	13	4	31	44

Psychological Aspect

Many people don't eat meat because of factory farming for the production of meat. In those places the animals are crated, crammed or confined in small spaces. They are often kept in conditions of utter deprivation, and are treated as little more than production machines. Farm animals are being pushed to their natural limits to maximise production here. Ask at the counter of your store where the meat is from and how the animals were reared.

F Interpret the chart.

G Make a list of rules that should be followed when we go shopping.

Example: *Always buy drinks in returnable bottles.*

H Comment: Factory farming is necessary to produce cheap meat. Do you agree or not? Give reasons for your answer.

The Future

Simple Present with a Future Meaning
We use the simple present when we talk about timetables, programmes (public transport, cinema etc.).
Example: *The lesson ends in ten minutes.   The train arrives at 10:30 a.m.*

Present Progressive with a Future Meaning
We use the present progressive to say what we have already arranged (future arrangements).
Example: *She is meeting my mother this afternoon.*

Going-To-Future
We use this future form to say what we have decided or intended to do,
Example: *I'm going to travel to France next week.*

and to describe something that is very likely to happen.
Example: *Look at the black clouds! It is going to rain.*

Will-Future
We use I will or I'll when we spontaneously decide something at the moment of speaking,
Example: *I'll cut next lesson.*

and we also use *will* when we predict a future happening which is not clearly foreseeable.
Example: *Perhaps he'll stay the whole week.*

A Simple Present with a Future Meaning –
A friend of yours wants to travel by plane
for the first time. Look at the timetable and
explain to him what the numbers mean.
Answer in full sentences.

Flight Number	Destination	Time of Departure	Boarding Time	Gate
148	Paris	8:15 a.m.	7:30 a.m.	B13
1. 234	Munich	11:30 a.m.	10:45 a.m.	A10
2. 569	Atlanta	3:20 p.m.	2:30 p.m.	C1
3. 450	Shanon	5:00 p.m.	4:15 p.m.	A15
4. 963	Brussels	6:15 p.m.	5:45 p.m.	B8

Example:
*Flight number 148 to Paris leaves at 8:15 a.m. The stewardess checks your boarding ticket
at 7:30 a.m. at gate B13.*

B Present Progressive with a Future Meaning –
Your friend Robert wants to go out with you but you are very busy. Look at your schedule
for the next days and explain to him why you have no time.
Robert: "I want to go out with you on Monday."
You: "Sorry, but I'm going to the hair-
dresser's then."
Robert: "Hmh, and what about Tuesday?"
You: "Not Tuesday, I ..."
Robert: "And Wednesday evening?"
You: "..."
Robert: "Your last chance is Thursday!"
You: "..."

5 Monday	6 Tuesday	7 Wednesday	8 Thursday
5:30 p.m. hairdresser	tennis	learn German	help Grandma

C Different ways of expressing future – which is correct?

Example: *"Did you phone grandmother?"*
- "Oh no, I'll phone her later."

1. The train from York is going to arrive/arrives at 10:30 a.m.
2. I can't help you this evening. I'm working/I'll work at Harrods.
3. "Look, the sun is shining." – "Oh great, I go/I'll go to the beach."
4. "Do you have any plans for your future?" – "I am studying/I am going to study biology."
5. We are going to the cinema this evening. The film is beginning/begins at 8:15 p.m.
6. I am not working/don't work tomorrow.
7. "Are you going out this evening?" – "No, I will watch/am watching TV."
8. I'm very hungry. I will buy/am buying a hamburger.

D Read the following sentences and complete them, using *will* or *going to*.
→ For rules see also page156
1. The bell rings. You open the door. The neighbour wants to speak to your father. You say:
"Just a moment. I ... (get him)."
2. It's a hot day. You have decided to go swimming. You tell your friend: "It's very nice today.
I ... (have a swim)."
3. You have lost your purse. Your friend says: "Don't worry. You ... (surely find it)."
4. You have got an invitation from a man you don't know very well. Your girlfriend asks:
"What have you decided about Mr Johnson's invitation? " You answer: "I ... (meet) him."

Vocabulary

boarding house ['bɔ:dɪŋ haʊs]	a house where people stay for a short time only	Pension

12.1 Different Ways of Life		
(to) murmur ['mɜ:mə]	to say something very quietly	murmeln
superior [su:'pɪərɪə]	someone who has more authority on the job	Vorgesetzter
promotion [prə'məʊʃn]	you get a more important job	Beförderung
urgently ['ɜ:dʒənt]	when something has to be dealt with as fast as possible	dringend
wage [weɪdʒ]	the money you get for your work	Lohn
cutlet ['kʌtlɪt]	a small piece of meat usually fried of grilled	Kotelett
(to) peel [pi:l]	to remove the skin of vegetables or fruit	schälen
cooker ['kʊkə]	large mostly electrical device in the kitchen used for cooking food; a stove	Herd
long jumper [lɒŋ 'dʒʌmpə]	an athlete who tries to jump as far as he can	Weitspringer
proudly [praʊd]	you feel glad about something good you have done	stolz
(to) promise ['prɒmɪs]	to say that you will do something definitely	versprechen
behaviour [bɪ'heɪvjə]	the way a person behaves	Verhalten

12.2 Are You an Environmentalist?		
means [mi:ns]		Mittel
destruction [dɪ'strʌkʃn]	the act of destroying something	Zerstörung
(to) support [sə'pɔ:t]	to want or help something/someone to succeed	unterstützen
greenhouse effect [gri:nhaʊs ɪ'fekt]		Treibhauseffekt
distant ['dɪstənt]	far away	entfernt
(to) destroy [dɪ'strɔɪ]	to ruin completely	zerstören
ozone layer ['əʊzəʊn 'leɪə]		Ozonschicht
CFC [si:efsi:]		Fluorchlorkohlenwasserstoff
lighter ['laɪtə]	a small device which produces a flame	Feuerzeug
non-returnable [nɒn rɪ'tɜ:nəbl]	things that can only be used once	Wegwerf-, Einweg-
traffic jam ['træfɪk dʒæm]	a long line of cars that can't move because the road is blocked	Verkehrsstau
species ['spi:ʃi:z]	class of plants or animals	Art, Spezies
(to) become extinct [ɪk'stɪŋkt]	no living members exist anymore	aussterben
capacity [kə'pæsɪtɪ]	the quantity of things	Fassungsvermögen
(to) admit [əd'mɪt]	you say that something is true	zugeben
(to) exaggerate [ɪg'zædʒəreɪt]	you make the thing you are talking about seem better, bigger, or worse than it actually is	übertreiben
sin [sɪn]	a bad and immoral behaviour	Sünde
algae ['ældʒi:]	green, slimy plants which live in the water	Algen
(to) apologize [ə'pɒlədʒaɪz]	to say 'Sorry'	sich entschuldigen
opinion poll [ə'pɪnjan pəʊl]	when several people are asked about their opinion	Meinungsumfrage

12.3 My Decisions as a Consumer		
trolley ['trɒlɪ]	a small cart where you put things in when you are shopping	Einkaufswagen
harm [hɑ:m]	bad influence	Schaden
pesticides ['pestɪsaɪds]	chemicals which farmers put on their crops to kill animals	Pestizide
(to) convince [kən'vɪns]	to make sure that something is true or necessary	überzeugen
ecological value [ˌi:kə'lɒdʒɪkl 'vælju:]		ökologischer Wert
(to) deny [dɪ'naɪ]	you say that it is not true	verneinen, ablehnen
retailer [ri:teɪlə]	a person or a business that sells goods to the public	Einzelhändler
mad-cow-disease [mæd kaʊ dɪ'zi:z]		Rinderwahnsinn, BSE
organic foods [ɔ:'gænɪk fu:ds]	foods grown without chemicals	biologisch-dynamisch erzeugte Lebensmittel
(to) harvest ['hɑ:vɪst]	to cut or pick crop, fruit or vegetables when they are ripe	ernten
(to) crate [kreɪt]		in Verschlägen halten
(to) cram [kræm]		mästen
(to) confine ['kɒnfaɪn]	to keep someone in prison	einsperren
utter deprivation ['ʌtə ˌdeprɪ'veɪʃn]		völlige Entbehrung
(to) rear [rɪə]	to bring someone up	aufziehen
factory farming ['fæktərɪ 'fɑ:mɪŋ]	when animals are reared in an unnatural way in narrow stables	Massentierhaltung
(to) predict [prɪ'dɪkt]	to say what will happen in the future	vorhersagen
destination [ˌdestɪ'neɪʃn]	the place to which someone/something is going	Bestimmungsort, Bestimmung

Revision IV (Unit 10 – 12)

Is School Too Boring?

1   "School is such a waste of time." (Lucy, 11)

"What is boring is the repetition of having to do the same
5   things every day, and sit through classes that you don't really enjoy." (Emily, 15)

"Most lessons teachers are telling us facts, which gets so bor-
10   ing that you lose concentration." (Christopher, 15)

These are just some of the comments on school made by British pupils to THE INDEPEN-
15   DENT recently.

A number of British education experts are concerned that school is not interesting enough. A new study has found
20   that more than half of the year-9 pupils are bored in some lessons. Professor Diana Montgomery who watched and analysed over 1000 different les-

25   sons said: "Some lessons are so boring that I do not know why all the children are not rioting."

Dull lessons are a serious problem. If children are bored, they do not learn ef-
30   fectively. Bright children can easily get bored if they are given tasks that are too easy. Slower learners lose interest if they don't fully understand what they are told to do.

35   So what makes some lessons dull and others enjoyable? The group of pupils interviewed by THE INDEPENDENT had plenty to say on the topic.

"I don't like teachers who talk too
40   much or read too much out of the textbook." (Ben, 13)

"I dislike copying work off the board, if it takes too long." (Jenny, 15)

"I enjoy group work and learning
45   games." (Lucy, 14).

"It is helpful to watch videos on the topic we're studying." (John, 15)

The pupils said that they liked lively teachers who have a good sense of hu-
50   mour and who make things easy to understand. Most pupils also seem to prefer strict teachers who make the class work.

"The boring teachers are those who never make you do any work." (Freddie,
55   12)

Professor Montgomery found that too many lessons were dominated by the teachers talking. In her opinion, teachers should give pupils opportunities to work
60   things out in pairs or small groups. Pupils should feel that what they are learning is relevant to their lives, now and in future.

Professor Montgomery: "School should help pupils to develop skills they need all
65   their lives, such as problem-solving, decision-making, team-work and communication skills."

(facts taken from Read On)

A Answer the following questions on the text.
1. What do the pupils say about school? Use the reported speech to answer.
2. Why are British education experts concerned about schools?
3. What does Professor Montgomery say about lessons?
4. What do the pupils say about their lessons? Write down all their comments.
5. What type of teachers do these pupils prefer?
6. What does Professor Montgomery suggest to teach in schools?

B Find the matching pairs of words and definitions.
1. lesson
2. repetition
3. education
4. humour
5. communication

a) consists of teaching people different subjects at school or college

c) a short period of time during which people are taught about a particular subject

e) something that has happened before or has been said before, happens again or is said again

b) the ability to see when something is funny and to say amusing things

d) the activity or the process of giving information to other people or to other living things

Pupils like to work things out in pairs or small groups.

C Write down your own definitions for the following words:
1. school
2. teacher
3. pupil
4. team-work
5. opinion

D Is school too boring? – Write a comment!
What do <u>you</u> think about school, lessons, and teachers? Write down your own opinion. Use the present tense (*I think that* …) Write about 150 words.

E If-clauses Type I – What will happen at school if …
→ For rules see page 161
Use if-clauses type I and form sentences.
1. to miss the bus/be too late
2. the teachers/to be ill/the pupils/to have a big party
3. to make a good exam/to study at university
4. to meet the headmaster/to be nervous
5. the teacher/to be angry/not to say a word

F If-clauses Type II – If I were a teacher …
Write down what you would do if you were a teacher!
1. If I were a teacher I would …
2. If I were a teacher …

Introducing a Person

John has just started to study at university. In the first few courses the students are asked to introduce themselves. To do this in an interesting way they have to interview their class neighbour, and introduce him or her to the class afterwards.

G Now it is your turn to introduce John. Use the following information about him. What tenses did you use? Say why.

'82	born in Leeds
'84–'86	kindergarten
'87–'83	primary school
'89	sister Jane born
'90———>?	play tennis
'91	dog "Sam" as a present
'93–2000	secondary school
'2000	A-level examination
'99 ———>?	girl-friend June
2000	move to Manchester
2000 ———>?	university

H Now work in pairs with a classmate and ask your partner about his or her life. Afterwards she or he has to do the same. Then introduce your partner to the class.

I   A quite normal day at school? – Writing a story

Have a close look at the following pictures. There you can see what happened in the class for
housekeeping last month. Now try to write a story about this.
Start with the following sentences:
*It was a quite normal day. The boys and girls of the 'Berufsfachschule Hauswirtschaft' were
in one of the kitchens, and they were preparing lunch …*

Activity/Methodenseiten

Role-Playing

There are some texts in your Englishbook which you could use for a role play. Have a look at the text about scenes in the life of Ryan, for example – page 47 ff.
If you want to do role-playing, there are several steps you should follow:

Step One
Decide which text you want to use for your role play.

Step Two
Find out how many actors you need for this. In our example you need an actor who plays Ryan. Then you need a waitress and some colleagues of the hotel staff. Somebody has to play the boss.

Step Three
Decide who wants to play which role. Important: Only choose pupils who want to play. Nobody should be forced to play. If you are not sure, why not just try it? You will at least make an interesting experience.

Step Four
Can you think of some material or items you might use to make your play more lively? Maybe you have got some plastic plates at home – why not bring them to school? Or – what can you use instead of porridge?

Step Five
Form three or four groups – one group for each actor that will take part in the role-playing later on. Go through the text again.

Each group has to form ideas what the actor could say. Make a list of those ideas. You are free to add something or to leave something out when you are playing your role. This list is only a help for the actor.

Step Six
Give the actors some time to coordinate their parts and to learn their roles.

Step Seven
Have you got anything you need? Start and play. Do it as freely as you can. The pupils who are not playing should observe the play and write down everything they notice.

Step Eight
The role play is over. Discuss what you have seen or heard. How did the actors feel? What was good? What could have been better?

Step Nine
You can play it again, this time with other actors. Compare the actors to each other.

Planning a Project

A good way to learn, to use and to present your knowledge of the English language is a practical project. The following method will help you to do this.

***Example:** An English Breakfast*

Breakfast is more than just eating food for most British people. It is a part of their way of life. Why not bring this aspect of British life into your school!
Such a project must be planned well, therefore here are five steps to help you. First it is important to find out if this project is suitable for your lessons. The following guide may be of some help to you.

Steps	Questions	Examples
Step One – **Setting Aims**	What are your reasons for doing such a project?	• use of the English language for vocational reasons • completing vocational knowledge • learning by practical experience • learning to organize something yourself

Step Two – **Collecting** **Ideas**	Which kind of lessons can be included in the project?	• nutrition (well-balanced nutrition, fibre)
		• practical domestic science (laying a table)
		• mathematics (calculation of energy in food, of costs)
		• English
		    ♦ collecting English menus (letters, e-mails, telephone, Internet)
		    ♦ informing/presenting (teachers, students, parents, other interested people)

	Who are your guests?	• teachers who speak English • a group of students • parents
	How can you create a British atmosphere?	• decorating the tables (blue and red napkins) • decorating the walls (posters with landmarks of Great Britain) • English newspapers
Step Three – **Making** **Decisions**	Prepare a plan of work: – What has to be done? – Who has to do it? – On what date has the task to be completed?	• Each student writes down what he or she expects from the project. • What food is going to be offered? • setting dates • calculating the costs
Step Four – **Checking** **the Manage-** **ment**	How are the plans carried out?	• presenting the project to the public • organising the layout of the room • carrying the plans through • creating a page for a school chronicle
Step Five – **Looking at** **the Results**	Was the project a success?	• Did all the students fulfill their tasks? • Was it worthwhile to invest work, time and money in the project? • experiences which have been learned and can be used for future projects? • reactions of the guests? • maybe even an evaluation with a video camera?

RESTAURANT

Breakfast

From the Serve-Yourself Buffet

Chilled Juices

Orange ● Apple

Assorted Yoghurts

Grapefruit Segments

Poached Figs In Syrup

Cereals Served With Chilled Milk

Cornflakes ● Muesli ● Fruit & Fibre

Brown Soda Bread ● Crispy Rolls ● Croissants

Brown Or White Toast

Waiter Service To Your Table

Country Style Breakfast:

Bacon, Sausage Pudding, Fried Egg, Sauté Of Mushrooms

Or

Grilled Fillet Of Plaice

Or

Continental Plate
Cheese, Ham, Salami, Sliced Tomato

Barry's Tea ● Hot Chocolate ● Coffee

£8.25 Adults   *£5.00 Children*

Example of a breakfast menu

Mind Mapping

What Is Mind Mapping?

This is a method which helps you to
- collect ideas,
- put them in the right order, and to
- summarize them.
- You can also learn vocabulary more easily that way!

Each mind map is individual.

There is no right or wrong.

Preparations

You need a large piece of paper and three or four pencils of different colours.
You also need a dictionary.

How to Do It

You write the central theme in the middle of your sheet of paper.

Then think of three or four main ideas. Write your main ideas around the central theme.

Write them in different colours.

Which other words go with your main ideas? Write those around your main ideas.

Combine your words with lines so that it may look like a tree.

Do it as shown below. The central theme in this example is 'work'.

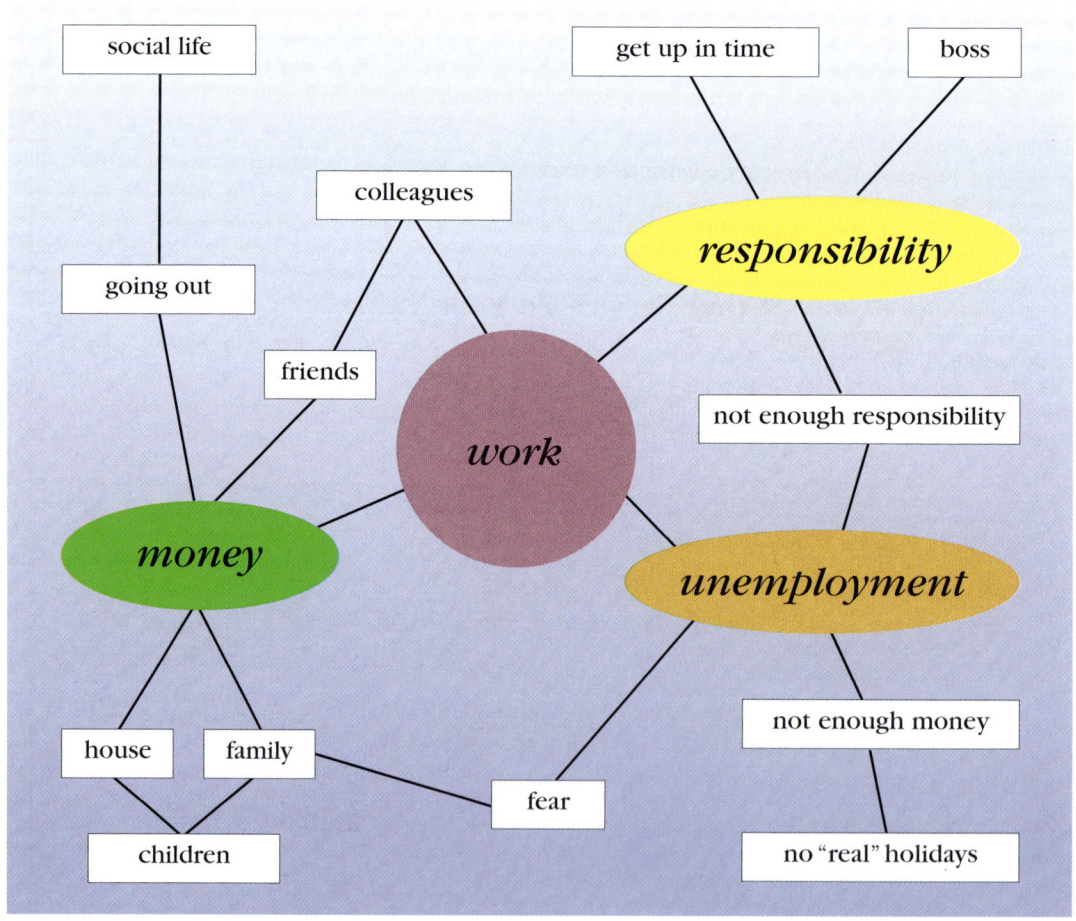

Now it's your turn. Do the same with another word. You can take 'love', for example.

Interpretation of Graphs

Whenever you are told to interpret graphs you have to take three steps.

Step One
Say in one or two sentences what the graph is about.

Example: *In the first graph the age of German people in the year 2001 is compared to the age of people in 2030 and 2050.*

Step Two
Compare the data that are given in the two graphs to each other.

Example: *In 2030 there will be fewer/more … than there were in 2001.*

Step Three
Think of the reasons for the different data. What are the consequences?

Example: *The reason that there will be fewer children and youngsters in the year 2030 is …/could be …*
That means … The consequences are …/could be …/will be …

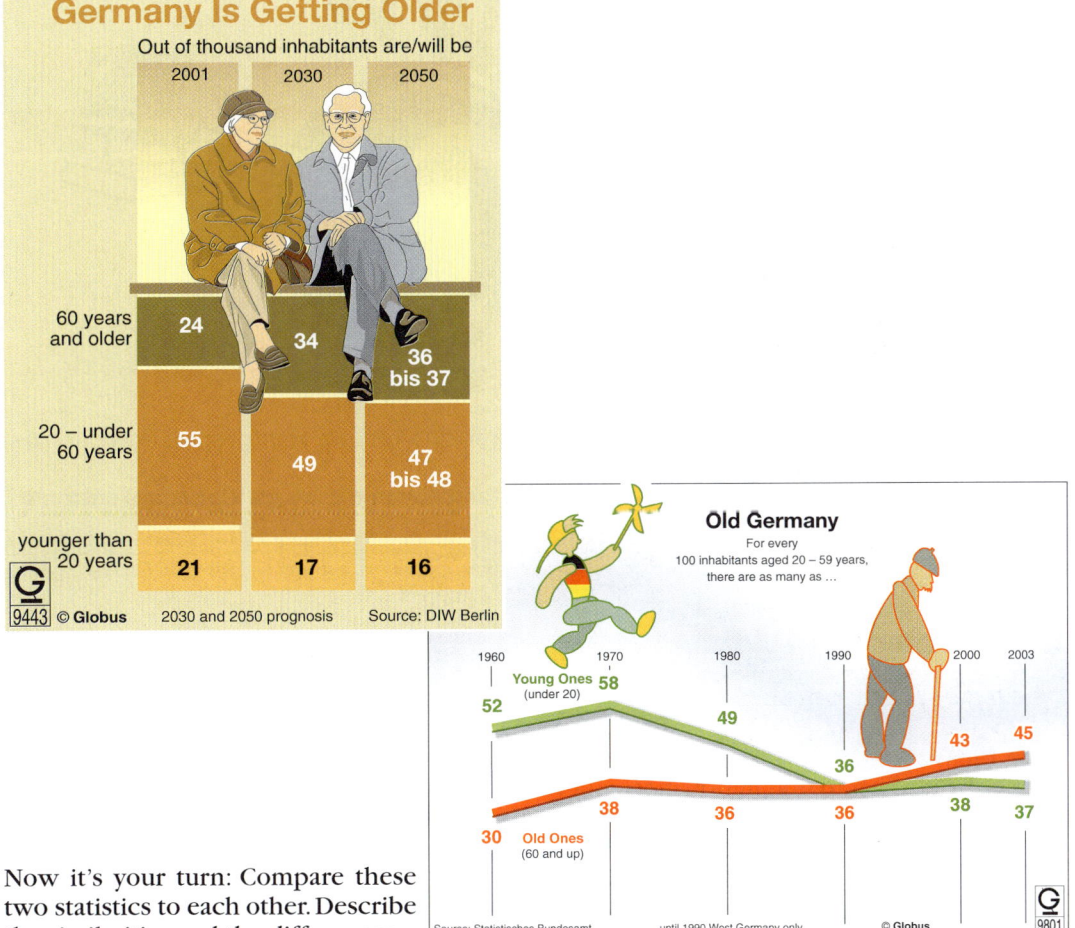

Now it's your turn: Compare these two statistics to each other. Describe the similarities and the differences.

Searching for Information in the Internet

Today everyone talks about the Internet and we find addresses everywhere: in advertisements, magazines, newspapers etc. Millions of computers are connected in the Internet, and there we can find all sorts of information.
But that is the problem: How can I find the information I need?

Preparations
1. Your school has got an Internet room that your class can use during your English lessons. Get the necessary information and make a date.
2. Make sure that you know a little bit about how to use a computer and about the secrets of the Internet.
3. Try to find some addresses of English or American newspapers or magazines, institutes, travel agencies etc.

How To Use the Internet
There are different possibilities to search the Internet:
1. You can use a search engine like
   www.yahoo.com,
   www.altavista.com
   or www.hotbot.com.
2. You can key in the full Internet address that you have found for example in a magazine.
3. In all homepages you can find 'links' (mostly underlined or coloured). When you activate those links you can get more information on other Internet sites.

Example:
You may want to get some information about Christmas customs in English-speaking countries. This is how you can start:
1. Work with the search engine 'www.yahoo.com' and key in the words 'Christmas customs'.
2. Or work with the following addresses:
   www.christmas.com
   www.santas.net
   www.christmasarchives.com
3. Compare your results.

More Ideas
1. Use the Internet to find information about new films, stars etc.
2. Imagine you want to travel to an English-speaking country. Get some information about the special area or the town you would like to travel to.

Analysing Advertisements

"I say, these ads on toothpaste are rubbish."

If you think the right place for your teeth is still your mouth and not your dentist's bucket …

… what do you do about it? Why don't you take

A smile makes friends …
and you can eat your T-bone steak
at your friend's barbecue.

… for a happy bite where things go right!

Look at this advertisement. To analyse it you can follow these steps.

Step One – Understanding the Advertisement
- Do you think this is a real advertisement? Why do you – why don't you?
- Do you think people will read this advertisement? Why will they – why won't they?
- Why does the reader automatically have to think that advertisements for toothpaste are not rubbish?
- How do the first picture and the text below go together?
- If the reader agrees with the text, what must he or she do?
- What is promised to those who use SMILEY ? (last line and picture)
- Describe the layout of the advertisement.

Step Two – Look at the AIDA-Rules of Advertising
- **A** – Attract attention
- **I** – Inspire conviction
- **D** – Direct desire
- **A** – Advise customers

How is this done in this advertisement?

Step Three – Why Don't You …
- look for advertisements in English magazines and find out which tricks they apply?
- design your own advertisement about …
  - a fridge?
  - a dishwasher or something else?

Having a Discussion

We are all individuals, and we all think differently about politics, religion, environment, leisure activities and so on. Consequently we very often discuss when we have a talk. But often discussions end in a quarrel.

Here are some rules to have a good discussion.

Preparations

1. Find one person to be the chairman of the discussion.
2. Form small groups. Only in groups with less than five people all participants have the chance to take part in the discussion equally.
3. Sit down in a circle so that all participants can see each other.
4. You might set a speaking time, and give one person the task to be the time controller.

How to Do It

1. The guide should start the discussion with a question or an example. Then he or she should call on the speakers.
2. The participants should listen to all arguments and put up their hand if they want to talk. Never interrupt a speaking person.
3. As a speaker you shouldn't talk too long, and you should concentrate on your main thoughts. Always be objective, and never become personal in your arguments.
4. The guide can summarize arguments from time to time and should make sure that the theme of the discussion is not lost.

Useful Expressions for Discussions

Here are some expressions to use for your arguments in a discussion:

Introducing the Topic
There are many points of view …
There are several questions to think about …
It is important to say …

Stating Points
I think …
In my opinion …
I am of the opinion …
My view is …

Stating Alternatives
On the other hand …
However …
Although …

Stating Results
As a result …
Because of this …

Closing the Discussion
It is clear that …
It seems that …

Preparing a Quiz

… is team work!

Would you like to prepare a quiz? In English? That would even be more fun! Well, what do you need for this?

Preparations

Before you can have an interesting quiz, you need …
- prizes,
- lots of questions on different subjects,
- material to make the questions more interesting for everybody,
- rules to say
  - what is allowed,
  - what is forbidden,
  - how you can score points,
- things with which you can measure points,
- funny games which the candidates must play if they do not know the right answer.

Form teams to prepare the quiz.

Prizes

- You could collect some money and buy something.
- You could prepare things in your cooking lessons: cakes, tarts, cookies, pots of jam, or make other things yourselves.
- You could look for sponsors.

Questions on Different Subjects

It may be difficult to choose subjects you have not talked about in your English lessons. It could be fun to think about subjects presented in this book. Examples:
- kitchen tools
- furniture
- types of homes
- food and spices
- jobs
- computer items
- cosmetics
but there can also be
- general knowledge (capital of France???)

Material

You can ask questions or just show things ("What is this?") or you can use pictures, charts or maps.

Rules

The quiz will be boring if someone takes a long time for thinking. You could have rules like:
- the fastest team wins
- there is a time limit (not more than 30 seconds for answering)
- wrong answers mean that the other groups get one point
- Decide: Are candidates allowed to speak German? What if they do?
- Decide: Are candidates allowed to use their hands and feet for explaining?
- What if someone else helps?

Things for Measuring Points

Everybody wants to see at any time how many points the teams have scored already and how much time is left to answer the question. You could
- prepare number boards,
- write on the blackboard,
- use score cards (from gym hall?),
- use a large stopwatch, if available.

Funny Games If Candidates Cannot Answer

Use your fantasy!

When everything has been prepared, form teams and select a quizmaster and an assistant. Make sure that the team members did not develop the questions they are being asked themselves!

How to Work with an English-English Dictionary

A dictionary can be a real friend. It can for example help you

A to pronounce a word correctly,
B to spell a word correctly or find irregularities,
C to find out what type of word or word class it is,
D to find out what meaning(s) a word has,
E to find the right preposition,
F to find, for example, the noun if you have the verb.

These are just some examples. For more information, consult the first pages of a good dictionary.

Pronunciation

The pronunciation is given behind the word. If you understand the special signs, called "Received Pronunciation" or "RP" in short, then you know how to pronounce a word correctly. To find out, look at this pronunciation table.

Consonants		
Symbol	**Keyword**	
p	pen	
b	back	
t	ten	
d	day	
k	key	
g	get	
f	fat	
v	view	
θ	thing	
ð	then	
s	soon	
z	zero	
ʃ	ship	
ʒ	pleasure	
h	hot	
x	loch	
tʃ	cheer	
dʒ	jump	
m	sum	
n	sun	
ŋ	sung	
w	wet	
l	let	
r	red	
j	yet	

Vowels			
		Symbol	**Keyword**
short		ɪ	bit
		e	bed
		æ	cat
		ɒ	dog (*BrE*)
		ʌ	but
		ʊ	put
		ə	about
		i	happy
		u	actuality
long		iː	sheep
		ɑː	father
		ɒː	dog (*AmE*)
		ɔː	four
		uː	boot
		ɜː	bird
diphthongs		eɪ	make
		aɪ	lie
		ɔɪ	boy
		əʊ	note (*BrE*)
		oʊ	note (*AmE*)
		aʊ	now
		ɪə	real
		eə	hair (*BrE*)
		ʊə	sure (*BrE*)
		uə	actual
		iə	peculiar

1. Read the words on the left, and train the consonants and the vowels.
2. Now get dictionaries from the school library and try to find out how you spell these words correctly:
   a) domestic
   b) bursar
   c) apron
   d) recipe
   e) alternative

Look at the balloon. The signs there are **RP**. Can you read what the policeman says?

/həˈləʊ, aɪ æm ə pəˈliːsmən. ðiː ˈɪŋglɪʃ pəˈliːsmən ɑː kɔːld bɒbi/

Special signs

ǀ	separates British and American pronunciations, British on the left, American on the right
/ˈ/	shows main stress
/ˌ/	shows secondary stress

Spelling Rules and Other Irregularities

Look for the following words. The dictionary may inform you about spelling and other irregularities.

1. one fly, two ???
2. You pay today, he ??? yesterday.
3. acceptable, ???-ly
4. information, plural ???
5. one box, two ???
6. one cactus, two ???
7. four, fourteen, 40 = ???

Finding Out the Type of Word or Word Class

The words in the dictionary are sometimes followed by abbreviations like *adj, adv, conj, n, prep, v*. What do those abbreviations mean? Can you make a list of the abbreviations and the meanings?

The abbreviation can be important for the meaning of a word. Try to translate the following words, **but be careful and look at the word class, or you will make mistakes**!

1. fast, adj
2. fast, v
3. fast, n
4. open, adj
5. open, v
6. open, n
7. saw, v (from see)
8. saw, n
9. saw, v

Finding Out the Right Meaning of a Word

If you look up a word you do not understand, the dictionary can give you

● one or more definitions behind the word,
● example sentences in which the word is used in a context,
● pictures.

There may be new words, which you do not understand either. Don't worry: If you learn vocabularies on a regular basis, you will get better day by day. Now try to find the German meanings of these words:

Some people who fast lose their weight rather slowly.

1. ladle, n (soup)
2. mustard, n (spice)
3. spice, v (food)
4. whisk, n (cream)
5. iron, v (clothes)
6. iron, n (for clothes)
7. sheet, n (bed)

Finding Out the Right Preposition

Sometimes we cannot just translate the German preposition into English. Verbs, nouns or adjectives may take **other** prepositions in English. Your dictionary informs you about the right preposition. Try to find the right propositions in the following text.

Mary has always been fond …[1] Jack. She was interested …[2] getting to know him since she first met him …[3] school. When school was over, she was looking …[4] to seeing him the next day. He felt a great admiration …[5] her as well. They fell in love …[6] each other, and she soon longed …[7] spend the rest of her life …[8] him. When they left school, he finally popped the question and she said "Yes, I will." Now she is married …[9] him, and they are happy ever after.

Finding Other Types of Words (Word Classes)

It can happen that you know the verb and look for the noun or the adjective. This is not that easy: ***Example:*** You *invest* money in a project, and this is an ??? (*investment*, n). Did you know that? Well, if you didn't, here the dictionary can help you as well. Just try it yourself. Can you find the right words?

1. employ, v (n = ?)
2. cook, n (v = ?)
3. ladle, n (v = ?)
4. contraceptive, n (adj = ?)
5. spice, v (n = ?)
6. duster, n (v = ?)
7. automatic, adj (adv = ?)

Talking Games

This game is an exercise in talking to people and using the English language by speaking as much as possible.

Two students form a team, one student is partner A, the other is partner B. Partner A reads his own part A out loud, while partner B looks up his B-part on page 147.

Together they answer the questions and work on the exercise given in the game.

Partner A

■ Game 1A (partner B takes Game 1B)

On the Phone

Who is that speaking, please? – This is …
Dictate these names to partner B.

1. Gina	2. Fiona
3. Ken	4. Jim
5. Maureen	6. Laura

Sometimes it is hard to understand people's surnames and write them correctly.
In that case you may ask: "How do you spell that, please?"
Dictate the following surnames to partner B. Spell the names, if he or she asks you to do so.
→ For spelling, refer to page 152

1. Hartnett	2. Kelly
3. Gordon	4. Meyrick
5. Pembroke	6. Crown
7. Brown	8. Marsh

Now write down what partner A dictates you. If you do not know how to write the name or surname, you can ask him or her to spell it.

■ Game 2A (partner B takes Game 2B)

Asking for Information about People

You need some information about these people – ask partner B to give it to you. Do that in full sentences.

◆ Stephen Miller: a) age? b) job? c) hobbies? d) address? e) phone number? f) e-mail address?
◆ Sara Celtenham: a) age? b) job? c) hobbies? d) address? e) phone number? f) e-mail address?

◆ Jodie Baker: a) age? b) school she goes to? c) future plans? d) part-time job? e) wage?

Now partner B asks you to give him/her information about the following people. Always answer in full sentences.

◆ Jack Smart: a) 22, b) cook, c) go-cart racing, chess, cinema, d) 14 Cheltenham Road, Norwich e) 832770, f) smart.jack@att.uk (@ = at) (. = dot)
◆ Liz Hornsby: a) 19, b) hotel clerk, c) riding, parties, books, d) 27 St David's Road, Bristol, e) 7321113 f) none
◆ Use the information of yourself/of a friend/of someone you know.

■ Game 3A (partner B takes Game 3B)

Where Is My Recipe?

You want to make an apple crumble, but you forgot some of the ingredients and how much you need of them. You phone partner B and ask him to get the missing information. And how exactly do you have to prepare it?

Ingredients
?? g apples

?? g soft brown sugar
$\frac{1}{2}$ teaspoon of ??? (spice)
?? of orange juice

For the Crumble
?? plain flour
50g ???
75 g ???
(which is sugar, which is butter?)
a pinch or a pint (??) of salt

Cook the apples in a ??? with ??? until ???.
Spread the crumble out with a ??? but do not press it down.
Bake the crumble for about ??? to ??? minutes. It will be ready when ???. The oven setting should be ??? °C, gas mark ???.
Serve the crumble with ??? or ???.

Now partner B rings you up. He does not exactly remember what he needs for "Pumpkin Gnocchi", the meal you brought home with you from your last holidays in Italy. Of course, now you can help him.

Ingredients
1 kg pumpkins
200 g flour
1 egg
crushed nutmeg
1 pinch of salt

For the Sauce
700 g chopped tomatoes
1 chopped onion
6 chopped basil leaves
olive oil
a pinch of salt

Peel the pumpkin, prepare the dough. Cut it into pieces and bake it at 160 to 180 °C for 40 minutes.
Fry the onions briefly in 2 tablespoons of oil, add the tomatoes and cook for 30 minutes. Oven setting: medium. Stir while cooking. Pass through a sieve and bring it to boil again.
Add the sauce and the basil shortly before you serve the dish.

Game 4A (partner B takes Game 4B)

Going for an Interview

You have read an advertisement that a hotel is looking for a trainee cook. Now you phone the hotel (partner B), and want to know more about the job:
- job?
- working hours?
- working time?
- shift work?
- working days per week?
- free weekends?
- pay?
- college?
- holidays?
- clothing?
- time of training?
- promotion prospects?

Now your old people's home is offering a job for a trainee old people's nurse.
You are interviewing a young woman who has some questions on the job. Please give her the information she wants.

- Job: helping old people to get along with their problems

Examples:
- *bring them their breakfast every morning*
- *tidy up their rooms*
- *give them the medicine the doctor prescribed ...*

- working hours: from 7 a.m. to 4 p.m.
- night shift: yes, once a week, from 7 p.m. to 7 a.m.
- free days: 1 day per week
- work at weekends: once a month
- pay: £80 per week for a start, later up to £120 per week at end of training
- holidays: 24 working days per year
- college: once a week, on Tuesdays
- length of training: 3 1/2 years

Game 5A (partner B takes Game 5B)

A Survey of a Market Research Institute

You (partner A) are working for a Market Research institute. The management of a department store want to get more information about their customers. So you ask the people (partner B) after they leave the store.
You want to find out:
- what the customer bought,
- how old she is,
- if she remembers what items she can buy in this store,
- what she thinks about the information she can get in this store,
- if the shop assistants are friendly and helpful,
- the reason why she can go shopping in the morning.

Now you are interviewed by partner B. Here are your details – tell the interviewer that …
- it took some time until you found what you were looking for,
- you go there perhaps once or twice a month,
- you think it's quite agreeable; your suggestion: a larger variety of clothes for young people,

- as to the special offers, yes;
- it took you some 30 minutes to find what you were looking for,
- the shop assistant helped you quite a lot and gave you some good advice.

Game 6A (partner B takes Game 6B)

Buying Electrical Household Equipment

You have the technical information about a washing machine. Your partner has also got some information about another washing machine. Try to find out which of the two machines is better, can hold more washing, is more economical etc.

Ask your partner for his technical data and then form sentences like: *"My washing machine needs less electricity than yours."*

You can use adjectives like: *much, easy to handle, wide, high, long, economic, little, slow, fast*

This list of adjectives is neither complete nor in the right order!

Super Wash 2000	
amount of washing	5 kg
control	fully automatic
spin drier speeds	400 to 1800 rpm
Consumption Data at 60 °C	
water	39 litres
power consumption	0.89 kWh
washing programmes	3
dimensions (height, width, length)	85 by 60 by 60 cm
price	£299.–

Discuss which washing machine you would prefer to buy.

You also want to buy a freezer. You have collected the technical data about the "Eco-Arctic

Eco-Arctic Super	
capacity	176 litres
control	fully electronic
warning	acoustic door and temperature alert
power consumption	208 kWh per year
defrosting	not mentioned in brochure
dimensions (height by width by length)	126 by 65.5 by 65 cm
price	£495.—

Super", and partner B has collected information about the "Freezer Freak 2001 S". Ask each other for the technical data, then form sentences and compare the freezers.

Game 7A (partner B takes Game 7B)

Getting and Giving Information about a Flat

You are a flat hunter. Phone a landlord (partner B) and try to get more information about the flat he advertised in the newspaper. Please, speak in full sentences, or the landlord will not give you the flat!

- carpets on the floor?
- get ground plan of the flat?
- see the flat?
- type of heating?
- extra rooms like cellar or attic?
- telephone outlet?
- place for drying washed clothes?
- next bus stop?
- shopping facilities near?

Now you are the one who offers a flat, and you have to answer questions on the phone. These are the answers:

- there is a hall, a bedroom, a living-room, a bathroom, a kitchen and a balcony
- kitchen and the bathroom: tiled; all the other rooms: stripped floor
- any time, give me a ring before you come
- £250 pcm
- no, extra costs for heating
- former lodger: £30 per month
- washing machine, dishwasher: just call a plumber; telephone: yes
- parking space: right in front of the house (if lucky)
- shopping centre: five minutes by bus

Game 8A (partner B takes Game 8B)

Getting an Idea of Computer Devices

Give a definition of a computer device to your partner. Partner B has a list of words which match your definitions, but they are not in the correct order. Decide if he gave you the wrong or the right term. You could say: *"Yes, I think that's right"* or *"No, I think it's a …"*

1. I need this for drawing something on the monitor.
2. This is used for getting pictures into the computer.
3. … a device for storing information on it and carrying it with you
4. … for storing large programmes
5. … surf … the net
6. … type … letters
7. … watch … input data
8. … calculate nutritional values
9. … design kitchens

Now you would like to know what the following things are for. Ask partner B for his information. He has a list of explanations which are not in the correct order, however. So do not believe everything he tells you!
1. What is a mouse (for)?
2. … a modem …?
3. … a printer …?
4. … a text processing programme … ?
5. … a CD-ROM … ?
6. … a file directory?
7. … multi-tasking?
8. … a layout?
9. … a preview?

Game 9A (**partner B** takes Game 9B)

Reported Speech Memory Game

Read the following sentences out loud to partner B. For the first one (“*I often go to a beauty farm*”), he must answer: “*You said learning English was great fun.*”
When you read your second sentence, he must put your first sentence into reported speech.
Now start reading, and give him some time to think.
1. I often go to a beauty farm.
2. I never eat pork.
3. Do you want to give up smoking?
4. You will be happier if you eat carrots.
5. Why do you eat hamburgers?
6. Stop making a fool of me!

Here are sentences that are already in reported speech – now do it the other way around.
1. You said that learning English was great fun.
2. You said you had eaten …
3. You said you couldn't …
4. You asked me if …

Partner B

 Game 1B (**partner A** takes Game 1A)

On the Phone

Who is that speaking, please? – This is …
Write down what partner A dictates you.
Then you dictate these names to your partner.
1. Liz   2. Peter
3. Sue   4. Jean
5. Michael   6. Samantha

Sometimes it is hard to understand people's surnames and write them correctly.
In that case you may ask: “How do you spell that, please?”
Write down what partner A dictates. If you do not know how to write the name or surname, you ask him or her to spell it.
Now dictate the following surnames to partner B. Spell the names, if he or she asks you to do so.
→ For spelling, refer to page 152.
1. Parker   2. Hewlett Packard
3. Lewis   4. Marleybone
5. Banks   6. Studebaker
7. Joyce   8. Yeats

 Game 2B (**partner A** takes Game 2A)

Asking for Information about People

Your English friend rings you and needs some information about these three people. Please help him/her, but you must answer in full sentences.
◆ Stephen Miller: a) 24 b) baker c) skating, hockey, judo d) 18 Bardwell Square, Stratford on Avon
e) 2214731 f) Steph.Miller@iol.uk (@ = at)
◆ Sara Celtenham: a) 29 b) domestic bursar c) tayloring, shopping, mountain climbing d) 49 Butcher's Lane, Liverpool
e) 8877794 f) Celtysar.ham@att.uk
◆ Jodie Baker: a) 16 b) Brunel College c) old people's nurse d) babysitting e) £2 per hour

Now you need some information about three other people. Ask partner B to give it to you. Do that in full sentences, please.

- Jack Smart: a) age? b) job? c) hobbies?
  d) address? e) phone number? f) e-mail
  address?
- Liz Hornsby: a) age? b) job? c) hobbies?
  d) address? e) phone number? f) e-mail
  address?
- Ask for partner A's own data or for A's
  friend or for someone he/she knows.

 **Game** 3B (**partner A** takes Game 3A)

Where Is My Recipe?

Your friend (partner A) phones you. She
wants to make an apple crumble, but she has
lost the recipe. Of course, you can help her.

Ingredients
900 g apples
50 g soft brown sugar
$1/2$ teaspoon of ground cinnamon (spice)
2 tablespoons of orange juice

For the Crumble
175 g plain flour
50g sugar
75 g butter
(which is sugar, which is butter?)
a pinch of salt (or do you want to kill your
guests?)

Cook the apples in a saucepan with the orange juice, cinnamon and brown sugar until soft.
Spread the crumble out with a fork but do not
press it down.
Bake the crumble for about 20 to 30 minutes.
It will be ready when the top has browned a
bit. The oven setting should be 200 °C, gas
mark 6.
Serve the crumble with hot custard or ice
cream.

When you visited partner A last time, she had
brought a new recipe from Italy – "Pumpkin
Gnocchi". You do not exactly remember what
you need for making pumpkin gnocchi. Parts
of the paper on which you wrote the recipe
are now unreadable. So you phone her to get
the missing information.

Ingredients
?? kg pumpkins
?? g flour
1 ???
crushed ???
1 pinch of ???

For the Sauce
?? g chopped tomatoes
1 chopped ???
6 chopped ???
olive ???
??? salt

Peel the pumpkin, prepare the dough. Cut it
into pieces and bake it at ??? °C for ??? minutes.
Fry the onions briefly in 2 tablespoons of oil,
add the tomatoes and cook them for ??? minutes. Oven setting: ??? Stir while cooking. Pass
through a sieve and bring it to boil again.
Add the sauce and the basil (when?).

 **Game** 4B (**partner A** takes Game 4A)

Going for an Interview

You have published an advertisement, saying
that your hotel is looking for a trainee cook.
Now a young man/woman is sitting in front of
you and wants to know more about the job.
Please answer his/her questions.

- job: helping to prepare the various meals
  in the hotel kitchen
- working hours: 8 hours per day, 40 hours
  per week
- working time:
- two shifts: morning shift – 6 a.m. to 2
  p.m., late shift – 6 p.m. to 2 a.m.
- working days per week: 5 days
- free weekends: every other weekend
- pay: £100 per week for a start, later up to
  £150 per week at end of training
- college: once a week, on Wednesdays
- holidays: 4 weeks per year
- clothing: provided by the hotel
- time of training: 3 to 5 years
- promotion prospects: junior cook usually
  after three years, it depends on how well
  you are doing

Now you are looking for an apprenticeship as a trainee old people's nurse. In an interview, you ask them (partner A) some questions about the job. Remember that someone who has no questions may be seen as an idiot …

- job?
- examples?
- working hours?
- night shift?
- free days?
- work at weekends?
- pay?
- holidays?
- college? How often?
- length of training?

Game 5B (partner A takes Game 5A)

A Survey of a Market Research Institute

When you (partner B) leave a department store, an interviewer (partner A) wants to ask you some questions. You are friendly and answer them, as you can win "half a washing machine or something like this."

This is what you can answer – but in full sentences!

- you found a pullover, a T-shirt and a pair of socks,
- you are ??? years old,
- they mainly sell clothes, toys, books, household equipment and food,
- some shop assistants: no idea; others: informed quite well,
- some shop assistants seem to prefer chatting to helping customers; they kill you with looks when you ask questions,
- you work the night shift this week.

Now you interview partner A. Promise him that he can win a long distance flight from Heathrow to Gatwick.
Try to find out:
- if he found what he was looking for,
- how often he goes shopping in this department store,
- what he thinks about the offers in this store,
- if he thinks the prices are okay,
- if he had problems to find what he was looking for,
- how good the advice was which the shop assistants gave him.

Game 6B (partner A takes Game 6A)

Buying Electrical Household Equipment

You have some technical information about a washing machine. Your partner has also got some information about another washing machine. Try to find out which of the machines is better, can hold more washing, is more economical etc.
Ask your partner for his technical data and then form sentences like: "*My washing machine needs less electricity than yours.*"
You can use adjectives like: *much, easy to handle, wide, high, long, economic, little, slow, fast*
This list of adjectives is neither complete nor in the right order!

Cleaning Mate 2020 de Luxe	
amount of washing	4.5 kg
control	half automatic
spin drier speeds	600 to 1500 rpm
Consumption Data at 60 °C	
water	49 litres
power consumption	0.95 kWh
washing programmes	4
dimensions (height, width, length)	85 by 60 by 60 cm
price	£286.--

Discuss which washing machine you would prefer to buy.

You also want to buy a freezer. You have collected the technical data about the "Freezer Freak 2001 S" and partner A has collected information about the "Eco-Arctic Super". Ask for the technical data, then form sentences and compare the freezers.

Freezer Freak 2001 S	
capacity	225 litres
control	fully electronic
warning	acoustic door and temperature alert
power consumption	329 kWh per year
defrosting	quick defroster system
dimensions (height by width by Length)	155 by 66 by 66 cm
price	£595.--

 **Game 7B** (**partner A** takes Game 7A)

Getting and Giving Information about a Flat

You are a landlord who offers a flat. Someone phones you (partner A) and wants to know more about the flat. You give him the information he needs. Since you want him to come and rent the flat, be friendly and answer in full sentences!
These are the answers to his questions:

- in the bedroom and in the living room; lino in the hall, tiled floors in kitchen and bathroom
- come and measure yourself
- tomorrow afternoon?
- gas central heating
- a 2 square metre partition in the cellar
- no problem!
- small place in the attic, buy a drier
- just round the corner
- a five-minute walk to a supermarket

Now you are a flathunter yourself, and you ask the landlord questions about a flat you are interested in:

- number of rooms?
- type of floor covering in the rooms?
- see the flat? when?
- rent – how high?
- rent exclusive or inclusive of heating charges?
- heating costs on the average?
- outlets for washing machine, dishwasher, telephone?
- parking space – where?
- shopping facilities near?

Game 8B (**partner A** takes Game 8A)

Getting an Idea of Computer Devices

Partner A gives you a definition of a computer device. You have a list of words that go with the definitions, but the list is not in the correct order. Find the terms which match his definitions.
1. I think that is … a spread-sheet programme
2. … a hard disk
3. … a flatbed scanner
4. … a mouse

5. … a monitor
6. … a drawing programme
7. … a keyboard
8. … a modem
9. … a disk

Partner A has heard some computer terms which he doesn't understand. He wants to know what they mean. Make sure that you are the expert who can explain. Here is a list of explanations, which is not in the correct order, however.
1. It's for getting your work on a sheet of paper.
2. … something you can see before you in-fix it into your file
3. … kind of a "bookcase" in which you for example store letters of the same type
4. … for large programmes which you can buy in computer shops
5. … an operation modus in which you can quickly change from one programme to another
6. … how you arrange text and pictures
7. … it connects your computer to the internet
8. write … letters and design … a nicer layout
9. … for moving the cursor more quickly

Game 9B (**partner A** takes Game 9A)

Reported Speech Memory Game

What did partner A say? For the first statement, you answer: "*You said learning English was great fun.*"
When partner A gives you his second statement, you report what he said in his first sentence etc.
1. You said that learning English was great fun.
2. You said you often …
3. You said you never …
4. You asked me if …

Now do it the other way around.
1. I ate two rolls this morning.
2. I simply cannot reduce my weight.
3. Have you ever eaten fat bacon?
4. All my friends are too fat.
5. When did you eat your last bar of chocolate?
6. Start thinking!

Unregelmäßige Verben

Infinitive	Past Tense	Past Participle	
to be	was, were	been	sein
to beat	beat	beaten	schlagen
to become	became	become	werden
to begin	began	begun	beginnen, anfangen
to bite	bit	bitten	beißen
to bleed	bled	bled	bluten
to blow	blew	blown	blasen
to break	broke	broken	brechen, zerbrechen
to bring	brought	brought	bringen, mitbringen
to build	built	built	bauen
to burn	burnt	burnt	brennen
to buy	bought	bought	kaufen
to catch	caught	caught	fangen, ergreifen
to choose	chose	chosen	wählen
to come	came	come	kommen
to cost	cost	cost	kosten
to cut	cut	cut	schneiden
to deal (with)	dealt	dealt	sich kümmern um, sich beschäftigen mit
to do	did	done	machen, tun
to draw	drew	drawn	zeichnen, malen
to dream	dreamt	dreamt	träumen
to drink	drank	drunk	trinken
to drive	drove	driven	(Auto) fahren
to eat	ate	eaten	essen
to fall	fell	fallen	fallen
to feel	felt	felt	fühlen
to fight	fought	fought	bekämpfen, kämpfen
to find	found	found	finden
to fly	flew	flown	fliegen
to forget	forgot	forgotten	vergessen
to forgive	forgave	forgiven	vergeben, verzeihen
to freeze	froze	frozen	frieren, gefrieren
to get	got	got	bekommen, kommen
to give	gave	given	geben
to go	went	gone	gehen, fahren
to grow	grew	grown	wachsen
to have	had	had	haben
to hear	heard	heard	hören
to hide	hid	hidden	(sich) verstecken
to hit	hit	hit	schlagen, stoßen
to hold	held	held	halten, abhalten
to hurt	hurt	hurt	(sich) verletzen
to keep	kept	kept	behalten, halten
to know	knew	known	wissen, kennen
to lead	led	led	führen
to learn	learnt	learnt	lernen
to leave	left	left	verlassen, abfahren
to lend	lent	lent	leihen, verleihen
to let	let	let	lassen
to lie	lay	lain	liegen
to lose	lost	lost	verlieren
to make	made	made	machen, anfertigen
to mean	meant	meant	bedeuten
to meet	met	met	treffen, begegnen
to pay	paid	paid	bezahlen
to put	put	put	setzen, legen, stellen
to read	read	read	lesen
to ride	rode	ridden	reiten, (Rad) fahren
to ring	rang	rung	klingeln, läuten
to rise	rose	risen	aufstehen, (Sonne) aufgehen
to run	ran	run	rennen, laufen

Infinitive	Past Tense	Past Participle	
to say	said	said	sagen
to see	saw	seen	sehen
to seek	sought	sought	suchen
to sell	sold	sold	verkaufen
to send	sent	sent	senden, schicken
to shake	shook	shaken	schütteln
to show	showed	shown	zeigen
to shut	shut	shut	schließen
to sing	sang	sung	singen
to sit	sat	sat	sitzen
to sleep	slept	slept	schlafen
to smell	smelt	smelt	riechen
to speak	spoke	spoken	sprechen
to spend	spent	spent	verbringen, ausgeben
to stand	stood	stood	stehen
to steal	stole	stolen	stehlen
to swim	swam	swum	schwimmen
to take	took	taken	nehmen, mitnehmen
to teach	taught	taught	lehren, unterrichten
to tear	tore	torn	zerreißen
to tell	told	told	erzählen
to think	thought	thought	denken
to throw	threw	thrown	werfen
to wake (up)	woke	woken	aufwachen
to wear	wore	worn	(Kleidung) tragen
to win	won	won	gewinnen
to write	wrote	written	schreiben

The English Alphabet

a [eɪ]   b [bi]   c [si]   d [di]   e [iː]   f [ef]

g [dʒiː]   h [eɪtʃ]   i [aɪ]   j [dʒei]   k [keɪ]   l [el]

m [em]   n [en]   o [əʊ]   p [pi]   q [kjuː]   r [aː]

s [es]   t [tiː]   u [juː]   v [viː]   w [dʌbljuː]   x [eks]

y [waɪ]   z [zed] (BrE)
    [ziː] (AmE)

Grammatikalischer Anhang

Present Progressive (Verlaufsform der Gegenwart)

Die Verlaufsform der Gegenwart wird immer mit einer von Form von *to be* gebildet. An das Verb wird ein *-ing* angehängt.

Aussagen und Verneinungen				
I	**am**			
He/She/It	**is**	(not)	bak**ing** a cake.	
We/You/They	**are**			

Die Verlaufsform wird immer dann gewählt, wenn eine Handlung noch im Verlauf ist, d.h. zum Zeitpunkt des Sprechens noch nicht abgeschlossen ist. – *I am preparing the meal*.
Die Verlaufsform wird ebenfalls angewendet, wenn eine Handlung vorübergehend ist, aber nicht unbedingt zum Zeitpunkt des Sprechens stattfindet. – *I am working in an ice café this week*.
Signalwörter: *at the moment, (just) now, look*
Verneinte Sätze werden gebildet, indem an die Form von *to be* ein *not* angehängt wird.

Ja-/Nein-Fragen			Kurzantworten	
Am	I		Yes, I am	No, I am not.
Are	you	bak**ing** a cake?	Yes, you are.	No, you are not.
Is	he/she/it		Yes, he/she/it is.	No, he/she/it is not.
Are	we/you/they		Yes, we/you/they are.	No, we/you/they are not.

Um Fragen zu bilden, wird die jeweilige Form *am/is/are* mit dem Subjekt getauscht.
In der Kurzantwort wird jeweils die Form von *to be* aus der Fragestellung wiederholt.

Simple Present (Einfache Gegenwart)

Aussagen			Verneinungen		
I/You	walk		I/You	do not (don't)	
He/She/It	walk**s**	home.	He/She/It	does not (doesn't)	walk home.
We/You/They	walk		We/You/They	do not (don't)	

Das Simple Present drückt aus, dass etwas regelmäßig geschieht bzw. regelmäßig nicht geschieht: *I go to school; I don't work at home;* etc.
Tatsachen werden ebenfalls in Simple Present ausgedrückt: *Peter lives in London*.
Diese Zeit wird auch verwendet, um auszudrücken, welchen Beruf, welches Hobby oder welche Fähigkeit jemand hat.
In den Aussagesätzen wird das Verb nicht verändert; bei *he/she* und *it* wird jedoch ein *-s* (*walks*) bzw. *-es* (*goes*) angefügt. Endet das Verb mit *o, s, sh, ch, x*, wird *-es* angehängt.
(Regel: He, she, it → s muss mit.)
Signalwörter: always, usually, sometimes, never etc.
Verneinte Sätze werden mit *do not/don't* bzw. *does not/doesn't* gebildet. Das Verb wird nicht verändert.

Ja-/Nein-Fragen		Kurzantworten	
Do	I live in London?	Yes, I do.	No, I don't.
	you live in London?	Yes, you do.	No, you don't.
Does	he/she/it live in London?	Yes, he/she/it does.	No, he/she/it doesn't.
Do	we/you/they live in London?	Yes, we/you/they do.	No, we/you/they don't.

Bei Ja-/Nein-Fragen wird *do* (bzw. *does* bei *he/she/it*) an den Satzanfang gestellt.
Die höfliche Antwort sollte niemals nur 'yes' oder 'no' lauten. Es muss stets heißen: *Yes, I do* bzw. *No, I don't*.

Der Gebrauch von "to do"

Wann wird *to do* verwendet?
- bei Verneinungen
- bei Fragen

– *I don't like Peter.*
– *Do you live in London?*

Do/does erscheint nur im Simple Present bzw als *did* im Past Tense.

– *Does Peter like you?*
– *Did you go to school yesterday?*

Ausnahmen:
- *To do* erscheint nicht in Fragesätzen, wenn eine Form von *to be* vorhanden ist.
- *To do* wird nicht verwendet, wenn bereits ein Hilfsverb wie *can, must, may, will, shall* vorhanden ist.

– *Are you at home?*
– *Why is he so late?*

– *Can I come home later? No, you can't.*
– *Must I really stay at home tonight? Yes, you must.*

- *To do* wird ebenfalls nicht verwendet, wenn nach dem Subjekt gefragt wird (wer oder was?). – *Who stays at home? Peter.*

Simple Past (Einfache Vergangenheit)

Bei regelmäßigen Verben wird ein *-ed* an das Verb gehängt (open → open**ed**)
Bei unregelmäßigen Verben wird die zweite Verbform benutzt (break → **broke**)
(→ Vgl. Liste der unregelmäßigen Verben auf Seite 151 f.)

Aussagen		
I/You/He/She/It We/You/They	**opened**	a bottle.
I/You/He/She/It We/You/They	**broke**	a plate.

Verneinungen werden mit *did not/didn't* gebildet. Das nachfolgende Verb erscheint daraufhin wieder in der Grundform.
Das Simple Past wird gebraucht, um auszudrücken, dass eine Handlung völlig abgeschlossen ist.
Signalwörter: last year, last month, two weeks ago, in 2004 etc.

Verneinungen		
I/You/He/She/It We/You/They	**did** not (didn't) **open**	a bottle.
I/You/He/She/It We/You/They	**did** not (didn't) **break**	a plate.

Achtung: An *he/she/it* wird im Simple Past kein *-s* angehängt!

Ja-/Nein-Fragen				Kurzantworten
Did	I/you/he/she/it we/you/they	**open**	a bottle?	Yes, I did. No, I didn't.
	I/you/he/she/it we/you/they	**break**	a plate?	Yes, we did. No, we didn't.

Bei Ja-/Nein-Fragen wird *did* an den Satzanfang gestellt.
Die Antwort lautet: *Yes, I did* oder *No, I didn't*.
Handelt es sich um Informationsfragen (when, why, were, how often etc.) wird das jeweilige Fragewort an den Anfang des Satzes gestellt: *When did you break the plate?*
Die Verwendung von *did* entspricht den Regeln der Verwendung von *do* bzw. *does*.

Past Progressive (Verlaufsform der Vergangenheit)

Aussagen und Verneinungen				
I	**was** (wasn't)			
You	**were** (weren't)	fry**ing**	meatballs	at that time.
He/She/It	**was** (wasn't)			
We/You/They	**were** (weren't)			

Das Past Progressive wird mit der zweiten Form von *to be* (= *was/were*) bzw. bei der Vernein-ung mit *wasn't/weren't* gebildet. An das Verb wird ein *-ing* angehängt.

Past Progressive wird immer dann benutzt, wenn es sich um eine Handlung handelt, die in der Vergangenheit im Verlauf war. Das Ergebnis ist unwichtig.

Ja-/Nein-Fragen					Kurzantworten
Was	I				Yes, I was. No, I wasn't.
	he/she/it	fry**ing**	meatballs	at that time?	
Were	you				Yes, you were. No, you weren't.
Were	we/you/they				Yes, we were. No, we weren't.

Bei Ja-/Nein-Fragen wird *was* bzw. *were* an den Satzanfang gestellt.

Present Perfect (Das Perfekt)

Aussagen und Verneinungen				
I	**have**			
You		(not)	**been**	to Ireland yet.
He/She/It	**has**			
We/You/They	**have**			

Das Present Perfect wird mit *have* (*have not*) bzw. *has* (*has not*) und der dritten Verbform gebildet.
Bei regelmäßigen Verben wird dazu ein *-ed* an das Verb gehängt. *work → worked*
Bei unregelmäßigen Verben wird die dritte Form des Verbs genommen. *go → went*
→ Vgl. hierzu die Liste der unregelmäßigen Verben auf S. 151.

Das Present Perfect wird benutzt, um auszudrücken, dass eine Handlung oder ein Zustand in der Vergangenheit begonnen wurde und nun bis in die Gegenwart oder darüber hinaus andauert oder Auswirkungen auf die Gegenwart hat.
So kann z. B ein sichtbares Ergebnis vorliegen: *I have painted my fence. Now it is blue*.

Das Present Perfect wird auch verwendet, um auszudrücken, dass sich etwas einmal, mehrmals oder nie <u>bis zum Zeitpunkt des Sprechens</u> ereignet hat: *I haven't been to Ireland yet.*

Signalwörter: so far, up to now

Ja-/Nein-Fragen				Kurzantworten	
Have	I			Yes, I have.	No, I haven't.
	you	**worked**	on the project?	Yes, you have.	No, you haven't.
Has	he/she/it			Yes, he/she/it has.	No, he/she/it hasn't.
Have	we/you/they			Yes, we/you/they have.	No, we/you/they haven't.

Past Perfect (Vollendete Vergangenheit)

Past Perfect					Past Tense			
After	I/you he/she/it we/you/they	**had**	**seen**	the accident	I/you he/she/it we/you/they		**called**	the police.

Das Past Perfect wird mit had (*had not/hadn't*) und der dritten Form des Verbs gebildet.

Das Past Perfect wird verwendet, um auszudrücken, dass zwei Handlungen aufeinander folgen. Beide haben in der Vergangenheit stattgefunden.
Die zeitlich weiter zurückliegende Handlungen wird in Past Perfect ausgedrückt: *After I **had** seen ....* (= erste Handlung)
Die darauf folgende Handlung wird in Past Tense ausgedrückt: *... I **called** the police.* (= zweite Handlung)
Signalwörter: when, after

Die Anwendung dieser Zeit entspricht dem deutschen Plusquamperfekt.

Future (Zukunft)

Es gibt mehrere Möglichkeiten, zukünftiges Geschehen oder zukünftige Handlungen auszu-drücken. Die beiden wichtigsten sind die **Going-To-Future** und die **Will-Future**.

● Going-To-Future
Das Going-To-Future wird mit *am/are/is* + *going to* + der Grundform des Verbs gebildet.

Going-To-Future				
I	**am**			
You	**are**	**going to**	**see**	the doctor.
He/She/It	**is**			
We/You/They	**are**			

Das Going-To-Future wird dann verwendet, wenn man etwas in naher Zukunft geplant hat oder es zu tun beabsichtigt (bzw. es nicht zu tun beabsichtigt):
*I **am** (not) **going** to tell you what I know.*

Das Going-To-Future wird ferner bei einem wahrscheinlich eintretenden zukünftigem Ereignis benutzt – wenn man es bereits vorhersehen oder erahnen kann:
*The chair **is going to** break if you don't stop moving on it.*

● Will-Future
Das Will-Future wird mit *will* (*will not/won't*) + der Grundform des Verbs gebildet.

Will-Future			
I/You He/She/It We/You/They	**will**	**see**	the doctor.

Das Will-Future wird verwendet, um einen spontanen Entschluss zum Ausdruck zu bringen:
*You are not able to do your homework? I **will help** you.*

Das Will-Future wird ferner verwendet, um ein künftiges Geschehen auszudrücken, das der Sprecher nicht beeinflussen oder nicht klar vorhersehen kann: *What **will** the world **be** like when I'm 64?*

Das Will-Future wird auch verwendet, um eine Vermutung über ein zukünftiges Ereignis auszu-drücken:
*I'm sure you **will be** able to understand these explanations.*

Die Verwendung der Simple-Form und der Progressive-Form bei verschiedenen Verbgruppen

Jedes Verb kann in der Simple-Form verwendet werden. Die meisten Verben können sowohl in der Simple-Form als auch in der Progressive-Form (mit *–ing*-Endung) erscheinen. Das zweite sind vor allem Verben, die Tätigkeiten (z. B. *read, play, sing* etc.) ausdrücken.

Folgende Verben können in der Regel nur in der Simple-Form verwendet werden:
Alle Formen von *to be, have (got), mean, look, seem, sound, need, want, like, dislike, love, hate, agree, doubt, remember, understand*

Verben der Sinneswahrnehmung (z.B. *hear, see, smell, taste, feel*) erscheinen in der Simple-Form: *This soup tastes good. (= Sinneswahrnehmung)*

Aber: *Smell, taste* und *feel* können auch Tätigkeitsverben sein und dann in der Progressive-Form erscheinen: *I am tasting the soup. (= aktive Handlung)*

Some und Any

Aussagen	Verneinungen	Fragen	Angebote/Bitten
I need **some** bread, butter and **some** tomatoes.	There isn't **any** butter left.	Is there **any** bread left? No, there isn't.	Can I have **some** cheese then, please?
No, you can't. Somebody must have eaten all our food, I'm afraid.	I haven't seen **anybody** in this house except you and me.	Can you think of **anybody** who is keen on our food?	No, you can't. But I can offer you **some** peanuts.
I want **something** real to eat!	But there isn't **anything** left!	Why isn't there **anything** to eat in the house?	What about **some** fast-food?

Some und *any* können sowohl bei zählbaren (z. B. *tomatoes*) als auch bei nicht zählbaren (z. B. *butter*) Begriffen stehen.
In Fragen und Verneinungen wird *any* verwendet.
Some wird in Aussagesätzen verwendet.
Some erscheint lediglich dann in Fragen, wenn man eine Bitte aussprechen oder etwas anbieten will.
Wie *some* und *any* werden auch die Zusammensetzungen *somebody, something* und *anybody, anything* verwendet.

Personal Pronouns (Personalpronomen)

Bei den Personalpronomen unterscheidet man zwischen Subjektpronomen, Objektpronomen, den besitzanzeigenden Fürwörtern und den rückbezüglichen Fürwörtern.
Pronomen ersetzen ein Hauptwort.

Nach dem Hauptwort wird mit "Wer oder was?" gefragt. Man kann z. B. sagen: ***Peter is nice.*** (Peter ist das Hauptwort.)
Man kann ebenfalls sagen: ***He is nice.***

Subject Pronouns (Subjektpronomen)			
Einzahl		**Mehrzahl**	
I	ich	we	wir
you	du	you	ihr
he/she/it	er/sie/es	they	sie

Ein Objekt ist der Satzteil, mit dem beschrieben wird, auf wen oder was eine Handlung oder ein Zustand ausgerichtet ist.
- *I like Peter*. (Wen mag ich?) *I like him*.
oder: *I like my room*. (Was mag ich?) *I like it*.

Object Pronouns (Objektpronomen – direktes Objekt)

Einzahl		Mehrzahl	
me	mir, mich	us	uns
you	dir, dich	you	euch
him	ihm, ihn	them	sie, ihnen
her	ihr, sie		
it	ihm, es		

Besitzanzeigende Fürwörter geben an, wem oder zu wem etwas gehört.
- *This is my room. Is this your handbag?*
Possessive Pronouns I stehen immer zusammen mit einem Hauptwort.

Possessive Pronouns I (besitzanzeigende Fürwörter)

Einzahl		Mehrzahl	
my	mein	our	unser
yours	dein, Ihr	your	euer, eure
his	sein	their	ihr
her	ihr		
its	sein		

Possessive Pronouns II stehen anstelle eines Hauptworts.
Man kann z. B. sagen: - *This room is my room.*
Oder: *This room is mine*.
- *Is this handbag your handbag?*
Oder: *Is this handbag yours?*

Man verwendet die Possessivpronomen II, wenn man das vorausgegangene Hauptwort nicht noch einmal wiederholen will.

Possessive Pronouns II (Possessivpronomen)

Einzahl		Mehrzahl	
my	mine	our	ours
yours	yours	your	yours
his	his	their	theirs
her	hers		
its	its		

Reflexivpronomen werden benutzt, um auf das Subjekt des Satzes zurückzuverweisen.
- *She enjoyed herself*. (Sie amüsierte sich.)
- *The children can take care of themselves*.
(Die Kinder können auf sich selbst aufpassen.)

Reflexive Pronouns (rückbezügliche Fürwörter)

Einzahl		Mehrzahl	
I	myself	we	ourselves
you	yourself	you	yourselves
he	himself	they	themselves
she	herself		
it	itself		

Adjectives (Adjektive – Wiewörter)

Adjektive beschreiben Eigenschaften oder Merkmale. Sie beschreiben, wie etwas ist:
The pretty girl oder *The girl is pretty*.

Die Steigerung von Adjektiven
Wie Adjektive gesteigert werden, hängt von der Endung und der Silbenzahl des Adjektivs ab. Die beiden Steigerungsstufen heißen Komparativ und Superlativ.

Bei einsilbigen Adjektiven wird *-er/-est* angehängt. Wenn ein einsilbiges Adjektiv auf einen Konsonanten (Mitlaut) endet, wird dieser verdoppelt: *hot - hotter - (the) hottest*

Zweisilbige Adjektive, die auf *-er, -ow, -le, -re* und *-y* enden, werden ebenfalls mit *-er/-est* gesteigert.
Das *-y* wird zu *-i*: *pretty - prettier - (the) prettiest*

Die meisten Adjektive mit zwei und mehr Silben werden mit *more/most* gesteigert. Das Adjektiv selbst verändert sich dann nicht: *expensive - more expensive - most expensive*

	Adjektiv	Komparativ	Superlativ
Einsilbige Adjektive	nice	nicer	(the) nicest
Adjektive, die auf *-y, -er, -ow, -le* oder *-re* enden	pretty	prettier	(the) prettiest
Adjektive mit zwei und mehr Silben	expensive	more expensive	(the) most expensive
Unregelmäßige Adjektive	good	better	(the) best
	bad	worse	(the) worst
	much/a lot of/some/many	more	(the) most
	far	further	(the) furthest

Vergleiche von Dingen oder Personen
Vergleiche können mit *-er/more … than* oder *(not) as … as* gebildet werden:
*I am taller **than** Peter but I am **not as tall as** Fred.*
*Butter is **more** expensive **than** milk.*
*Cheese is **as** expensive **as** butter.*

Adverbs (Adverbien – Umstandswörter)

Adverbien beschreiben, unter welchen Umständen etwas geschieht oder nicht geschieht. Die wichtigsten sind die Häufigkeitsadverbien und die Adverbien der Art und Weise.
Adverb (lat.): dem Verb hinzugefügt

● Adverbs of Frequency (Häufigkeitsadverbien)
Häufigkeitsabverbien sind z. B. *always, usually, regularly, seldom, never*

Achtung: Im Gegensatz zum Deutschen stehen die Häufigkeitsadverbien <u>vor</u> dem Vollverb.
Deutsch: *Ich trinke immer Kaffee.*   Englisch: *I always drink coffee.*

    ↑   ↑   ↑   ↑

  Verb   Adverb   Adverb Verb

Aber: Bei den Formen von *to be* stehen diese Adverbien – genauso wie im Deutschen – <u>nach</u> dem Hilfsverb: *Peter is never ill.*

● Adverbs of Manner (Adverbien der Art und Weise)
Adverbien der Art und Weise beschreiben beispielsweise Tätigkeiten genauer.
In der Regel werden diese Adverbien durch ein Anhängen von *-ly* an das Adjektiv gebildet:
successful – successfully   quick – quickly
Endet das Adjektiv bereits auf *-y*, wird *-ily* angehängt: *easy – easily*

Man kann die Art und Weise z. B. wie jemand schreibt durch diese Adverbien genauer umschreiben: *He writes slowly. He writes quickly.*

Keine Regel ohne Ausnahmen!
- Die Adverbien *hard, early* und *fast* sind identisch mit den Adjektiven und werden nicht verändert:
  *He is a **hard** worker, he works **hard**.*
- Das Adverb von *good* ist *well: She writes well.*
- Nach den Verben *be, feel, look* und *seem* folgen keine Adverbien, sondern Adjektive: *You look good.*

Hier wird ein Zustand beschrieben.

The Passive Voice (Das Passiv)

Ein Aktivsatz drückt aus, wer oder was eine Handlung durchführt: *The robot ..., Caren ...* Das Subjekt des Aktivsatzes wird zum Objekt des Passivsatzes.

Aktivsatz		
The robot	**cooks**	the meal.
Caren	**started**	the toaster.
↑		↑
Subjekt		Objekt

Ein Passivsatz hebt die Person oder die Sache hervor, mit der etwas geschieht: *The meal ..., the toaster ...*

Wer oder was die Handlung veranlasst hat, ist oft unbekannt oder uninteressant.

Das Passiv wird mit einer Form von *to be* + der dritten Form des Verbs gebildet.

Passivsatz		
The meal	**is cooked**	by the robot.
The toaster	**was started**	(by Caren).
↑		↑
Subjekt (ehemaliges Objekt)		Objekt (ehemaliges Subjekt)

Reported Speech (Indirekte Rede)

In der indirekten Rede wird einem Dritten erzählt, was jemand gesagt, geschrieben oder gedacht hat.

Direkte Rede	Indirekte Rede
Susan: **I'm** too fat. The boys don't like **me**.	Pam: Susan thinks that **she** is too fat, and that the boys don't like **her**.

● Die Verschiebung der Zeiten

Wenn das einleitende Verb wie im obigen Beispiel im Simple Present steht *(thinks),* ändern sich die Zeiten in der Umwandlung von der direkten zur indirekten Rede nicht. In allen anderen Fällen müssen in der indirekten Rede andere Zeiten als in der direkten Rede verwendet werden, vgl. Tabelle:

● Veränderungen der Personalpronomen

I, you (Singular) we, you (Plural) ▶ he, she they

● Veränderungen der Possessivpronomen

my, your (Singular) our, your (Plural) ▶ his, her their

Direkte Rede	Indirekte Rede
Simple Present I **eat** too much chocolate.	Simple Past She said that she **ate** too much chocolate.
Present Progressive Mark **is cooking** a soufflé.	Past Progressive Carol told me that Mark **was cooking** a soufflé.
Past Tense We **bought** a pullover.	Past Perfect She said that they **had bought** a pullover.
Present Perfect We **have** never **been** to London.	Past Perfect We were told that they **had** never **been** to London.
Will-Future I **will train** every day.	*Would* + Grundform des Verbs He remarked that he **would train** every day.

Relative Pronouns (Relativpronomen)

Mit Relativpronomen werden Relativsätze ein-
geleitet.
Relativsätze haben die Funktion, ein Substan-
tiv näher zu beschreiben.
Die Pronomen *who* oder *that* beziehen sich
auf Personen, *which* oder *that* auf Tiere und
Dinge.
Im Zweifelsfall ist immer *that* das richtige Relativpronomen.

Personen	Tiere und Dinge
Mark, **who** was ill, had to go to the hospital.	The ambulance, **which** came to Mark's house, took him to the hospital.

Who, which oder *that* können entfallen, wenn sie die Stelle des Objekts im Relativsatz ein-
nehmen: *This is the hospital (that/which) Mark went to yesterday.*
– *This is the hospital Mark went to yesterday.*

If-Clauses Type I (Bedingungssätze Typ I)

If-Sätze des Typs I beschreiben Bedingungen,
unter denen etwas <u>sehr wahrscheinlich</u> erfüllt
wird oder sehr wahrscheinlich nicht erfüllt
wird. Die Eintrittswahrscheinlichlichkeit des
Gesagten liegt bei ca. 80 Prozent.
Im If-Satz steht das Simple Present, im Hauptsatz steht das Will-Future.

If-Satz	Hauptsatz
If I **don't sleep** now,	I **will be** tired tomorrow.
If Mark's temperature **falls**,	I **will not call** the doctor.

Der Hauptsatz kann dem If-Satz auch vorangestellt werden: *I will be tired tomorrow, if I don't
sleep now.* Der If-Satz wird vom Hauptsatz durch ein Komma getrennt.

If-Clauses Type II (Bedingungssätze Typ II)

If-Sätze des Typs II beschreiben Bedingungen,
unter denen etwas <u>vielleicht</u> eintreten könnte
oder auch nicht eintreten könnte. Die
Wahrscheinlichkeit, dass dieses geschieht
bzw. nicht geschieht liegt bei ca. 20 Prozent.
Im If-Satz steht das Simple Past – es hat hier
aber nichts mit der Vergangenheit zu tun –, im
Hauptsatz steht *would, could* oder *might* + Grundform des Verbs.
Achtung: Im If-Satz darf niemals *would* stehen!

If-Satz	Hauptsatz
If I **had** a car,	I **would invite** you for a trip.
If Gina **passed** her exam,	she **could work** as a student nurse.

If-Clauses Type III (Bedingungssätze Typ III)

If-Sätze des Typs III beschreiben Bedingungen, unter denen etwas <u>hätte</u> eintreten oder
auch nicht eintreten können. Dies ist jedoch
nicht geschehen. Die Wahrscheinlichkeit des
Eintretens liegt nur noch bei 0 Prozent.
→ Er ist nicht zum Konzert gegangen, folglich
  hat er sie auch nicht getroffen.

If-Satz	Hauptsatz
If I **had been** to the concert,	I **would have met** you.
If the bus-driver **had seen** the traffic light,	he **would not have killed** the dog.

Im If-Satz steht das Past Perfect, im Hauptsatz steht *would, could* oder *might* + *have* + die dritte
Form des Verbs.

Gerunds: Using Verbs As Nouns
(Gerundien: Verben können als Substantive benutzt werden)

Die *ing*-Form eines Verbs kann als Substantiv benutzt werden: *Das Schwimmen* …
Diese Form kann dann sowohl als Subjekt als auch als Objekt des Satzes verwendet werden.

ing-Form als Subjekt	*ing*-Form als Objekt
Swimming is fun for most people.	Some people don't like swimming.

→ Für Ausnahmen bei der Bildung der *ing*-Form vgl. Seite 156, "Die Verwendung der Simple-Form und der Progressive-Form bei verschiedenen Verbgruppen".

Quantifiers (Mengenangaben)

Many	= viele	much	= viel
a few	= einige wenige	a little	= (ein) wenig
more	= mehr	less	= weniger
fewer	= weniger(e)	more	= mehr
a lot of	= recht viele		

zählbar	nicht zählbar
Many girls believe cooking is fun.	They believe that there is not **much** work to do.
Only **a few** girls think that it is an awful job.	They think there is only **a little** to do.
There are **more** girls who like cooking.	Women who stay at home earn **less** money than those who go out to work.
There are **fewer** girls who don't like it.	
A lot of men think to keep a household isn't difficult.	Usually men earn **more** money than women.

> Many people waste much time for earning a little money, but who counts time and money?

Must/Have to (müssen)

Sowohl ‚*must*' als auch ‚*have to*' bedeuten *müssen*. Es gibt jedoch Unterschiede in der Bedeutung.

Must
‚*Must*' drückt eine dringende Verpflichtung aus, die a) von einem selbst oder b) von anderen Personen ausgeht, und die man unbedingt einhalten sollte.
Zu a) *I must get my hair cut. / I must see the doctor.* (Verpflichtung, die man sich selbst auflegt, und die man unbedingt einhalten will)
Zu b) *You must go to the Empire State Building when you are in New York.* (dringende Empfehlung, die von anderen Personen ausgeht)

‚*Must not*' bedeutet nicht, dass man etwas nicht muss, sondern dass etwas nicht erlaubt ist.
You must not walk over the grass. (Sie dürfen nicht über den Rasen laufen.)
‚*Must*' bzw. ‚*must not*' wird nur in der Gegenwart (Present Tense) benutzt. In der Vergangenheit (Simple Past) wird aus ‚*must*' – ‚*had to*'.

Have to
‚*Have to*' ist allgemeiner gehalten und weniger dringlich in der Aussage als ‚*must*'. Es handelt sich meistens um Anordnungen oder Anweisungen, die ganz allgemein einzuhalten sind.
When you are in Britain, don't forget that you have to drive on the left.

Bei Fragen wird die Umschreibung mit ‚*do*' gebildet.
Do I have to wear a special cloth for that event?

Grundwortschatz

Diese Liste enthält cirka 750 Grundwörter, die in Living Together als bekannt vorausgesetzt werden. Nicht aufgeführt, jedoch vorausgesetzt sind internationale Wörter (Taxi, Fax, TV usw.) und einige sehr elementare Wörter, wie Pronomen, Zahlen und Tage.

a lot	viel/e, sehr	beach	Strand	(to) check	(über)prüfen
a. m.	vor 12:00 Uhr mittags	beautiful	schön	cheese	Käse
		because	weil	child	Kind
about	über, etwa, circa	bed	Bett	chips	Pommes frites
		bedroom	Schlafzimmer	chocolate	Schokolade, Praline
above	über, oben, obenstehend	beef	Rindfleisch		
		beer	Bier	(to) choose	wählen, aussuchen
accident	Unfall	before	bevor, zuvor		
address	Adresse	(to) begin	anfangen, beginnen	church	Kirche
advantage	Vorteil			cigarette	Zigarette
adventure	Abenteuer	beginning	Anfang	cinema	Kino
after	nach	behind	hinter, hinten	circle	Kreis
afternoon	Nachmittag	below	unter, unten	city	Stadt
again	wieder	between	zwischen	class	(Schul-)Klasse, Unterricht
against	gegen, an	bicycle	Fahrrad		
age	Alter	bike	Fahrrad (Kurzform)	classroom	Klassenraum, Klassenzimmer
air	Luft				
airport	Flughafen	bird	Vogel	clean	sauber
all	alle	birthday	Geburtstag	clever	klug
alone	alleine	black	schwarz	(to) climb	klettern
along	entlang, weiter, vorwärts	blood	Blut	clock	Uhr
		boat	Boot, Schiff	(to) close	schließen
also	auch, außerdem	body	Körper	closed	geschlossen
always	immer	book	Buch	clothes	Kleidung, Kleider
America	Amerika	both	beide		
American	Amerikaner/-in, amerikanisch	bottle	Flasche	coat	Mantel
		box	Kästchen	coffee	Kaffee
angry	verärgert	boy	Junge	cold	kalt, auch: Erkältung
animal	Tier	boyfriend	fester Freund		
(to) answer	beantworten, auch als Substantiv: Antwort	branch	Ast	college	(Berufs-)Fach-schule, Fach-hochschule, Universität
		bread	Brot		
		(to) break	brechen, kaputt machen		
any	irgendetwas, irgendwelche	breakfast	Frühstück	colour	Farbe
		bridge	Brücke	(to) come	kommen
anyone	jemand, jeder	(to) bring	bringen, mitbringen, holen	(to) compare	vergleichen
anything	etwas			concert	Konzert
apple	Apfel			(to) continue	fortsetzen
arm	Arm	Britain	Großbritannien	(to) cook	kochen, als Substantiv: Koch/Köchin
(to) arrive	ankommen	British	britisch		
(to) ask	fragen, bitten	brother	Bruder		
at	in, an, bei, auf, zu … hin	brown	braun	corner	Ecke
		(to) build	bauen	(to) correct	berichtigen
at home	zu Hause	bus	(Linien-)Bus	(to) cost	kosten
at once	sofort	but	aber, sondern, als	country	Land
at the moment	im Augenblick			cousin	Cousin, Cousine
aunt	Tante	butcher	Fleischer/-in		
Austria	Österreich	(to) buy	kaufen	cow	Kuh
Austrian	Österreicher/-in	by	bis, durch, per, von, an … vorbei	crazy	verrückt
autumn, auch: fall	Herbst			cream	(Schlag-)Sahne, Creme
away	weg				
awful	schrecklich	cake	Kuchen, Torte, Gebäckstück	cross	Kreuz
back	Rücken, auch: zurück			(to) cry	weinen, auch: schreien
		calculator	Taschenrechner		
bacon	Schinkenspeck	can	können	cup	Tasse
bad(ly)	schlecht, schlimm	cannot = can not	nicht können	cupboard	Schrank
		car	Auto	dad	Papa, Vater
bag	Sack, Packung, Tasche	careful	vorsichtig, sorgfältig	(to) dance	tanzen
				dangerous(ly)	gefährlich
baker	Bäcker/-in	(to) carry	tragen	dark	dunkel
banana	Banane	cat	Katze	date	Datum, auch: Verabredung
bank	Bank, auch: Ufer	(to) catch	fangen		
bath	Bad, auch: Badewanne	central	zentral, Zentral-, mittlere/r/s	daughter	Tochter
				day	Tag
bathroom	Badezimmer	chair	Stuhl	dear	liebe, lieber
(to) be	sein	chance	Gelegenheit	death	Tod
(to) be able to	können	(to) change	(sich) (ver)ändern	(to) decide	(sich) entschei-den
(to) be right	Recht haben				

(to) describe	beschreiben	fly	Fliege	(to) hope	hoffen
desk	Schreibtisch	(to) fly	fliegen	horse	Pferd
dictionary	Wörterbuch	(to) follow	folgen	hospital	Hospital, Krankenhaus
(to) die	sterben	food	Essen, Nahrung, Lebensmittel	hot	heiß, warm
difference	Unterschied			hotel	Hotel
difficult	schwer, schwierig	foot	Fuß	hour	Stunde
		football	Fußball	house	Haus
dinner	Abendessen	for	für	how	wie
dirty	schmutzig	(to) forget	vergessen	how many	wie viele
(to) do	tun, machen	fork	Gabel	how much	wie viel
doctor	Arzt, Ärztin	form	Form, Formular, als Verb: bilden	hungry	hungrig
dog	Hund			husband	(Ehe-)Mann
door	Tür	France	Frankreich	ice	Eis
double	Doppel-...	free	kostenlos, frei	ice-cream	Speiseeis
down	nach unten, hin-/herunter, unten	French	französisch	idea	Idee, Gedanke, Vorstellung
		friend	Freund/-in		
		from	von, aus	if	wenn, falls
dress	Kleid	front	Vorderseite, Vorderteil	ill	krank
(to) drink	trinken, als Substantiv: Getränk			important	wichtig
		fruit	Obst, Frucht	impossible	unmöglich
(to) drive	fahren	full	voll	in	in, auf, hinein, herein
driver	Fahrer/-in	funny	komisch		
during	während	furniture	Möbel	industry	Industrie
each	jede/r/s	future	Zukunft	interesting	interessant
ear	Ohr	game	Spiel	into	in ... hinein
early	früh	garden	Garten	Italy	Italien
east	Osten, Ost-, nach Osten	German	deutsch	jacket	Jacke, Jackett
		Germany	Deutschland	job	Arbeit, Aufgabe
easy (easily)	einfach, leicht	(to) get	bekommen, auch: werden	joke	Witz, Scherz
(to) eat	essen, fressen			just	nur, gerade
egg	Ei	girl	Mädchen	key	Schlüssel
emergency	Notfall, Not-	girlfriend	feste Freundin	(to) kill	töten, umbringen
empty	leer	(to) give	geben, schenken		
English	englisch			kilometre	Kilometer
(to) enjoy	genießen	glad	froh, glücklich	kitchen	Küche
enough	genug	(to) go	gehen, auch: fahren	knife	Messer
Europe	Europa			(to) know	kennen, wissen
European	europäisch, Europäer/-in	good	gut	label	Aufkleber, Etikett
		goodbye	auf Wiedersehen		
evening	Abend			lamb	Lamm
every	jede/r/s	government	Regierung	lamp	Lampe
everyone	jede/r/s, alle	granddad	Opa	language	Sprache
everything	alles	granddaughter	Enkelin	large	groß
everywhere	überall, überallhin	grandfather	Großvater	last	letzte/r/s
		grandma	Großmama	late	spät
example	Beispiel	grandmother	Großmutter	(to) laugh	lachen
(to) excuse	entschuldigen	grandparents	Großeltern	lazy	faul
exercise	Übung	great	toll	(to) learn	lernen
(to) expect	erwarten	green	grün	(to) leave	abreisen, weggehen, verlassen
expensive	teuer	group	Gruppe		
(to) explain	erklären	(to) grow	wachsen		
eye	Auge	guest	Gast		
face	Gesicht	guitar	Gitarre	left	linke/r/s, links
factory	Fabrik	hair	Haar	leg	Bein
false	falsch	hairdresser	Friseur/-in	lesson	(Schul-)Stunde
family	Familie	half	Hälfte	(to) let	lassen
family name	Familienname	ham	Schinken	letter	Buchstabe, auch: Brief
far	weit	hand	Hand		
farm	Bauernhof	happy	glücklich, zufrieden	(to) lie	lügen, auch: liegen
farmer	Bauer, Bäuerin				
fast	schnell	(to) have	haben	life	Leben
father	Vater	head	Kopf	lift	Aufzug
(to) fight	kämpfen	health	Gesundheit	like	wie
(to) find	finden	healthy	gesund	(to) like	mögen, gern haben
finger	Finger	(to) hear	hören		
(to) finish	beenden, abschließen	heart	Herz	line	Linie, Zeile
		heavy	schwer	(to) list	auflisten
first	erste/r/s	height	Höhe	(to) listen	zuhören
first name	Vorname	hello	hallo	(to) listen to	hören, sich anhören
fish	Fisch	help	Hilfe, helfen		
flat	flach	here	hier	little	klein, wenig
flat	Wohnung	high	hoch	(to) live	leben, wohnen
flight	Flug	holiday	Ferien, Urlaub, auch: Feiertag	long	lang
floor	Etage, auch: Fußboden			(to) look	sehen, schauen
		home	Zuhause	(to) look at	sich anschauen

(to) look for	suchen (nach)	o'clock	(fünf usw.) Uhr	present	Geschenk
(to) lose	verlieren	odd	ungerade	pretty	hübsch
lot	Menge	of	von	problem	Problem
loud	laut	(to) offer	anbieten,	(to) produce	herstellen
(to) love	lieben		Angebot	programme	Programm
low	niedrig	office	Büro	progress	Fortschritt
lucky	Glücks-,	often	oft, häufig	pub	Wirtshaus,
	glücklich	old	alt		Kneipe
lunch	Mittagessen	on	auf, an	pullover	Pullover
mad	verrückt	onion	Zwiebel	pupil	Schüler
magazine	Zeitschrift,	only	nur	(to) put	setzen, stellen,
	Magazin	(to) open	offen,		legen
mail	Post		aufmachen	quarter	Viertel
(to) make	tun, machen,	opinion	Meinung	queen	Königin
	bilden	opposite	gegenüber,	question	Frage
man	Mann		Gegenteil	quick(ly)	schnell
manager	Leiter/-in	or	oder	quiet	ruhig
many	viele	other	andere/r/s	quite	ziemlich
margarine	Margarine	out	draußen,	railway	Eisenbahn
(to) marry	heiraten		hinaus, heraus	rain	Regen, als Verb:
match	Streichholz	over	über		regnen
may	dürfen, können	(to) own	besitzen	(to) read	lesen
maybe	vielleicht	p. m.	nach 12:00 Uhr	real	echt, wirklich
meaning	Bedeutung,		mittags	reason	Grund
	Sinn	page	Seite	red	rot
meat	Fleisch	(to) paint	streichen, malen	(to) remember	sich erinnern,
(to) meet	(sich) treffen,	pair	Paar		daran denken
	(sich) begeg-	palace	Palast	rent	Miete
	nen	pan	Pfanne, Topf	(to) rent	mieten
middle	Mitte	paper	Papier	(to) repair	reparieren
mile	Meile	parent	Elternteil	(to) repeat	wiederholen
milk	Milch	park	Park	rest	Pause
million	Million	(to) park	parken	rice	Reis
minute	Minute	part	Teil	rich	reich
(to) miss	verpassen,	party	Party, Fest	(to) ride	reiten
	auch: vermissen	passport	(Reise-)Pass	right	rechts, auch:
mistake	Fehler	(to) pay	bezahlen		richtig
moment	Moment	pea	Erbse	river	Fluss
money	Geld	peace	Frieden	road	Straße
month	Monat	pen	Füllfederhalter,	roll	Brötchen
moped	Moped, Mofa		Kugelschreiber	roof	Dach
morning	Morgen	pence	Pence (briti-	room	Zimmer, Raum,
mother	Mutter		sche Währung)		Platz
mountain	Berg	people	Leute,	round	rund, um (…
mouth	Mund		Menschen		herum)
(to) move	(sich) bewegen	perhaps	vielleicht	(to) run	laufen, rennen
much	viel	person	Mensch, Person	sad	traurig
music	Musik	phone	Telefon, als	safe(ly)	sicher
must	müssen		Verb: anrufen	salad	Salat
name	Name	photo	Foto	sale	Verkauf,
nearly	beinahe, fast	phrase	Redewendung		Ausverkauf
necessary	notwendig,	piano	Klavier	salt	Salz
	nötig	picture	Bild	same	gleiche/r/s,
neck	Hals	piece	Stück, Teil		der-, die-,
(to) need	brauchen	place	Platz, Ort		dasselbe
neighbour	Nachbar	plan	Plan, planen,	sandwich	Sandwich
nervous	nervös		vorhaben	(to) say	sagen
never	nie, niemals	plane	Flugzeug	school	Schule
new	neu	plate	Teller	science	Wissenschaft
newspaper	Zeitung	(to) play	spielen	sea	Meer
next	nächste/r/s	please	bitte	season	Jahreszeit
nice	schön, nett	(to) please	gefallen	second	zweite/r/s
night	Nacht	pleased	froh, erfreut	second	Sekunde
nobody	niemand	police	Polizei	secret	geheim
noise	Lärm	policeman	Polizist	(to) see	sehen
none	keine/r/s	policewoman	Polizistin	(to) seem	scheinen
nonsense	Unsinn	pop music	Popmusik	(to) sell	verkaufen
normal	normal, üblich	post	Post	(to) send	senden,
north	Norden, Nord-	poster	Plakat		schicken
nose	Nase	postman	Briefträger	sentence	Satz
not	nicht	postwoman	Briefträgerin	serious	ernsthaft
nothing	nichts	potato	Kartoffel	ship	Schiff
(to) notice	bemerken	pound	Pfund (Sterling)	shop	Laden, Geschäft
now	nun, jetzt		(britische	shopping	einkaufen
number	Nummer, Zahl		Währung)	short	kurz, klein

Grundwortschatz

(to) shout	rufen, schreien
(to) show	zeigen
shower	Dusche
(to) shut	schließen
side	Seite, Rand
sight	Anblick, auch: Sehvermögen
silly	dumm
since	seit
(to) sing	singen
sister	Schwester
(to) sit	sitzen
size	Größe
(to) sleep	schlafen
slow(ly)	langsam
small	klein
(to) smile	lächeln
(to) smoke	rauchen
snow	Schnee
so	also
sofa	Sofa
soft	leise, weich
some	einige, etwas
somebody	jemand
someone	jemand
something	etwas
sometimes	manchmal
son	Sohn
soon	bald
sorry	traurig
south	Süden, Süd-
(to) speak	sprechen, reden
spoon	Löffel
square	Quadrat
(to) stand	stehen
(to) start	beginnen
station	Bahnhof
(to) stay	bleiben, übernachten
still	immer noch
(to) stop	(an)halten
story	Erzählung, Geschichte
stranger	Fremde, Fremder
street	Straße
strong	stark
student	Student/-in
suddenly	plötzlich
sugar	Zucker
suitcase	Koffer
summer	Sommer
sun	Sonne
supermarket	Supermarkt
sure	sicher, freilich
surname	Nachname
survey	Umfrage
sweets	Süßigkeiten
(to) swim	schwimmen
Switzerland	Schweiz
table	Tisch, Tabelle
(to) take	nehmen, bringen
(to) talk about	sprechen (über)
tall	groß
tax	Steuer
tea	Tee, (frühes) Abendbrot
teacher	Lehrer/-in
telephone	Telefon
television	Fernsehen, Fernseher
(to) tell	sagen, erzählen
temperature	Temperatur
terrible	schrecklich
than	als
(to) thank	danken, sich bedanken
thank you, thanks	danke
that	dies, der, die, das, jene/r/s
then	dann
there	dort, dorthin
there are	es gibt
these	diese
thick	dick
thief	Dieb
thin	dünn
thing	Sache, Ding
(to) think	denken, glauben, meinen
this	dies, diese/r/s
those	jene
through	durch … hindurch, durch
ticket	(Fahr-)Karte, Ticket
time	Zeit, Mal, Uhrzeit
timetable	Fahrplan, Stundenplan
tired	müde
to	zu, nach, in, um zu
today	heute
toe	Zehe
together	zusammen
tomorrow	morgen
tonight	heute Abend
too	zu, auch
town	Stadt
traffic	(Straßen-)Verkehr
train	Zug
tram	Straßenbahn
(to) translate	übersetzen
transport	Vekehrsmittel
(to) travel	reisen
tree	Baum
trouble	Schwierig- keiten
trousers	Hose
true	richtig, wahr
(to) try	probieren, versuchen
tube	U-Bahn
typical	typisch
ugly	hässlich
uncle	Onkel
under	unter
(to) understand	verstehen, begreifen
unhappy	unglücklich
unit	Lektion
until	bis
unusual(ly)	ungewöhnlich
up	oben, nach oben
US(A)	die Vereinigten Staaten (von Amerika)
(to) use	verwenden
usual(ly)	gewöhnlich
vegetable	Gemüse
very	sehr
visit	Besuch, als Verb: besuchen
(to) wait (for)	warten (auf)
waiter	Kellner
waitress	Kellnerin
(to) walk	Spaziergang, (zu Fuß) gehen
wall	Wand, Mauer
(to) want	wollen
warm	warm
(to) wash	(sich) waschen
watch	Armbanduhr
(to) watch	(zu)sehen, beobachten
water	Wasser
way	Weg, Art und Weise
(to) wear	tragen
weather	Wetter
week	Woche
weekend	Wochenende
(to) welcome	willkommen heißen
well	gesund
west	Westen, West-
what	was, welche/r/s
wheel	Rad
when	wenn, als, wann
where	wo, wohin
which	welche/r/s
while	während
white	weiß
who	wer, der, die
whom	wen, wem
why	warum
wife	Ehefrau
(to) win	gewinnen, siegen
wind	Wind, als Verb: spulen
window	Fenster
wine	Wein
winter	Winter
with	mit
without	ohne
woman	Frau
wonderful	wunderbar, wundervoll
word	Wort
work	Arbeit, arbeiten, funktionieren, klappen
world	Welt
(to) write	schreiben
wrong	falsch
year	Jahr
yellow	gelb
yesterday	gestern
young	jung
zoo	Zoo

Alphabetisches Vokabelverzeichnis

AmE = American English, BrE = British English

Vokabel	Erstes Vor-kommen in	Übersetzung	Vokabel	Erstes Vor-kommen in	Übersetzung
A			(to) be disabled	(unit 8)	behindert sein
an abbreviation	(unit 6)	Abkürzung	(to) be disappointed	(unit 4)	enttäuscht sein
absorbency	(unit 3)	Aufnahmefähigkeit	(to) be divorced	(unit 2)	geschieden sein
abuse	(unit 11)	Missbrauch	(to) be grateful	(unit 8)	dankbar sein
accomodation	(unit 6)	Unterkunft	(to) be hygienic	(unit 8)	hygienisch sein
acrylic	(unit 3)	Acryl	(to) be lucky	(unit 2)	Glück haben
an actor (male),	(activity)	Schauspieler,	(to) be over	(unit 5)	vorbei sein
actress (female)		Schauspielerin	(to) be overweight	(unit 4)	übergewichtig sein
actual value	(unit 9)	Zufuhr, Istwert	(to) be paralysed	(unit 8)	gelähmt sein
ad (AmE), advert (BrE)	(activity)	Kurzform für Annonce	(to) be patient	(unit 8)	geduldig sein
admiration	(activity)	Bewunderung	(to) be pregnant	(unit 4)	schwanger sein
(to) admit	(unit 12)	zugeben	(to) be ready for	(unit 5)	bereit sein
an advertisement	(unit 10)	Werbung	something		
advertising business	(activity)	Reklame-Geschäft	(to) be sensitive	(unit 8)	sensibel sein
an advice	(unit 5)	Rat	(to) be short of money	(unit 2)	mit dem Geld knapp
(to) advise	(activity)	beraten			sein
(to) agree	(unit 3)	(jemandem)	(to) be unable	(unit 8)	unfähig sein
		zustimmen	(to) be unemployed	(unit 2)	arbeitslos sein
aim	(activity)	Ziel	(to) be upset	(unit 4)	bestürzt sein
algae	(unit 12)	Algen	(to) be well	(unit 1)	gut gehen, gesund sein
(to) allow	(unit 11)	erlauben	(to) beat the rent	(unit 6)	die Miete
almonds	(unit 10)	Mandeln	down		herunterhandeln
an alternative	(unit 1)	Möglichkeit,	(to) become extinct	(unit 12)	aussterben (Arten)
		Alternative	bedsitter (or: bedsit)	(unit 6)	Wohnschlafzimmer,
an ambulance	(unit 11)	Notarztwagen			Einzimmerapartment
amount of washing	(talking	Wäschemenge	bedsore	(unit 8)	Druckgeschwür;
	games)				Decubitus
anorexia nervosa	(unit 11)	Magersucht	behaviour	(unit 12)	Verhalten
an apartment	(unit 6)	Wohnung	besides	(revision I)	neben, außerdem
(AmE); flat (BrE)			bills (or: extra costs,	(unit 6)	Nebenkosten
(to) apologize	(unit 12)	entschuldigen	extras)		
appearance	(unit 10)	Aussehen, auch:	bits and pieces	(unit 5)	Scherben
		Auftreten	(to) bleach	(unit 3)	bleichen
appendicitis	(unit 11)	Blinddarmentzündung	blood clotting	(unit 11)	Blutverdickung
an application	(unit 5)	Bewerbungsschreiben	blood pressure	(unit 9)	Blutdruck
(to) apply	(activity)	anwenden	blouse	(unit 3)	Bluse
an appointment	(unit 9)	Verabredung	boarding house	(unit 12)	Pension
an apprenticeship	(unit 8)	Ausbildung	boring	(unit 2)	langweilig
an apron	(unit 1)	Schürze	brackets	(unit 5)	Klammern (im Text)
Are you kidding?	(unit 4)	Machst du dich lustig?	brave	(unit 4)	tapfer (nicht: brav)
		Machst du Scherze?	break	(revision I)	Pause
assorted	(activity)	verschiedene, eine	(to) break up with	(unit 4)	eine Freundschaft
		Auswahl von	someone		beenden
at least	(unit 6)	wenigstens	breath	(unit 11)	Atem
at once	(unit 11)	sofort	(to) breed	(unit 2)	züchten
attention	(activity)	Aufmerksamkeit	bright	(revision IV)	intelligent
an attic	(talking	Bodenkammer,	(to) brush	(unit 11)	bürsten
	games)	Speicher, Dachboden	bucket	(activity)	Eimer
(to) attract	(activity)	anziehen	bulk rubbish	(unit 6)	Möbel vom Sperrmüll
(to) avoid	(unit 4)	verhindern	furniture		
			by the way	(unit 1)	übrigens
B			by 6 o'clock	(unit 5)	bis spätestens sechs
(to) ban	(unit 11)	verbannen			Uhr
banner	(revision II)	Transparent, Banner	by 10 p.m.	(unit 6)	bis (spätestens)
bar	(unit 3)	Strich, Balken			22:00 Uhr
bargain	(unit 3)	Gelegenheitskauf			
basil leaves	(talking	Basilikumblätter	**C**		
	games)		calf (sg.), calves (pl.)	(unit 11)	Wade
bath salts	(unit 7)	Badezusatz, Badesalz	canned	(unit 10)	in Dosen verpackt
bathing suit	(unit 10)	Badeanzug	caterer	(unit 1)	Verpflegungs-
(to) be addicted to	(unit 11)	abhängig sein von			dienstleister
(to) be ambitious	(unit 5)	ehrgeizig sein	catering	(unit 1)	Verpflegung von Fir-
(to) be awake	(unit 11)	wach sein			men, Veranstaltungen
(to) be concerned	(revision IV)	besorgt sein	capacity	(unit 12)	Fassungsvermögen,
(to) be confused	(unit 6)	verwirrt sein			Kapazität
(to) be curious	(unit 4)	neugierig sein	cardigan	(unit 3)	Strickjacke
			(to) care	(unit 3)	pflegen

Alphabetisches Vokabelverzeichnis

Vokabel	Erstes Vorkommen in	Übersetzung	Vokabel	Erstes Vorkommen in	Übersetzung
carpenter	(unit 4)	Zimmermann	**D**		
carpet	(unit 6)	Teppich	(to) damage something	(unit 4)	etwas beschädigen
(to) carry out	(activity)	durchführen	decision	(activity)	Entscheidung
(to) cause	(unit 3)	verursachen	(to) decorate	(activity)	schmücken, dekorieren
cellar	(talking games)	Keller	definitely	(unit 4)	ganz bestimmt
cereals	(unit 9)	Cerealien, Getreideflocken	degree	(unit 3)	Grad
			delay	(unit 7)	Verspätung
CFC	(unit 12)	FCKW – Fluorchlorkohlenwasserstoff	delicious	(unit 1)	köstlich, lecker
			(to) deliver newspapers	(revision I)	Zeitungen austragen
change	(unit 3)	Wechselgeld			
(to) chat	(unit 10)	plaudern	dentist	(activity)	Zahnarzt, -ärztin
cheese platter	(unit 6)	Käseplatte	(to) deny	(unit 12)	verneinen, ablehnen
chef	(unit 1)	Koch, Küchenchef	department	(unit 1)	Abteilung
cheque	(unit 3)	Scheck	department store	(unit 1)	Warenhaus
(to) chill	(activity)	kühlen	deposit required	(unit 6)	Mietkaution/Hinterlegung erforderlich
chlorine	(unit 3)	Chlor, auch: chlorhaltig			
chopped	(unit 10)	gehackt, zerkleinert	(to) deserve something or someone	(unit 4)	jemand oder etwas verdienen (aber: Geld verdienen – to earn money)
chopping block	(unit 5)	Hackklotz			
chronicle	(activity)	Chronik			
classmate	(unit 4)	Klassenkamerad			
clatter	(unit 5)	Geklirr	desire	(activity)	Wunsch, Verlangen
cleansing agents	(unit 6)	Reinigungsmittel	destination	(unit 7)	Zielort
Clonakilty Pudding	(activity)	(englisches Gericht)	(to) destroy	(unit 12)	zerstören
clothes factory	(unit 2)	Textilfabrik	destruction	(unit 12)	Zerstörung
(to) collect	(unit 11)	sammeln	detached house	(unit 6)	Einzelhaus, Einfamilienhaus
College of Further Education	(unit 2)	Berufsbildende Schule (Bezeichnung in Great Britain)			
			devil	(revision III)	Teufel
			(to) die	(unit 1)	sterben
			(to) dig the weeds	(unit 2)	Unkraut jäten
comment	(revision IV)	Äußerung	(to) direct	(activity)	lenken
commercial	(unit 1)	Werbespot	(to) discuss	(unit 2)	diskutieren
(to) commit suicide	(unit 8)	Selbstmord begehen	dish	(unit 12)	Gericht
(to) complain about something	(unit 11)	über etwas klagen	distance	(unit 6)	Entfernung
			distant	(unit 12)	entfernt
complete	(unit 1)	vollständig (als Verb: to complete = vervollständigen)	(to) distinguish	(unit 11)	unterscheiden
			(to) do the garden	(unit 2)	den Garten machen/pflegen
compress	(unit 7)	Kompresse, Wickel	doctor's assistant	(unit 12)	Arzthelfer/-in
conceited	(revision II)	eingebildet	domestic science	(unit 2)	Hauswirtschaft
(to) concentrate (on)	(unit 6)	sich konzentrieren	(to) dominate	(revision IV)	bestimmen
(to) condemn	(unit 10)	verurteilen	(to) drop someone or something	(unit 8)	jemanden oder etwas fallen lassen
consciousness	(unit 9)	Bewusstsein			
consonant	(activity)	Konsonant	(to) drown	(unit 1)	ertrinken
constable	(unit 1)	Polizist	(to) dry clean	(unit 3)	chemisch reinigen
consumption data	(talking games)	Verbrauchsdaten	dull	(revision IV)	langweilig
			(to) dust	(unit 6)	staubwischen
(to) contain	(unit 3)	enthalten, aufweisen			
contraceptive	(activity)	Verhütungsmittel	**E**		
control	(talking games)	Steuerung	ecological value	(unit 12)	ökologischer Wert
			education	(unit 9)	Bildung
control of temperature	(unit 4)	Temperaturmethode	elderly	(unit 6)	ältlich
conviction	(activity)	Überzeugung	an emergency case	(unit 11)	Notfall
(to) convince someone	(unit 12)	jemanden überzeugen	(to) employ someone	(unit 3)	jemanden beschäftigen
			an employer	(unit 5)	Arbeitgeber
cooker	(unit 12)	Herd	(to) ensure	(unit 3)	sichern
cottage	(unit 6)	kleines Landhaus	enthusiastic	(unit 6)	begeistert
craftsman	(unit 6)	Handwerker	an envelope	(unit 5)	Briefumschlag
crash barrier	(revision II)	Sicherheitsabsperrung	environment	(unit 3)	Umwelt
(to) create	(activity)	herstellen	environmentalist	(unit 10)	Umweltschützer
crowded	(unit 10)	überfüllt	equipment	(unit 6)	Ausstattung
crushed nutmeg	(talking games)	geriebene Muskatnuss	an essay	(unit 7)	Aufsatz, Zeitschriftenartikel
culinary art	(unit 5)	Kochkunst	evaluation	(activity)	Auswertung
customer	(unit 3)	Kunde	an event	(unit 7)	Ereignis
cut	(unit 4)	Einschnitt, Schnitt (als Verb: to cut = schneiden)	every now and then	(unit 2)	ab und zu
			exactly	(unit 8)	genau
			(to) exaggerate	(unit 12)	übertreiben
cute	(revision II)	süß, niedlich	exciting	(unit 1)	aufregend, spannend
cutlet	(unit 12)	Kotelett	an exhibition	(unit 7)	Ausstellung
			an experience	(unit 2)	Erfahrung
			(to) express	(unit 7)	ausdrücken
			extremely	(revision II)	äußerst

Vokabel	Erstes Vor-kommen in	Übersetzung	Vokabel	Erstes Vor-kommen in	Übersetzung
F			Hell, no!	(unit 2)	Zur Hölle, nein!
fabric	(unit 3)	Gewebe	herb	(unit 7)	Kraut, Kräuter
fabric conditioner	(unit 3)	Weichspülmittel	herbal garden	(unit 7)	Kräutergarten
fair pay	(unit 2)	angemessene Bezahlung	hernia	(unit 11)	Leistenbruch
(to) fall asleep	(revision I)	einschlafen	hint	(unit 5)	Tipp, Ratschlag
fashion	(unit 1)	Mode	hole	(unit 6)	hier: Bruchbude (eigentlich: Loch)
fellow students	(unit 2)	Mitschüler	holly	(unit 7)	Stechpalme
fever	(unit 11)	Fieber	home remedy	(unit 7)	Hausmittel
fibre	(unit 10)	Ballaststoff	honest	(unit 10)	ehrlich
fig	(activity)	Feige	(to) hoover	(unit 6)	staubsaugen
fillet	(activity)	Filet	hot	(revision II)	heiß, auch: toll
finally	(unit 4)	schließlich, endlich	hotel lounge	(unit 5)	Hotelsalon
fingernail	(unit 4)	Fingernagel	hotel staff	(activity)	die Mitarbeiter eines Hotels
fish fingers	(unit 6)	Fischstäbchen	household chores	(unit 2)	Hausarbeiten
flat-hunting	(unit 6)	Wohnungssuche	housekeeper	(unit 2)	Hauswirtschafter/-in
flight	(unit 7)	Flug	housekeeping	(unit 5)	Hauswirtschaft
fluid	(unit 11)	Flüssigkeit	housewarming party	(unit 6)	Kistenparty, Einzugsparty
foam	(unit 4)	Schaum (Spermizid)	however	(revision I)	jedoch
fool	(unit 4)	Dummkopf	(to) hug someone	(unit 11)	jemanden umarmen
for ages	(unit 4)	seit Ewigkeiten	(to) hurt someone	(unit 5)	jemanden verletzen
(to) force one's way	(unit 5)	sich seinen Weg bahnen	hygienic hat	(unit 2)	Kopftuch
freedom	(unit 6)	Freiheit	hysteria	(revision II)	Hysterie
fridge	(unit 6)	Kühlschrank	**I**		
frog	(unit 11)	Frosch	illogical	(unit 11)	unlogisch
furious	(unit 5)	wütend	(to) improve	(unit 9)	verbessern
furnished	(unit 6)	möbliert	an improvement	(unit 3)	Verbesserung
G			in brackets	(unit 5)	in Klammern
gap	(unit 4)	Lücke	in common	(unit 2)	gemeinsam
generous	(unit 10)	großzügig	(to) include	(unit 6)	einschließen
gentle	(unit 3)	sanft	(to) increase	(unit 8)	hier: an Gewicht zunehmen
(to) get a divorce	(unit 4)	sich scheiden lassen	indifference	(unit 5)	Gleichgültigkeit
(to) give someone a hand	(activity)	jemandem helfen	(to) infer	(revision II)	schließen, folgern
a glass (of stout etc.)	(unit 7)	0,284 Liter (britische Maßeinheit)	an ingredient	(unit 1)	Zutat
(to) go abroad	(unit 8)	ins Ausland gehen	an inhabitant	(activity)	Einwohner
graph	(activity)	Schaubild, Diagramm	an injection	(unit 9)	Spritze
greenhouse effect	(unit 12)	Treibhauseffekt	(to) inspire	(activity)	auslösen
(to) grind; ground; ground	(unit 1)	mahlen, zermahlen	insulation	(unit 6)	Isolation
ground plan	(unit 6)	Grundrisszeichnung einer Wohnung	intention	(unit 8)	Absicht
(to) guarantee	(unit 9)	garantieren	(to) interrupt	(unit 9)	unterbrechen
guide	(activity)	Führer	(to) invent	(unit 9)	erfinden
guideline	(unit 3)	Richtlinie	invisible	(unit 9)	unsichtbar
H			an invitation	(unit 1)	Einladung
hairy	(unit 2)	haarig (auch: unangenehm)	IQ	(revision II)	Intelligenzquotient
ham	(activity)	Schweineschinken	(to) iron	(unit 3)	bügeln
hand of a clock	(unit 5)	Zeiger einer Uhr	irregularities	(activity)	Unregelmäßigkeiten
(to) handle something	(unit 3)	behandeln	an item	(unit 3)	Sache, Gegenstand
(to) hang about	(unit 8)	herumlümmeln	**J**		
hardness in the water	(unit 3)	Wasserhärte	jam	(unit 1)	Marmelade
harm	(unit 12)	Schaden	juice	(unit 10)	Saft
harmful	(unit 3)	schädlich	**K**		
(to) have a bad conscience	(unit 2)	ein schlechtes Gewissen haben	kidneys	(unit 11)	Nieren
(to) have a week off	(unit 8)	eine Woche dienstfrei haben	kitchenette	(unit 6)	Kochnische
(to) have arguments	(unit 8)	Streit haben	knowledge	(unit 7)	Kenntnis, Wissen
head teacher	(revision I)	leitender Lehrer	**L**		
heart attack	(unit 11)	Herzinfarkt	lady teacher (AmE)	(unit 8)	Kinderpflegerin
heartily	(unit 7)	herzlich	lager	(unit 7)	helles Bier
heatstroke	(unit 11)	Hitzschlag	lake	(unit 1)	See
height, width, length	(unit 9)	Höhe/Größe, Breite, Tiefe	landing	(unit 6)	Treppenabsatz
hell	(unit 6)	Hölle	landlady	(unit 6)	Vermieterin
			landlord	(unit 6)	Vermieter
			landmark	(activity)	Wahrzeichen (eines Landes etc.)
			laundry	(unit 3)	(Schmutz-)Wäsche
			laundry basket	(unit 6)	Wäschekorb

169

Alphabetisches Vokabelverzeichnis

Vokabel	Erstes Vor- kommen in	Übersetzung	Vokabel	Erstes Vor- kommen in	Übersetzung
lavatory	(unit 6)	Toilette, Waschraum	not to care about	(unit 4)	sich nicht kümmern um
(to) lay out	(activity)	gestalten			
(to) lay the table	(unit 5)	den Tisch decken	not to stop asking	(unit 4)	immer wieder fragen
layout	(activity)	Gestaltung	nurse	(unit 1)	Krankenschwester
leaflet	(revision I)	Flugblatt, Handzettel	nursery nurse	(unit 8)	Kinderpflegerin, Erzieherin
leafy greens	(unit 10)	grünes Blattgemüse			
lean	(unit 10)	mager	nursery school	(unit 8)	Kindergarten
leisure activities	(activity)	Freizeitaktivitäten	nutrients	(unit 9)	Nährstoffe
leisure centre	(unit 10)	Freizeitzentrum			
less well-paid	(revision I)	weniger gut bezahlt	nutrition	(activity)	Ernährung, auch: Fach Ernährungslehre
lighter	(unit 12)	Feuerzeug			
likely	(unit 7)	wahrscheinlich	nutritional value	(unit 10)	Nährwert
lino	(talking games)	Linoleum	nutritive	(unit 9)	Ernährungs-
lively	(activity)	lebensnah, lebendig	**O**		
liver cirrhosis	(unit 11)	Leberzirrhose	an odd job	(unit 2)	Gelegenheitsarbeit
living space	(unit 6)	Wohnraum	old couple	(unit 2)	ein altes Paar
location	(unit 6)	Ort, Wohnort	old people's home	(unit 7)	Altenheim
lodger	(unit 6)	Mieter	old people's nurse	(unit 7)	Altenpflegerin, Altenpfleger
long jumper	(unit 12)	Weitspringer			
long-term effects	(unit 11)	Langzeitwirkung	on time	(unit 7)	pünktlich
low income	(unit 8)	geringes Einkommen	once	(unit 4)	einmal
(to) lower	(unit 3)	hier: herabsetzen, verringern	one's own four walls	(unit 6)	die eigenen vier Wände
			opinion poll	(unit 12)	Meinungsumfrage
lung cancer	(unit 11)	Lungenkrebs	opportunity	(revision IV)	Gelegenheit
			organic foods	(unit 12)	biologisch-dynamisch erzeugte Lebensmittel
M					
mad-cow-disease	(unit 12)	Rinderwahnsinn	Ouch!	(unit 6)	Aua!
mainly	(activity)	hauptsächlich	"out of the saucepan into the fire"	(unit 6)	"vom Regen in die Traufe kommen" (Redewendung)
maisonette	(unit 6)	Einliegerwohnung			
majority	(unit 7)	Mehrheit			
(to) make a promise	(unit 4)	ein Versprechen machen	overweight	(unit 10)	Übergewicht
			ozone layer	(unit 12)	Ozonschicht
(to) make friends	(activity)	Freunde schaffen			
male nurse	(unit 8)	Krankenpfleger	**P**		
management	(activity)	Leitung	panic attacks	(unit 11)	Panikattacken
mania	(revision II)	Manie, Rausch	participant	(activity)	Teilnehmer
marginal	(revision II)	hier: schwach durchschnittlich	partition	(talking games)	Vorschlag
mark	(revision I)	Note	part-time job	(revision I)	Teilzeitarbeit
maths	(unit 4)	Mathematik	(to) pass through a sieve	(talking games)	durch ein Sieb passieren
mature	(unit 4)	reif, erwachsen			
means	(unit 12)	Mittel	(to) peel	(unit 12)	schälen
meantime	(unit 9)	Zwischenzeit	per cent (BrE), percent (AmE)	(unit 11)	Prozent
measurement	(unit 7)	Maßeinheit			
meatballs	(unit 6)	Frikadellen	personally	(unit 11)	persönlich
men's wear	(unit 3)	Männerkleidung	pessary	(unit 4)	Pessar/Diaphragma
mental breakdown	(unit 11)	Nervenzusammenbruch	pesticides	(unit 12)	Pestizide
mews	(unit 6)	zur Wohnung umgebauter Stall	pharmacy	(unit 7)	Apotheke
			physical strength	(unit 8)	körperliche Stärke
midnight	(unit 11)	Mitternacht	piece of clothing	(unit 2)	ein Stück Kleidung
minimum criteria	(unit 6)	Mindestkriterien, -eingabedaten	pill	(unit 4)	(Anti-Baby-) Pille
			a pint	(unit 7)	0,568 Liter (britische Maßeinheit)
mistletoe	(unit 7)	Mistel (-zweig)			
(to) moan	(unit 5)	maulen	plaice	(activity)	Scholle
molasses	(unit 10)	Melasse, Zuckersirup	plenty of	(unit 4)	genügend viele
monarchy	(unit 7)	Monarchie	plum pudding	(unit 7)	Plumpudding
(to) move into	(unit 1)	einziehen (in Wohnung)	plump	(unit 10)	mollig
			(to) poach	(activity)	dünsten
(to) mow the lawn	(unit 2)	Rasen mähen	(to) polish	(unit 5)	polieren
(to) murmur	(unit 12)	murmeln	poor	(revision I)	hier: dürftig, schlecht
mushrooms	(activity)	Pilze	porridge	(unit 5)	Haferflockensuppe
			power consumption	(talking games)	Stromverbrauch
N					
napkin	(activity)	Serviette	practical experience	(unit 7)	praktische Erfahrung
narrow	(unit 4)	eng	pregnancy	(unit 4)	Schwangerschaft
national anthem	(unit 7)	Nationalhymne	presentation	(unit 7)	Darbietung, Vorstellung
nightmare	(unit 5)	Alptraum	(to) press	(unit 11)	pressen, drücken
noise	(unit 5)	Lärm	(to) prevent	(unit 8)	verhindern
nominal value	(unit 9)	Bedarfszahl, Sollwert	prewash	(unit 3)	Vorwäsche
non-returnable	(unit 12)	Wegwerf-	privacy	(unit 6)	Ungestörtheit
			probably	(unit 4)	wahrscheinlich

Vokabel	Erstes Vor-kommen in	Übersetzung	Vokabel	Erstes Vor-kommen in	Übersetzung
(to) promise	(unit 12)	versprechen	skills	(unit 1)	Fähigkeiten, Kenntnisse
promotion	(unit 12)	Beförderung	skirt	(unit 3)	Rock
(to) pronounce	(activity)	(ein Wort) aussprechen	slice of bread	(unit 11)	Brotscheibe
pronunciation	(activity)	Aussprache	slim	(unit 10)	schlank
proper	(unit 1)	richtig	slippery	(unit 4)	rutschig, glatt
property	(unit 6)	Eigentum, Besitz	(to) soak	(unit 3)	einweichen
property type	(unit 6)	Wohnungstyp	social allowance	(unit 2)	Sozialfürsorge
(to) protect	(unit 3)	schützen	soda bread	(activity)	mit Backsoda
proudly	(unit 12)	stolz			gebackenes Brot
(to) provide	(unit 10)	hier: liefern	solvent	(unit 3)	Lösungsmittel
pub	(unit 7)	Gaststätte	somewhere else	(unit 2)	woanders
public	(activity)	Öffentlichkeit	sorrow	(unit 4)	Traurigkeit
(to) publish	(revision I)	veröffentlichen	(to) sound good	(unit 2)	gut klingen
pure	(unit 3)	rein, pur	source	(unit 10)	Quelle
purse	(unit 4)	Portemonnaie,	spare time	(unit 1)	Freizeit
		Handtasche	sparingly	(unit 10)	sparsam
Q			species	(unit 12)	Arten, Spezies
quarrel	(activity)	Streit	spelling	(unit 1)	Schreibweise
(to) quit	(unit 5)	kündigen, aufhören	(to) spend; spent; spent	(unit 5)	(Zeit) verbringen, auch: (Geld) ausgeben
			spin drier speeds	(talking games)	Schleuderdrehzahlen
R					
raining very hard	(unit 1)	sehr stark regnen	(to) squeeze out	(unit 6)	auspressen
ready-to-serve meal	(unit 10)	Fertiggericht	staff entrance	(unit 5)	Personaleingang
reason	(unit 3)	Grund, Ursache	stain	(unit 3)	Fleck
recently	(revision IV)	kürzlich	starchy foods	(unit 10)	stärkereiche
receptionist	(unit 5)	Empfangsdame, Portier			Lebensmittel
recipe	(unit 1)	(Koch-)Rezept	statistics	(unit 8)	Statistik
(to) reduce	(unit 3)	reduzieren	(to) stay awake	(unit 11)	wach bleiben
refusal	(unit 5)	Ablehnung	steam bath	(unit 9)	Dampfbad
regularly	(unit 11)	regelmäßig	sterile	(unit 9)	steril
relative	(unit 11)	Verwandter, Verwandte	sticky-out ears	(revision II)	abstehende Ohren
(to) relax	(unit 1)	(sich) entspannen	(to) stir while cooking	(talking games)	während des Kochens umrühren
relevant	(revision IV)	von Bedeutung			
remark	(unit 7)	Bemerkung	stomach	(unit 11)	Magen
rental period	(unit 6)	Mietzeitraum	stout	(unit 7)	dunkles Starkbier
resident	(unit 8)	Bewohner, Heiminsasse	(to) straighten out	(unit 6)	gerade machen,
responsibility	(unit 5)	Verantwortung			strecken
responsible	(unit 8)	verantwortlich,	strange	(unit 1)	fremdartig,
		verantwortungsvoll			merkwürdig
restless	(unit 11)	ruhelos, schlaflos	(to) strengthen muscles	(unit 11)	Muskeln stärken
retailer	(unit 12)	Einzelhändler	strict	(revision IV)	streng
(to) return	(unit 6)	hier: wiedergeben, anzeigen	stripped floor	(unit 6)	Fußboden ohne Auslegware
(to) ring someone (up)	(unit 1)	jemanden anrufen	suburb	(unit 10)	Vorort
(to) riot	(revision IV)	randalieren	(to) succeed (in)	(unit 8)	Erfolg haben,
rubber	(unit 4)	Gummi			gewinnen
rubbish	(activity)	Quatsch, Unsinn	success	(activity)	Erfolg
rubbish tip	(unit 2)	Müllhalde	successful	(unit 7)	erfolgreich
rule	(unit 3)	Regel	suggested	(unit 9)	vorgeschlagen
S			suit	(unit 3)	Anzug
(to) sacrifice	(revision I)	opfern	suitable	(activity)	passend
sales	(unit 3)	Schlussverkauf	(to) summarize	(activity)	zusammenfassen
sauté	(activity)	kurz Angebratenes	superior	(unit 12)	Vorgesetzte,
(to) save money	(unit 2)	Geld sparen			Vorgesetzter
scones	(unit 1)	Waffeln, Hörnchen	supply	(unit 9)	Versorgung (als Verb:
(to) scream	(unit 11)	schreien			to supply – versorgen)
(to) scrub	(unit 5)	schrubben	support	(activity)	Unterstützung
search engine, browser	(activity)	Suchmaschine	(to) support	(unit 8)	unterstützen
secure	(unit 4)	sicher	suppository	(unit 4)	Zäpfchen (Spermizid)
seeds	(unit 10)	Samen	surprise	(unit 1)	Überraschung
segments	(activity)	Teilstücke	survey	(unit 3)	Untersuchung,
(to) select	(unit 10)	auswählen			Umfrage
semi-detached house	(unit 6)	Doppelhaushälfte	sweater	(unit 3)	Pullover
senseless	(unit 4)	sinnlos	(to) sweep	(unit 5)	fegen
(to) separate	(unit 3)	sich trennen, scheiden	syrup	(unit 10)	Sirup
(to) serve food	(unit 2)	Essen servieren			
sick-room	(unit 9)	Krankenzimmer	**T**		
(to) sigh	(unit 4)	seufzen	(to) take after someone	(revision II)	jemandem ähnlich sein
silk	(unit 3)	Seide			
similarity	(activity)	Ähnlichkeit	(to) take exams	(unit 8)	Examen machen
sin	(unit 12)	Sünde			

Alphabetisches Vokabelverzeichnis

Vokabel	Erstes Vor-kommen in	Übersetzung	Vokabel	Erstes Vor-kommen in	Übersetzung
(to) take part in	(unit 1)	teilnehmen an	**U**		
talented	(revision I)	talentiert, begabt	unbelievable	(unit 11)	unglaublich
(to) talk over	(unit 6)	darüber reden, durchsprechen	uncontrollably	(unit 11)	unkontrollierbar
			unfortunately	(unit 7)	unglücklicherweise
task	(activity)	Aufgabe	unhelpful	(revision II)	nicht hilfsbereit
tasteful	(unit 10)	geschmackvoll	urgently	(unit 12)	dringend
team	(unit 2)	Mannschaft			
(to) tease	(revision II)	quälen, hänseln	**V**		
temptation	(revision I)	Versuchung	vegetarian	(unit 10)	Vegetarier/-in
terraced houses	(unit 6)	Reihenhäuser	veneral disease	(unit 4)	Geschlechtskrankheit
thumb	(unit 11)	Daumen	vocational school	(unit 4)	berufsbildende Schule
(to) thunder	(unit 5)	donnern	vowel	(activity)	Vokal
(to) tidy up	(unit 2)	aufräumen			
(to) tie	(unit 1)	etwas binden	**W**		
tight clothes	(unit 10)	engsitzende Kleidung	wage	(unit 12)	Lohn
tiled	(talking games)	gefliest	wardrobe	(unit 3)	Kleiderschrank
			waste	(unit 3)	Verschwendung, auch: Abfall
tiles	(unit 6)	Fliesen, Kacheln			
tongue	(unit 11)	Zunge	wealth	(revision I)	Reichtum
tonsilitis	(unit 11)	Mandelentzündung	wealthy	(unit 10)	reich
tooth (sg.), teeth (pl.)	(unit 8)	Zahn, Zähne	web site	(unit 6)	Internetseite
(to) toss and turn	(unit 11)	sich hin- und herwälzen	weight	(unit 9)	Gewicht
			whole grain	(unit 10)	Vollkorn
towel	(unit 11)	Handtuch	widow	(unit 6)	Witwe
traffic jam	(unit 12)	Verkehrsstau	window pane	(unit 6)	Fensterscheibe
training	(unit 5)	Ausbildung	wooden	(unit 5)	hölzern
tray	(unit 2)	Tablett	(to) work on shifts	(unit 8)	im Schichtdienst arbeiten
(to) treat	(unit 5)	jemanden behandeln			
trip	(revision I)	Ausflug	(to) worry	(unit 11)	sich Sorgen machen
trolley	(unit 12)	Einkaufswagen	(to) wrap	(unit 3)	einpacken
tub	(unit 3)	Wanne			
tumble-dryer	(unit 3)	Wäschetrockner	**Y**		
turkey	(unit 7)	Truthahn	youth hostel	(unit 6)	Jugendherberge
(to) turn down	(unit 6)	hier: leiser drehen			
twice	(unit 4)	zweimal			

Bildquellenverzeichnis